Financial Management

Financial Management

Jensen Helberg

Larsen & Keller
www.larsen-keller.com

Financial Management
Jensen Helberg
ISBN: 978-1-64172-618-4 (Hardback)

Larsen & Keller
Published by Larsen and Keller Education,
5 Penn Plaza,
19th Floor,
New York, NY 10001, USA

Cataloging-in-Publication Data

Financial management / Jensen Helberg.
p. cm.
Includes bibliographical references and index.
ISBN 978-1-64172-618-4
1. Finance--Management. 2. Business enterprises--Finance.
3. Corporations--Finance. I. Helberg, Jensen.
HG4026 .F56 2021
658.15--dc23

For more information regarding Larsen and Keller Education and its products, please visit the publisher's website www.larsen-keller.com

Table of Contents

Preface

The planning, controlling and organizing of financial activities is termed as financial management. A few activities which fall under this category are procurement of funds as well as their utilization. Financial management is involved in the application of the principles of management to the financial resources of an enterprise. It primarily focuses on ratios, debts and equities. Some of the major objectives of this field are profit maximization, wealth maximization, maintenance of proper cash flow and minimization on capital cost. A few of its allied fields are investment management, managerial finance and corporate finance. This book elucidates the concepts and innovative models around prospective developments with respect to financial management. It picks up individual branches and explains their need and contribution in the context of a growing economy. For someone with an interest and eye for detail, this textbook covers the most significant topics in the field of financial management.

Given below is the chapter wise description of the book:

Chapter 1- The branch of business administration which is involved in the research for determining the capital to be obtained by a company for funding its assets is known as financial management. It is also involved in the maximizing of the value of the firm for the stockholders. This chapter has been carefully written to provide an easy introduction to the varied facets of financial management such as its features and functional areas.

Chapter 2- The system which facilitates the exchange of funds between investors, lenders and borrowers is termed as the financial system. Some of the components of financial systems are financial markets, financial instruments and financial services. This chapter discusses the different aspects of these components of financial systems in detail.

Chapter 3- The formal records of the financial activities and position of entities such as a person or business are known as financial statements. The process of analyzing and reviewing a firm's financial statements for the purpose of making informed business decisions is termed as financial statement analysis. The topics elaborated in this chapter will help in gaining a better perspective about the different types of financial statements and their analysis.

Chapter 4- The methods through which a company finances its assets by a combination of debt, equity or hybrid securities is known as capital structure. Some of the theories related to capital structure are net income approach, net operating income approach and Modigliani-Miller approach. This chapter discusses in detail these theories related to capital structure and its management.

Chapter 5- The process which is used by businesses for determining which of the proposed fixed asset purchases to accept and which ones to decline is known as capital budgeting. Some of its objectives are selecting profitable projects and capital expenditure control. This chapter closely examines these key objectives of capital budgeting to provide an extensive understanding of the subject.

Chapter 6- The process which is used to determine an asset's present value is known as valuation. Some of its fundamental concepts are the time value of money, bond valuation and equity valuation. The topics elaborated in this chapter will help in gaining a better perspective about these key concepts of valuation.

Chapter 7- The management of finance in an international business environment is known as international financial management. It is mainly involved in trading and making money through the exchange of foreign currency. All the diverse aspects of international financial management such as the international monetary system and foreign exchange market have been carefully analyzed in this chapter.

Indeed, my job was extremely crucial and challenging as I had to ensure that every chapter is informative and structured in a student-friendly manner. I am thankful for the support provided by my family and colleagues during the completion of this book.

Jensen Helberg

1

Financial Management: An Introduction

The branch of business administration which is involved in the research for determining the capital to be obtained by a company for funding its assets is known as financial management. It is also involved in the maximizing of the value of the firm for the stockholders. This chapter has been carefully written to provide an easy introduction to the varied facets of financial management such as its features and functional areas.

Finance

Finance means the study of managing money and finding the required funds. The very foundation of the economic world is Finance. Its components are financial service and financial instruments. Basically, finance is about acquiring funds and their optimal management with respect to businesses. Capital, funds, money, and amount are a few abstractions of finances however they all have their separate entity. In order to enhance business development one must study and understand the concepts of finance thoroughly. The definition of Finance has always observed that it is subjected to improvisations.

Examples of Financing Activities

When a company borrows money for the short-term or long-term, and when a corporation issues bonds or shares of its common or preferred stock and receives cash, the proceeds will be reported as positive amounts in the cash flows from financing activities section of the SC3. A positive amount informs the reader that cash was received and thereby increased the company's cash and cash equivalents.

When a company repays the principal portion of its short-term or long-term loans, redeems any of its bonds payable, purchases its owns shares of capital stock (treasury stock), or pays dividends on its capital stock, the amount of cash used will be reported as negative amounts in the cash flows from financing activities section of the SCF. The negative amount informs the reader that cash was used and thereby reduced the company's cash and cash equivalents.

Features of Finance

- Channelizing Funds: It is well established fact that financial system is a critical element of any economy. Financial sector and financial markets perform the essential function of channelling funds from people who have saved surplus funds by spending less than their income to people who have a shortage of investible funds because their plans to spend exceed their income.

- Acquisition, Allocation and Utilization of Funds: Finance as a function deals with acquisition, allocation and utilization of funds. A business must ensure that adequate funds are available from the right sources at the right cost at the right time. It needs to decide the mode of raising fund, whether it is to be through the issue of securities or lending from the bank. Once funds are acquired the funds have to be allocated to various projects and services and finally the objective of the business is to earn profits which on a very large extent depend upon how effectively and efficiently allocated funds are utilized. Proper utilization of funds is based on sound investment decisions, proper control and asset management policies and efficient management of working capital.
- Maximization of Shareholder's Wealth: The objective of any business is to maximize and create wealth for the investors, which is measured by the price of the share of the company. The price of the share of any company is a function of its present and expected future earnings. Finance helps in defining policies and ways to maximize the earnings.
- Financial Management: Maximization of economic welfare of its owners is the accepted financial objective of the firm. Hence, the objectives of finance are to ensure adequate and regular supply of funds to the business and provide a fair rate of return to the suppliers of capital. Finance helps by ensuring efficient utilization of capital and available resources according to the principles of profitability, liquidity and safety. It provides a definite system for internal investment, financing and internal controls. And finally attempts to minimize cost of capital by developing a sound and economical combination of corporate securities.

Categories of Finance

Finance can be broken into three different sub categories: public finance, corporate finance and personal finance. All three of which would contain many sub-categories:

- Public Finance: Public Finance is a part of study of Economics. It borders on the fields of government and political science. Public finance is the study of the financial activities of governments and public authorities. Public finance describes finance as related to sovereign states and sub-national entities (like states/provinces) and related public entities (e.g. municipal corporations) or agencies. It describes and analyses the expenditures of governments and the techniques used by governments to finance these expenditures. It is concerned with the identification of required expenditure of a public sector entity and sources of revenue and the budgeting process. Public finance analysis helps us to understand why certain services have come to be supplied by government, and why governments have come to rely on particular types of taxes.
- Corporate Finance: Corporate finance is the task of providing the funds for a corporation's activities by raising and administering funds. Corporate finance aims at studying the funding of assets from various sources like market, general public, or various financial institutions. In this process corporate finance aims to balance risk and profitability, while attempting to maximize an entity's wealth and the value of its stock. The importance of corporate finance is underlined by economic and social significance in terms of increase

in public responsibility as the organization grows and wide distribution of the corporate ownership in the process separating ownership from management.

- Personal Finance: Personal finance refers to the financial decisions which an individual must make to plan for his future. These decisions include obtaining monetary resources, planning application of income, budgeting, deciding on amounts and mode of saving, and decisions around spending monetary resources over time. During this process one is expected to take into account various financial risks and future life events that may impact current income levels or projected incomes and must plan for them.

Other Categories of Classification of Finance

- Direct and Indirect Finance. The finance could be of two types:
    - Direct Finance: In this case the borrower directly borrow funds from the lender in the financial markets by selling them securities (also called financial instruments), which are claim on the borrower's future income/assets or reserves and entitle the borrower with partial ownership if the funds have be raised using equity.
    - Indirect Finance: In this case the role of channelizing the funds from the savers to borrowers is done through financial intermediaries (example commercial banks).
- Short Term and Long Term Finance: Money is needed to setup any kind of business. A business owner can look for the investors to invest money in the business and this money can be borrowed for short term or long term.
    - Long Term Finance: Long term finance is generally used for investment in fixed assets such as land and building, plant and machinery etc. and is not repayable with in short period of time.
    - Short Term Finance: Short term finance is used for investment in working capital. It is used to meet the short term needs of the business. It may be repayable in short term or on demand as in case of a cash credit account. Short term loans are usually repayable within a period of one to three years.
- Sources of Finance: The sources of funds can be broadly divided into owned capital and borrowed funds.
    - Owned Capital: Owned capital is the money brought in by the businessman himself and sometimes referred to as capital or equity capital.
    - Borrowed Capital: Borrowed capital is the money advanced by outside agencies like banks, financial institutions etc. generally in the form of loan.

Principles of Finance

Principles act as a guideline for the investment and financing decision. Financial managers take operating, investment and financing decisions, some of this related to the short term and some long term. The six Principles of Finance Every one Need to know whether it is for individual or organization.

There are six basic principles of finance everyone needs to know:

- The Principle of Risk and Return.
- The Principle of the Time Value of Money.
- The Principle of Cash Flow.
- The Principle of Profitability and liquidity.
- Principles of diversity.
- The Hedging Principle of Finance.

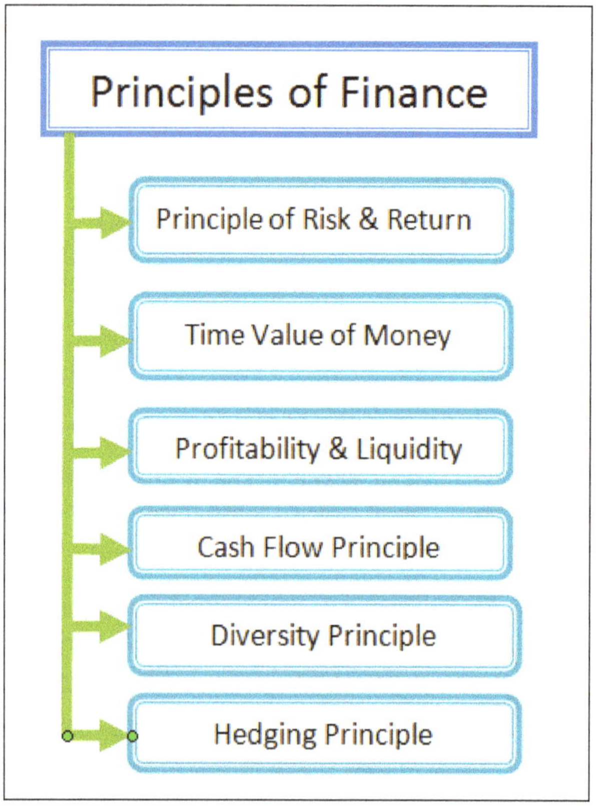

Six Principles of Finance.

The Principle of Risk and Return: This principle indicates that investors have to conscious both risk and return, because higher the risk higher the rates of return and lower the risk, lower the rates of return. For business financing, we have to compare the return with risk. To ensure optimum rates of return investors need to measure risk and return by both direct measurement and relative measurement.

The Principle of Time Value of Money: This principle is concerned with the value of money, that value of money is decreased when time passes. The value of dollar 1 of the present time is more than the value of dollar 1 after some time or years. So before investing or taking funds, we have to think about the inflation rate of the economy and the required rate of return must be more than the inflation rate so that return can compensate for the loss incurred by the inflation.

Cash Flow Principle: This principle mainly discusses the cash inflow and outflow, more cash inflow in the earlier period is preferable than later cash flow by the investors. This principle also follows the time value principle that's why it prefers earlier more benefits rather than later years benefits.

The Principle of Profitability and Liquidity: This principle is very important from the investor's perspective because the investor has to ensure both profitability and liquidity. Liquidity indicates the marketability of the investment i.e. how much easy to get cash by selling the investment. On the other hand, investors have to invest in a way that can ensure the maximization of profit with a moderate or lower level of risk.

The Principles of Diversity: This principle helps to minimize the risk by building an optimum portfolio. The idea of portfolio is, never put all your eggs in the same basket because if it falls then all of your eggs will break, so put eggs by separating in a different basket so that your risk can be minimized. To ensure this principle investors have to invest in risk-free investment and some risky investment so that ultimately risk can be lower. Diversification of investment ensures minimization of risk.

Hedging Principle of Finance: Hedging principle indicates us that we have to take a loan from appropriate sources, for short-term fund requirement we have to finance from short-term sources and for long-term fun requirement we have to manage fund from long-term sources. For fixed asset financing is to be done from long-term sources.

Financial Management

Financial management may be defined as planning, organising, directing and controlling the financial activities of an organisation. Financial activities deal with not only the procurement and utilisation of funds but also with the assessing of needs for funds, raising required finance, capital budgeting, distribution of surplus, financial controls, etc.

In this broader view, the central issue of financial policy is the wise use of funds and the central process involved is a rational matching of the advantage of potential uses against the cost of alternative potential sources so as to achieve the broad financial goals which an enterprise sets for itself.

In addition to raising funds, financial management is directly concerned with production, marketing and other functions within an enterprise whenever decisions are made about the acquisition or distribution of funds."

Objectives of Financial Management

Financial management is one of the functional areas of business. Therefore, its objectives must be consistent with the overall objectives of business. The overall objective of financial management is to provide maximum return to the owners on their investment in the long-term.

This is known as wealth maximisation. Maximisation of owners' wealth is possible when the capital invested initially increases over a period of time. Wealth maximisation means maximising the market value of investment in shares of the company.

Wealth of shareholders = Number of shares held × Market price per share.

In order to maximise wealth, financial management must achieve the following specific objectives:

- To ensure availability of sufficient funds at reasonable cost (liquidity).
- To ensure effective utilisation of funds (financial control).
- To ensure safety of funds by creating reserves, re-investing profits, etc. (minimisation of risk).
- To ensure adequate return on investment (profitability).
- To generate and build-up surplus for expansion and growth (growth).
- To minimise cost of capital by developing a sound and economical combination of corporate securities (economy).
- To coordinate the activities of the finance department with the activities of other departments of the firm (cooperation).

Profit Maximisation

Very often maximisation of profits is considered to be the main objective of financial management. Profitability is an operational concept that signifies economic efficiency. Elements of Financial Management Some writers on finance believe that it leads to efficient allocation of resources and optimum use of capital.

It is said that profit maximisation is a simple and straightforward objective. It also ensures the survival and growth of a business firm. But modern authors on financial management have criticised the goal of profit maximisation.

Elements of Financial Management

- Investment decisions includes investment in fixed assets (called as capital budgeting). Investment in current assets are also a part of investment decisions called as working capital decisions.
- Financial decisions: They relate to the raising of finance from various resources which will depend upon decision on type of source, period of financing, cost of financing and the returns thereby.
- Dividend decision: The finance manager has to take decision with regards to the net profit distribution. Net profits are generally divided into two:
    - Dividend for shareholders: Dividend and the rate of it has to be decided.
    - Retained profits: Amount of retained profits has to be finalized which will depend upon expansion and diversification plans of the enterprise.

The financial management is generally concerned with procurement, allocation and control of financial resources of a concern. The objectives can be:

- To ensure regular and adequate supply of funds to the concern.

- To ensure adequate returns to the shareholders this will depend upon the earning capacity, market price of the share, expectations of the shareholders.
- To ensure optimum funds utilization. Once the funds are procured, they should be utilized in maximum possible way at least cost.
- To ensure safety on investment, i.e, funds should be invested in safe ventures so that adequate rate of return can be achieved.
- To plan a sound capital structure-There should be sound and fair composition of capital so that a balance is maintained between debt and equity capital.

Features of Financial Management

Estimating Financial Requirements

The first task of a financial manager is to estimate short-term and long-term financial requirements of his business. For this purpose, he will prepare a financial plan for present as well as for future. The amount required for purchasing fixed assets as well as needs of funds for working capital will have to be ascertained.

The estimations should be based on sound financial principles so that neither there are inadequate nor excess funds with the concern. The inadequacy of funds will adversely affect the day-to-day working of the concern whereas excess funds may tempt a management to indulge in extravagant spending or speculative activities.

Deciding Capital Structure

The capital structure refers to the kind and proportion of different securities for raising funds. After deciding about the quantum of funds required it should be decided which type of securities should be raised. It may be wise to finance fixed assets through long-term debts. Even here if gestation period is longer, then share capital may be most suitable.

Long-term funds should be employed to finance working capital also, if not wholly then partially. Entirely depending upon overdrafts and cash credits for meeting working capital needs may not be suitable. A decision about various sources for funds should be linked to the cost of raising funds.

If cost of raising funds is very high then such sources may not be useful for long. A decision about the kind of securities to be employed and the proportion in which these should be used is an important decision which influences the short-term and long-term financial planning of an enterprise.

Selecting a Source of Finance

After preparing a capital structure, an appropriate source of finance is selected. Various sources, from which finance may be raised, include: share capital, debentures, financial institutions, commercial banks, public deposits, etc.

If the concern does not want to tie down assets as securities then public deposits may be a suitable source. If management does not want to dilute ownership then debentures should be issued in preference to shares. The need, purpose, object and cost involved may be the factors influencing the selection of a suitable source of financing.

Scope or Content of Finance Function	
1.	Estimating financial requirements.
2.	Deciding capital structure.
3.	Selecting a source of finance.
4.	Selecting a pattern of investment.
5.	Proper cash management.
6.	Implementing financial control.
7.	Proper use of surpluses.

Selecting a Pattern of Investment

When funds have been procured then a decision about investment pattern is to be taken. The selection of an investment pattern is related to the use of funds. The funds will have to be spent first on fixed assets and then an appropriate portion will be retained for working capital.

Even in various categories of assets, a decision about the type of fixed or other assets will be essential. While selecting a plant and machinery, even different categories of them may be available. The decision-making techniques such as Capital Budgeting, Opportunity Cost Analysis etc. may be applied in making decisions about capital expenditures.

While spending on various assets, the principles of safety, profitability and liquidity should not be ignored. A balance should be struck even in these principles. One may not like to invest on a project which may be risky even though there may be more profits.

Proper Cash Management

Cash management is also an important task of finance manager. He has to assess various cash needs at different times and then make arrangements for arranging cash.

Cash may be required to:

- Purchase raw materials,
- Make payments to creditors,
- Meet wage bills;
- Meet day-to-day expenses.

The usual sources of cash may be:

- Cash sales,
- Collection of debts,
- Short- term arrangements with banks etc.

The cash management should be such that neither there is a shortage of it and nor it is idle. Any shortage of cash will damage the creditworthiness of the enterprise. The idle cash with the business will mean that it is not properly used.

It will be better if Cash Flow Statement is regularly prepared so that one is able to find out various sources and applications. If cash is spent on avoidable expenses then such spending may be curtailed. A proper idea on sources of cash inflow may also enable to assess the utility of various sources. Some sources may not be providing that much cash which we should have thought. All this information will help in efficient management of cash.

Implementing Financial Controls

An efficient system of financial management necessitates the use of various control devices.

Financial control devices generally used are:

- Return on investment,
- Budgetary Control,
- Break Even Analysis,
- Cost Control,
- Ratio Analysis and
- Cost and Internal Audit.

Return on investment is the best control device to evaluate the performance of various financial policies. The higher this percentage better may be the financial performance. The use of various control techniques by the finance manager will help him in evaluating the performance in various areas and take corrective measures whenever needed.

Proper use of Surpluses

The utilisation of profits or surpluses is also an important factor in financial management. A judicious use of surpluses is essential for expansion and diversification plans and also in protecting the interests of shareholders. The ploughing back of profits is the best policy of further financing but it clashes with the interests of shareholders.

A balance should be struck in using funds for paying dividend and retaining earnings for financing expansion plans, etc. The market value of shares will also be influenced by the declaration of dividend and expected profitability in future.

A finance manager should consider the influence of various factors, such as;

- Trend of earnings of the enterprise,
- Expected earnings in future,
- Market value of shares,

- Need for funds for financing expansion, etc. A judicious policy for distributing surpluses will be essential for maintaining proper growth of the unit.

Functional Areas of Financial Management

Determining Financial Needs

A finance manager is supposed to meet financial needs of the enterprise. For this purpose, he should determine financial needs of the concern. Funds are needed to meet promotional expenses, fixed and working capital needs. The requirement of fixed assets is related to the type of industry.

A manufacturing concern will require more investments in fixed assets than a trading concern. The working capital needs depend upon the scale of operations, larger the scale of operations, the higher will be the needs for working capital. A wrong assessment of financial needs may jeopardise the survival of a concern.

Selecting the Sources of Funds

A number of sources may be available for raising funds. A concern may resort to issue of share capital and debentures. Financial institutions may be requested to provide long-term funds. The working capital needs may be met by getting cash credit or overdraft facilities from commercial banks. A finance manager has to be very careful and cautious in approaching different sources.

The terms and conditions of banks may not be favourable to the concern. A small concern may find difficulties in raising funds for want of adequate securities or due to its reputation. The selection of a suitable source of funds will influence the profitability of the concern. This selection should be made with great caution.

Financial Analysis and Interpretation

The analysis and interpretation of financial statements is an important task of a finance manager. He is expected to know about the profitability, liquidity position, short-term and long-term financial position of the concern. For this purpose, a number of ratios have to be calculated.

The interpretation of various ratios is also essential to reach certain conclusions. Financial analysis and interpretation has become an important area of financial management.

Cost-volume-profit Analysis

Cost-volume-profit analysis is an important tool of profit planning. It answers questions like, what is the behaviour of cost and volume? At what point of production a firm will be able to recover its costs? How much a firm should produce to earn a desired profit? To understand cost- volume profit relationship, one should know the behaviour of costs.

The costs may be subdivided as fixed costs, variable costs and semi-variable costs. Fixed costs remain constant irrespective of changes in production. An increase or decrease in volume of production will not influence fixed costs.

Variable costs, on the other hand, vary in direct proportion to change in production. Semi-variable costs remain constant for a period and then become variable for a short period. These costs change with the change in output but not in the same proportion.

The first concern of a finance manager will be to recover all costs. He will aspire to achieve break-even point at the earliest. It is a point of no-profit no-loss. Any production beyond break-even point will bring profits to the concern.

The volume of sales, to earn a desired profit, can also be ascertained. This analysis is very helpful in deciding the volume of output or sales. The knowledge of cost-volume profit analysis is essential for taking important decisions about production and profits.

Functional Area of Financial Management	
1.	Determining financial needs.
2.	Selecting the source of funds.
3.	Financial analysis and interpretation.
4.	Cost – volume – profit analysis.
5.	Capital budgeting.
6.	Working capital management.
7.	Profit planning and control.
8.	Dividend policy.

Capital Budgeting

Capital budgeting is the process of making investment decisions in capital expenditures. It is an expenditure the benefits of which are expected to be received over a period of time exceeding one year. It is an expenditure incurred for acquiring or improving the fixed assets, the benefits of which are expected to be received over a number of years in future.

Capital budgeting decisions are vital to any organisation. An unsound investment decision may prove to be fatal for the very existence of the concern.

The crux of capital budgeting is the allocation of available resources to various proposals. The crucial factor which influences the capital budgeting decision is the profitability of the prospective investment.

For making correct capital budgeting decisions, the knowledge of its techniques is essential. A number of methods like payback period method, rate of return method, net present value method, internal rate of return method and profitability index method may be used for making capital budgeting decisions.

Working Capital Management

Working capital is the life blood and nerve centre of a business. Just as circulation of blood is essential in the human body for maintaining life, working capital is essential to maintain the smooth running of business. No business can run successfully without an adequate amount of working capital.

Working capital refers to that part of the firm's capital which is required for financing short- term or current assets such as cash, receivables and inventories. It is essential to maintain a proper level of these assets. Finance manager is required to determine the quantum of such assets. Cash is required to meet day-to-day needs and purchase inventories etc.

The scarcity of cash may adversely affect the reputation of a concern. The receivables management is related to the volume of production and sales. For increasing sales, there may be a need to give more credit facilities. Though sales may go up but the risk of bad debts and cost involved in it may have to be weighed against the benefits.

Inventory control is also an important factor in working capital management. The inadequacy of inventory may cause delays or stoppages of work. Excess inventory, on the other hand, may result in blocking of money in stocks, more costs in stock maintaining etc. Proper management of working capital is an important area of financial management.

Profit Planning and Control

Profit planning and control is an important responsibility of the financial manager. Profit maximisation is, generally, considered to be an important objective of a business. Profit is also used as a tool for evaluating the performance of management. Profit is determined by the volume of revenue and expenditure. Revenue may accrue from sales, investments in outside securities or income from other sources.

The expenditures may include manufacturing costs, trading expenses, office and administrative expenses, selling and distribution expenses and financial costs. The excess of revenue over expenditure determines the amount of profit.

Profit planning and control directly influence the declaration of dividend, creation of surpluses, taxation etc. Break-even analysis and cost-volume-pro fit relationship are some of the tools used in profit planning and control.

Dividend Policy

Dividend is the reward of the shareholders for investments made by them in the shares of the company. The investors are interested in earning the maximum return on their investments whereas management wants to retain profits for further financing. These contradictory aims will have to be reconciled in the interests of shareholders and the company.

The company should distribute a reasonable amount as dividends to its members and retain the rest for its growth and survival. A dividend policy is influenced by a number of factors such as magnitude and trend of earnings, desire and type of shareholders, future requirements of the company, government's economic policy, taxation policy, etc.

Dividend policy is an important area of financial management because the interests of the shareholders and the needs of the company are directly related to it.

Basic Factors Influencing Financial Decisions

External Factors

External factors refer to environmental factors within which a business enterprise has to operate. These factors are beyond the control and influence of the management. A wise management adopts policies that will be most suited to the present and prospective socio-economic and political conditions of the country.

The following external factors enter into decision making process:

State of Economy

At a time when the entire economy is enveloped into state of uncertainty and there is no ray of hope of recovery in the ensuing years, and considerable amount of risk is associated with investment it would be worthwhile on the part of a finance manager neither to take up new investment activities nor to carry further the expansion programmes.

On the contrary, if it is found that the economy is likely to recover from the current gloomy state of affairs, the finance manager should not miss the chance of exploiting investment opportunities. For that matter, he should after evaluating the economic viability of project in hand; select the most profitable project in advance so that when the opportunity crops up the same is seized upon.

Economic condition of the country influences financing decision also. In times of prosperity when investors have keen desire to invest more and more savings the firm can garner desired amount of funds from the market by floating securities. But it should be remembered that the firm will have to offer higher interest rate (dividend rate) because interest rates tend to harden under pressure of demand.

This would consequently increase cost of capital of the firm. To minimise cost of financing finance manger should insist more on debenture financing as benefits on trading on equity would tend to minimise cost. In times of depression, raising outside capital poses grave problem. Under such condition, greater emphasis should be laid on internal financing and for that purpose reserve position of the company will have to be strengthened.

Dividend policy of a firm should also be attuned to changing economic conditions. If it lurks that the business is entering upon a period of depression, conservatism should be followed, for the business may need all of its cash resources to carry it safely through the period of decline until its sales soar. During boom period there is tendency among firms to offer higher dividend rate to mobilise funds from the market.

The management is, therefore, constrained to declare dividend at higher rate. This should not pose any financial problem before the management since earning of the firm improves sharply in times of prosperity. There is also a strong possibility for the management to adopt conservative dividend policy during boom periods so that the firm may get sufficiently large amount of resources to finance growth requirements.

Structure of Capital and Money Markets

Where institutional structure of capital and money markets is well developed and organised with a multitude of financial institutions supplying long-term as well as short-term financial assistance and investors are venture some evincing keen interest in security dealings in stock market, business entrepreneurs will not have to encounter much problem in procuring even substantially large amount of capital.

Various alternate sources are available and businessmen have a freedom to decide about the optimal financing mix so that cost of capital is reduced. Furthermore, the firm's ability to adjust sources of funds in response to major changes in need for funds increases.

Not only does it enable entrepreneurs to use the type of funds that is most readily available at a given period of time but it also enhances their bargaining power when dealing with a prospective supplier of funds.

In the absence of organised capital market entrepreneurs find it difficult to procure large amount of resources from the market. They have to raise capital from closely held circles. In such a state of affairs, policy of internal financing is pursued so as to enable the firm to draw upon its resources in times of need for funds.

Taxation Policy

Taxation is the most predominant factor influencing business decisions since it takes away bigger slice of business income. While deciding to invest in projects, a finance manager has to keep in view the existence of tax incentives.

Further, a finance manager, has to decide as to which method of depreciation should be followed that may reduce tax burden. There are numerous methods of charging depreciation, important being Straight Line method, Straight Line method. Diminishing Balance method and Annuity method.

From the stand point of taxation, Straight Line method is very useful since in this method depreciation is charged at twice the normal depreciation rate which ultimately reduces the tax liability. It may be argued in this regard that tax savings generated in the initial years because of charging depreciation at higher rate will be compensated by the increased tax liability in the subsequent years when depreciation will be charged at lower rate.

However, on a closer scrutiny it would appear that the present value of tax savings in initial years would always be higher than the present value of the additional tax liability in the subsequent years. Thus taxation influences the choice of method of depreciation.

Likewise, tax liability of a firm fluctuates depending upon method of inventory valuation. There are different methods of inventory valuation, viz., LIFO, FIFO. A finance manager must ascertain in advance as to which method will be helpful in minimising the tax burden.

Taxation also influences the capital structure decision. Other things being equal, debt financing is always cheaper from taxation point of view because interest on debt is a tax deductible expenditure while dividends are not.

Taxation enters into dividend decision too. High corporate tax rates lower the amount of earnings left for dividend distribution which, in consequence, tend to lower dividend rate. However, recent studies have revealed that high rates would not necessarily influence dividend rate particularly when tax burden is shifted on consumers.

Requirements of Investors

While taking financing decision a finance manager should also give due consideration to the requirements of potential investors. There may be different types of investors with varying degree of safety, liquidity and profitability notions.

Investors who are conservative and liquidity conscious would like to hold such securities as may assure them certainty of return and return of principal amount after the stipulated period of time. There may be, on the other hand, investors who are not as liquidity conscious, venturesome and who have greater preference for profitability.

Such type of investors would prefer to invest their savings in equities. Thus, the management seeking to raise substantially large amount of capital for this undertaking has to issue different types of securities so as to cater to as large a number of investors as may be possible.

Further, investors' psychology changes with the variation in economic and business conditions. In times of economic turmoil and business depression even venturesome investors would like to hold senior securities while during the period of economic prosperity shares receive premium even at the hands of those investors who are not so venturesome. Finance manager should, therefore, be well aware of the prevailing temper of the investing class.

Dividend policy must be geared to investors in general and existing stockholders and potential stockholders in particular. This helps in maximisation of the market value of the firm. Problem of ascertaining optimum allocation of business earnings between retention and dividends because of the diverse investment goals, tax brackets and alternate investment opportunities of the current and potential investors may prompt management to rationalize the soundness of such other factors as influence dividend policy as risk avoidance or maintenance of market price.

Lending Policy of Financial Institutions

Lending policy of financial institutions may also influence investment decisions of a firm. If financial institutions follow the policy of concessional financing to priority projects and decide to grant loans to non- priority projects on a very strict terms and conditions, naturally the finance manager while taking investment decisions would provide greater weightage to the former group of projects in relation to the later ones, if other things remain the same.

Further, while deciding about the sources of funds that have to be tapped for raising capital, lending policy of the financial institutions should be carefully examined. Sometimes, financial institutions grant financial assistance on such terms and conditions as may not be acceptable to the management.

The finance manager must, therefore, make suitable adjustment in financing mix of the firm in such ways as to conform to the desired pattern. The finance manager will have, therefore, to examine into the expediency of getting loans from the institutions under the afore-stated condition.

Internal Factors

Internal factors refer to those factors which are related with internal conditions of the firm such as nature of business, size of business, expected return, cost and risk, asset structure of business, structure of ownership, expectations about regular and steady earnings, age of the firm, liquidity in company funds and its working capital requirements, restrictions in debt agreements, control factor and attitude of the management.

Within the economic and legal environment of the country finance manager must take financial decision, keeping in mind the numerous characteristics of the firm.

Nature of Business

Nature of business may influence the pattern of investment in a firm, firm's make-up of capitalisation and the firm's dividend policy. In manufacturing and public utility concerns bulk of the funds have to be employed in acquiring fixed assets while in trading concerns substantially large amount of funds is invested in current assets, and fixed assets claim a nominal proportion.

As among manufacturing industries, fixed assets requirements in capital goods industries would always be higher than in consumer goods industries.

Impact of nature of business activities on make-up of capitalisation should also be closely examined. It is generally found that firms engaged in production of staple goods will have stability in their level of earnings as demand of their products is very likely to be uniformly steady both in times of business depression and boom. In view of this, they could place heavier reliance on debt for acquiring additional funds for the business.

Contrary to this, level of business earnings is fluctuating in the case of industrial undertakings engaged in production of non-essential products because demand of their products changes in consonance with economic oscillations. Management of such companies would not choose to burden themselves with fixed charges.

Similarly, public utility concerns and industrial concerns manufacturing essential products because of their steady and slow rising earnings may pursue liberal dividend policy to declare higher dividend rate. But trading concerns and those dealing in luxurious products would be committing blunder in pursuing such dividend policy.

Prudent dividend policy in such concerns is one that lays more emphasis on greater retention of earnings so that the firm could build huge reserves in periods of prosperity and the same could be utilised to maintain dividend rate at times when earnings of the firm nose-dive.

Size of Business

Firms engaged in the same line of activity may have different investment patterns depending primarily on the scale of their operations. Relatively larger amounts of funds are required to acquire fixed assets in larger concerns because these companies automate their process of production which smaller firms cannot afford.

Furthermore, small firms with their limited amount of capital can carry on their affairs by renting or leasing plant and equipment and building while larger firms usually construct their own buildings to house the factory and acquire plant and machinery to carry on production work.

Smaller firms because of their poor credit position have limited access to capital and money market in contrast to their larger counterparts. Investors are usually averse to invest in shares and debentures of smaller organisations. Furthermore, these smaller organisations do not have adequate amount of fixed assets to offer as security for securing loan. This is why management in the smaller organisations has to arrange capital from closely held circles.

Even if smaller firms are in comfortable position to raise equity share capital, their owners would be hesitant to place issues for public offering with a view to maintaining their control over the organisation. On the contrary, larger concerns find it easier to procure needed funds from different sources of capital and money markets.

Management in such concerns, therefore, considers it useful to employ more and more doses of debt to meet business requirements since this course of action would tend to reduce the cost of capital.

Dividend decision of a firm is also influenced by its size. Because of difficult access to external sources of financing, smaller organisations have to depend on internal sources of financing and for that matter the management may pursue conservative dividend policy to retain larger proportion of business earnings.

The management does not encounter any problem in persuading the shareholders who are few in number to agree to their policy. The shareholders should also have no objection in such policy because this will help minimize their tax liability. However, in larger concerns having large number of shareholders the management cannot always adopt a particular policy because wishes of the shareholders would not be common.

Expected Return, Cost and Risk

Major factors influencing investment decision are expected return on the project, its cost and the risk associated with the project. Where dispersion of outcomes is known and all projects are equal in risk, finance manager would naturally go for that investment proposal which leads to highest revenues in relation to cost.

Where different projects have varying degrees of riskiness, allowance will have to be made for the absorption of risk. This is usually done by adjusting the discount rate, i.e., rate of interest which is employed to discount future net cash flows of the project to present values.

Thus, the greater the dispersion of outcomes, higher the discount rate is employed which means that returns will be reduced at a higher rate because of the allowance made for the risk assigned to the eventuality of their realisation.

For a risk-less investment, risk-free discount rate is employed. As risk increases, higher and higher discount rates are employed. In this way after making appropriate adjustments for risk factor final course of action is chosen.

A finance manager should take into consideration earning prospects of investment projects in hand while taking dividend decision. Supposing a firm has large number of investment projects with vast earning potentialities sufficient to exhaust its earnings and the shareholders of the firm have strong preference for current dividends a finance manager in such situation must impress upon the shareholders about the strong need to retain more and more earnings and pursue strict dividend policy.

However, where the projects in hand promise only normal return, the management should follow liberal dividend policy to keep up with preferences of shareholders. Contrary to this, if the shareholders are indifferent between dividends and capital gains a finance manager must accept all those investment projects that would carry income above the break-even point and funds for these projects should be arranged out of retained earnings.

Asset Structure of Firm

Firms with sufficient amount of fixed assets must rely on debt to take advantage of cheaper source of financing. For example, public utilities and steel companies can depend heavily on debentures for raising capital as they can mortgage their assets for securing loan.

But trading concerns whose assets are mostly receivables and inventory values which are dependent on the continued profitability of the firm should place less reliance on long-term debt and should depend more on short-term debt for their financial requirements.

Structure of Ownership

In private companies whose ownership is concentrated in a few hands the management can find it easier to persuade the owners to accept strict dividend policy in the interest of the firm. But in public limited companies having large number of shareholders with varying desires the finance manager must insist on the pursuance of liberal dividend policy.

Probabilities of Regular and Steady Earnings

While planning about the make-up of capitalisation and deciding about the relationship between debt and equity the finance manager must visualize the trends of earnings of the firm for the past few years. Where the firm's past earnings have been reasonably stable and the same tendency is likely to continue in future, reliance on debt may be desirable.

Where earnings of the firm have been irregular in the past but when averaged over a period of years give a fair margin over the preferred stock dividend, the management may issue preferred shares to raise funds. When earnings of the firm fluctuated violently in the past and the future earnings cannot be predicted with reasonable certainty, it will incur risk in issuing debt.

Accordingly, common stock must be issued. When earning of the firm fluctuated violently in the past and the future earnings cannot be predicted with reasonable certainty, it will incur risk in issuing debt. Accordingly, common stock must be issued.

Degree of stability in level of earnings is a potent factor influencing dividend policy. But such a policy will prove dangerous to companies whose earnings are subject to great fluctuations. In such companies it would be prudent to declare lower dividend rate even when the business earnings are fairly high in order to use them to maintain the dividend rate in times of adversities.

Age of the Firm

Investors are generally loath to employ their funds in new ventures because of relatively greater risks involved. Lenders too feel shy of lending because of their poor capital base. Consequently, new enterprises have to encounter considerable problems in assembling funds from the market. They approach underwriters and stock brokers and pay them higher commission and brokerage for sale of their securities.

Thus, a new firm will have small share of debt in its total capitalisation. Even if new enterprises are in comfortable position to garner funds by issue of debentures, a finance manager should, as far as possible, avoid bringing in heavy dose of debt, for in that case a large chunk of business income might be eaten away by interest on loans leaving a little amount for dividend distribution and retention for further financing.

The company's ability to raise funds by means of debt in the ensuing years might be circumscribed by restriction in debt covenants. In sharper contrast to this, existing ventures may not face considerable problem in raising funds from the market because of high credit standing in market.

Such concerns usually float debentures for their additional long-term financial requirements with a view to reaping benefit of trading on equity. They also draw upon a part of the reserves built out of the past earnings for covering their additional financial needs. Thus, there is every likelihood of relatively greater amount of dilution of debt in the capitalisation of older firms.

Age of the firm goes far to determine its dividend policy. A new and growing concern whose access to capital market is limited must follow strict dividend policy to keep away a larger portion of the business earnings for financing growth requirements. Existing ventures, however, need not follow such policy.

Liquidity Position of the Firm and its Working Capital Requirements

A finance manager must consider cash position of the firm and firm's needs for funds to meet maturing obligations and working and fixed capital requirements while taking dividend decisions. Dividends are generally paid out of cash. Care should, therefore, be exercised by the finance manager to make sure that cash is readily available to distribute dividends.

Availability of large surplus does not always mean the availability of cash in the firm particularly when a large amount of sale has been done on credit. By the time sale proceeds tied in receivables are collected the firm may need funds to buy materials to process production. Thus, despite the presence of profit and even the availability of cash, working capital requirements of the firm may be so imminent that may warrant the pursuance of conservative dividend policy.

Again, if a company has sufficient amount of cash resources in hand at the time when some loans taken in the past are due it would be advisable to finance manager to conserve cash to meet the past obligations and adjust dividend pattern accordingly.

In many cases firms rely on their earnings for financing the acquisition of fixed assets. In such circumstances too the management must not be liberal in dividend distribution at least for some years even though a sizeable profit has been earned.

Restrictions in Debt Agreements

The provisions of debt contracts should be carefully examined while deciding about forms of raising capital and establishing dividend policy since most indentures contain provisions that prevent the use of additional debt or issue of debentures of the earlier type.

They also restrict the payment of dividends and sometimes disallow their payment until certain conditions are fulfilled. Needless to say, finance manager should make available to the Board of Directors a brief of all contractual provisions that affect the capital structure and dividends in any way.

Management Attitude

Financial decisions are influenced by the attitude of the management. Management attitudes that most directly influence the choice of financing and dividend policy are those concerning control of the enterprise and risk.

Management desiring to maintain control of the firm would like to raise additional funds needed by means of debentures and preferred stock which do not affect controlling position of the management in the firm. However, if company borrows more than what can be serviced by it; there is every risk of losing all control to creditors. It is; therefore, better to sacrifice a measure of control by some additional equity financing rather run the risk of all control to creditors by bringing in additional doses of debt. In such a situation, finance manager should not be very much liberal in dividend distribution.

Management attitude towards risk also determines the pattern of capitalisation of the firm. Conservative management would always prefer to tread on beaten path and would always avoid incurring fixed obligations for raising additional capital even though recourse to debt financing may be advantageous.

References

- What-is-finance-meaning-definition-examples, finance: wikifinancepedia.com, Retrieved 31 March, 2019
- Financing-activities-cash-flow-statement-2: accountingcoach.com, Retrieved 14 July, 2019
- What-is-finance-meaning-definition-features-of-finance, finance-domain, domain-knowledge: technofunc.com, Retrieved 17 May, 2019
- Principles-of-finance, academic-study: ordnur.com, Retrieved 19 April, 2019
- Financial-management-its-definition-meaning-and-objectives-discussed, financial-management: yourarticlelibrary.com., Retrieved 5 February, 2019
- Financial-management: management studyguide.com, Retrieved 26 July, 2019
- Top-7-features-of-financial-management: businessmanagementideas.com, Retrieved 21 May, 2019
- Top-8-functional-areas-of-financial-management, functional-areas, financial-management: businessmanagementideas.com, Retrieved 8 January, 2019
- Financial-decisions-concept-and-factors-influencing-it, financial-decisions, financial-management: yourarticlelibrary.com, Retrieved 13 May, 2019

2

The Financial System

The system which facilitates the exchange of funds between investors, lenders and borrowers is termed as the financial system. Some of the components of financial systems are financial markets, financial instruments and financial services. This chapter discusses the different aspects of these components of financial systems in detail.

A financial system is a set of institutions, such as banks, insurance companies, and stock exchanges, that permit the exchange of funds. Financial systems exist on firm, regional, and global levels. Borrowers, lenders, and investors exchange current funds to finance projects, either for consumption or productive investments, and to pursue a return on their financial assets. The financial system also includes sets of rules and practices that borrowers and lenders use to decide which projects get financed, who finances projects, and terms of financial deals. Like any other industry, the financial system can be organized using markets, central planning, or some mix of both.

Financial markets involve borrowers, lenders, and investors negotiating loans and other transactions. In these markets, the economic good traded on both sides is usually some form of money: current money (cash), claims on future money (credit), or claims on the future income potential or value of real assets (equity). These also include derivative instruments. Derivative instruments, such as commodity futures or stock options, are financial instruments that are dependent on an underlying real or financial asset's performance. In financial markets, these are all traded among borrowers, lenders, and investors according to the normal laws of supply and demand.

In a centrally planned financial system (e.g., a single firm or a command economy), the financing of consumption and investment plans is not decided by counterparties in a transaction but directly by a manager or central planner. Which projects receive funds, whose projects receive funds, and who funds them are determined by the planner, whether that means a business manager or a party boss.

Most financial systems contain elements of both give-and-take markets and top-down central planning. For example, a business firm is a centrally planned financial system with respect to its internal financial decisions; however, it typically operates within a broader market interacting with external lenders and investors to carry out its long term plans.

At the same time, all modern financial markets operate within some kind of government regulatory framework that sets limits on what types of transactions are allowed. Financial systems are often strictly regulated because they directly influence decisions over real assets, economic performance, and consumer protection.

Financial Institutions

A financial institution (FI) is a company engaged in the business of dealing with financial and monetary transactions such as deposits, loans, investments, and currency exchange. Financial institutions encompass a broad range of business operations within the financial services sector including banks, trust companies, insurance companies, brokerage firms, and investment dealers. Virtually everyone living in a developed economy has an on-going or at least periodic need for the services of financial institutions.

How Financial Institutions Work

Financial institutions serve most people in some way, as financial operations are a critical part of any economy, with individuals and companies relying on financial institutions for transactions and investing. Governments consider it imperative to oversee and regulate banks and financial institutions because they do play such an integral part of the economy. Historically, bankruptcies of financial institutions can create panic.

Types of Financial Institutions

Financial institutions offer a wide range of products and services for individual and commercial clients. The specific services offered vary widely between different types of financial institutions.

Commercial Banks

A commercial bank is a type of financial institution that accepts deposits, offers checking account services, makes business, personal, and mortgage loans, and offers basic financial products like certificates of deposit (CDs) and savings accounts to individuals and small businesses. A commercial bank is where most people do their banking, as opposed to an investment bank.

Banks and similar business entities, such as thrifts or credit unions, offer the most commonly recognized and frequently used financial services: checking and savings accounts, home mortgages, and other types of loans for retail and commercial customers. Banks also act as payment agents via credit cards, wire transfers, and currency exchange.

Investment Banks

Investment banks specialize in providing services designed to facilitate business operations, such as capital expenditure financing and equity offerings, including initial public offerings (IPOs). They also commonly offer brokerage services for investors, act as market makers for trading exchanges, and manage mergers, acquisitions, and other corporate restructurings.

Insurance Companies

Among the most familiar non-bank financial institutions are insurance companies. Providing insurance, whether for individuals or corporations, is one of the oldest financial services. Protection of assets and protection against financial risk, secured through insurance products, is an essential service that facilitates individual and corporate investments that fuel economic growth.

Brokerage Firms

Investment companies and brokerages, such as mutual fund and exchange-traded fund (ETF) provider Fidelity Investments, specialize in providing investment services that include wealth management and financial advisory services. They also provide access to investment products that may range from stocks and bonds all the way to lesser-known alternative investments, such as hedge funds and private equity investments.

Financial Markets

A financial market is a market, or an arrangement or an institution that facilitates the exchange of financial instruments and securities. These instruments include shares, stocks, bonds, debentures, commercial papers, bills, cheques etc. The price of these instruments is determined by the laws of demand and supply in the market.

Concept of Financial Market

To understand the structure and the importance of financial markets, we must first understand their role in our economy. Now every economy has two basic sectors when it comes to funds – savings and investment. Savings is what we refer to when individual households save money. And investment is the capital that industries require to start and run their businesses.

Now the economy must provide a link between savings and investments. One obvious way to convert savings into investment is via banks. Alternatively, savings can be turned into investments through financial markets. Households will use their savings to buy financial instruments and commodities such as shares, stocks, debentures etc. This is the whole concept of the financial market.

This way a financial market serves an allocate function and mobilize idle funds to be put to more productive use. When the allocation of funds is done well, there are some added benefits, such as,

- The rate of return on their savings will be higher for householders, than what a bank offers.
- The resources will be invested in firms that have high productivity and show great promise in the economy.

Functions of Financial Markets

- Mobilizing Funds: In a successful economy, money should never sit idle. Investors that have savings must be linked with industries that require investment. So financial markets will enable this transaction, where investors can invest their savings according to their choices and risk assessment. This will utilize idle funds and the economy will boom.
- Price Determination: The financial commodities traded in a financial market get their prices from the rules of demand and supply. The investors or the household are the suppliers of the funds, and the industries are the ones demanding them. The interaction between the two and other market factors will help determine the prices.

- Liquidity: The instruments sold in the financial market tend to have high liquidity. This means at any given time the investors can sell their financial commodities and convert them to cash in a very short period. This is an important factor for investors who do not want to invest long term.
- Easy Access: Both investors and industries need each other. The financial market provides a platform where both the buyers and sellers can find each other easily without spending too much time, money or effort.

Spot Market

The spot market is a commodity or security market where goods, both perishable and non-perishable are sold for money and delivered immediately or within a short span of time. Contracts traded on a spot market are also in effect instantly. The spot market is also recognized as the cash market or physical market. The purchases are settled in cash at the current prices fixed by the market as opposed to the price at the time of distribution. An example of a spot market commodity that is often sold is crude oil. It is sold at the existing prices, and physically supplied later.

A commodity is basic goods, which is substitutable with other similar commodities. Some examples of commodities are grains, gold, oil, electricity and natural gas. Technology has entered the market with commodities such as mobile minutes and bandwidth. Commodities are standardized, and are essential to meet the specific standards to be traded on the spot market. The world spot market or foreign currency trading is a vast spot market. It is the simultaneous exchange of one nation's currency with another. The way it works is through a stakeholder choosing a currency pair.

Types of Spot Market

The spot market which is also called the cash market is a financial market, in which the financial commodities and instruments are transacted for instantaneous delivery. It contrasts with a futures market in which distribution or delivery is owed at a later date. A spot market can be:

- Exchange: It is also called an organized market where the security or commodity is traded on an exchange using and changing the current market price.
- Over the counter (OTC): In OTC, the trades are based on contracts which are done openly between two parties, and not subject to the guidelines of an exchange. The contract terms are approved between the parties and might be non-standard.

Example: Spot markets differ from futures markets in that delivery takes place immediately. For example, if you wish to purchase Company XYZ shares and own them immediately, you would go to the cash market on which the shares are traded. If you wanted to buy gold on the spot market, you could go to a coin dealer and exchange cash for gold.

The foreign exchange (FOREX) market is one of the largest spot markets in the world. People and companies all over the world are constantly exchanging one currency for another as transactions occur all over the globe.

Importance of Spot Market

It is important to know the difference between the spot market and the futures market, as well as the difference between spot prices and futures prices. This difference known as the time spread is important economically because it illuminates the market's expectations about futures prices.

For the most part, spot markets are influenced solely by supply and demand, whereas futures markets are also influenced by expectations about future prices, storage costs, weather predictions (for perishable commodities in particular), and a host of other factors.

Futures Market

Futures markets trade futures contracts. A futures contract is an agreement between a buyer and seller of the contract that some asset--such as a commodity, currency or index--will bought/sold for a specific price, on a specific day, in the future (expiration date). For example, if someone buys a July crude oil futures contract (CL), they are saying they will buy 1,000 barrels of oil from the seller at the price they pay for the futures contract, come the July expiry. The seller is agreeing to sell the buyer the 1,000 barrels of oil at the agreed upon price.

Day traders don't trade futures contracts with the intent of actually taking possession of (if buying) or distributing (if selling) the physical barrels of oil. Rather, day traders make money on the price fluctuations that occur after taking a trade. For example, if a day trader buys a natural gas futures contract (NG) at 2.065, and sells it later in the day for 2.105, they made a profit. The price of a futures contract is constantly moving as new buy and sell transactions occur.

Futures contracts are traded by both day traders and longer-term traders, as well as by non-traders with an interest in the underlying commodity. For example, a grain farmer might sell a futures contract to guarantee that he receives a certain price for his grain, or a livestock farmer might buy a futures contract to guarantee that she can buy her winter feed supply at a certain price. Either way, both the buyer and the seller of a futures contract are obligated to fulfil the contract requirements at the end of the contract term. Day traders are not so concerned about these obligations because they do not hold the futures contract position until it expires. All they have to do to realize a profit or loss on their position is make an offsetting trade. For example, if they buy 5 futures contracts, they need to sell those 5 futures contracts before expiry.

Characteristics of Futures Market

- Contract Grades and Prices: The contract grades of a product (that is the grades that may be delivered in the futures market) are the grades specified by the rules of the Produce Exchange for delivery on future contract. The grade is not specified in the individual contracts.
- Unit of Sale: The rules of the Various Exchanges specify the units for which future contracts shall be made.
- Time of Delivery: Future contracts are generally made for certain future months. For example, in October, future contracts may be made for December or May. The delivery month

selected for future trading are based on harvest periods and the movement of the grain traded in the marketing channels.

- Actual Delivery vs. Settlement of the Money Differences: Future contracts made upon an exchange contemplate an actual delivery of goods. The buyer has the right to demand the delivery of actual goods and the seller has the right to deliver them. But most are settled through a clearing house operated in connection with the exchange by a settlement based on money differences between the original contract price and the current price at the time of settlement.

Forward Market

A forward market is an over-the-counter marketplace that sets the price of a financial instrument or asset for future delivery. Forward markets are used for trading a range of instruments, but the term is primarily used with reference to the foreign exchange market. It can also it can also apply to markets for securities and interest rates as well as commodities.

A forward market leads to the creation of forward contracts. While forward contracts, like futures contracts, may be used for both hedging and speculation, there are some notable differences between the two. Forward contracts can be customized to fit a customer's requirements, while futures contracts have standardized features in terms of their contract size and maturity. Forwards are executed between banks or between a bank and a customer; futures are done on an exchange, which is a party to the transaction. The flexibility of forwards contributes to their attractiveness in the foreign exchange market.

Pricing

Prices in the forward market are interest-rate based. In the foreign exchange market, the forward price is derived from the interest rate differential between the two currencies, which is applied over the period from the transaction date to the settlement date of the contract. In interest rate forwards, the price is based on the yield curve to maturity.

Foreign Exchange Forwards

Interbank forward foreign exchange markets are priced and executed as swaps. This means that currency A is purchased vs. currency B for delivery on the spot date at the spot rate in the market at the time the transaction is executed. At maturity, currency A is sold vs. currency B at the original spot rate plus or minus the forward points; this price is set when the swap is initiated. The interbank market usually trades for straight dates, such as a week or a month from the spot date. Three- and six-month maturities are among the most common, while the market is less liquid beyond 12 months. Amounts are commonly $25 million or more and can range into the billions.

Customers, both corporations and financial institutions such as hedge funds and mutual funds, can execute forwards with bank counter-party either as a swap or an outright transaction. In an outright forward, currency A is bought vs. currency B for delivery on the maturity date, which can be any business day beyond the spot date. The price is again the spot rate plus or minus the forward points, but no money changes hands until the maturity date. Outright forwards are often for odd dates and amounts; they can be for any size.

The most commonly traded currencies in the forward market are the same as on the spot market: EUR/USD, USD/JPY and GBP/USD.

Non-deliverable Forwards

Currencies for which there is no standard forward market can be traded via a non-deliverable forward. These are executed off-shore to avoid trading restrictions, are only executed as swaps and are cash-settled in dollars or euros. The most commonly traded currencies are the Chinese remnimbi, South Korean won, and Indian rupee.

Financial Instruments

Financial instruments are legal agreements that require one party to pay money or something else of value or to promise to pay under stipulated conditions to counterparty in exchange for the payment of interest, for the acquisition of rights, for premiums, or for indemnification against risk. In exchange for the payment of the money, the counterparty hopes to profit by receiving interest, capital gains, premiums, or indemnification for a loss event.

A financial instrument can be an actual document, such as a stock certificate or a loan contract, but, increasingly, financial instruments that have been standardized are stored in an electronic book-entry system as a record, and the parties to the contract are also recorded.

Some common financial instruments include checks, which transfer money from the payer, the writer of the check, to the payee, the receiver of the check. Stocks are issued by companies to raise money from investors. The investors pay for the stock, thereby giving money to the company, in exchange for an ownership interest in the company. Bonds are financial instruments that allow investors to lend money to the bond issuer for a stipulated amount of interest over a specified period.

Financial instruments can also be used by traders to either speculate about future prices, index levels, or interest rates, or some other financial measure, or to hedge financial risk. The 2 parties to these kinds of instruments are speculators and hedgers. Speculators attempt to predict future prices or some other financial measure, then buying or selling the financial instruments that would yield a profit if their view of the future should be correct. In other words, speculators bet about future prices or some other financial measure. For instance, if a speculator thought that the price of XYZ stock was going to go up, then he could buy a call option for the stock, which would be profitable if the stock does go up. If the option expires worthless, then the loss to the speculator is less than the loss that would have been incurred from actually owning the stock. Hedgers attempt to mitigate financial risk by buying or selling the financial instruments whose value would vary inversely with the hedged risk. For instance, if the owner of XYZ stock feared that the price might go down, but didn't want to sell before a specific time for tax purposes, then she could buy a put on the stock that would increase in value as the stock declined in value. If the stock goes up, then the put expires worthless, but the loss of the put premium would probably be less than the loss incurred if the stock declined.

Types of Financial Instruments

There are many types of financial instruments. Many instruments are custom agreements that the parties tailor to their own needs. However, many financial instruments are based on standardized contracts that have predetermined characteristics.

Some of the most common examples of financial instruments include the following:

- Exchanges of money for future interest payments and repayment of principal.
  - Loans and Bonds: A lender gives money to a borrower in exchange for regular payments of interest and principal.
  - Asset-Backed Securities: Lenders pool their loans together and sell them to investors. The lenders receive an immediate lump-sum payment and the investors receive the payments of interest and principal from the underlying loan pool.
- Exchanges of money for possible capital gains or interest.
  - Stocks: A company sells ownership interests in the form of stock to buyers of the stock.
  - Funds: Includes mutual funds, exchange-traded funds, real estate investment trusts, hedge funds, and many other funds. The fund buys other securities earning interest and capital gains which increases the share price of the fund. Investors of the fund may also receive interest payments.
- Exchanges of money for possible capital gains or to offset risk.
  - Options and Futures: Options and futures are bought and sold either for capital gains or to limit risk. For instance, the holder of XYZ stock may buy a put, which gives the holder of the put the right to sell XYZ stock for a specific price, called the strike price. Hence, the put increases in value as the underlying stock declines. The seller of the put receives money, called the premium, for the promise to buy XYZ stock at the strike price before the expiration date if the put buyer exercises her rights. The put seller hopes that the stock stays above the strike price so that the put expires worthless. In this case, the put seller gets to keep the premium as a capital gain.
  - Currency: Currency trading, likewise, is done for capital gains or to offset risk. It can also be used to earn interest, as is done in the carry trade. For instance, if a trader believed that the Euro was going to decline with respect to the United States dollar, then he could buy dollars with Euros, which is the same thing as selling Euros for dollars. If the Euro does decline with the respect to the dollar, then the trader can close the position by buying more Euros with the dollars received in the opening trade.
  - Swaps: Swaps are an exchange of interest rate payments calculated as a percentage of a notional principal that is paid at periodic intervals. One leg of the swap pays a fixed

rate of interest and the other leg pays a floating rate of interest. However, only the net amount is exchanged. For instance, if the interest based on the floating rate is $1000 greater than the interest based on the fixed-rate on a payment date, then the party receiving the fixed rate would pay $1000 to the party receiving the floating rate. The receiver of the fixed rate of interest enters into the swap usually to offset risk while the receiver of the floating rate generally hopes to profit from changes in the market interest rate. Usually, the floating rate is calculated as a spread above LIBOR or some other benchmark, such as Treasuries with comparable terms. If both legs of the swap pay in the same currency, and the swap is known as an interest rate swap, since both the fixed-rate and the floating rate are paid in the same currency. By contrast, a currency swap is the exchange of interest rate payments paid in different currencies, so the net amount is calculated based on the exchange rate on the payment date.

- Exchanges of money for protection against risk.
    - Insurance: Insurance contracts promise to pay for a loss event in exchange for a premium. For instance, a car owner buys car insurance so that he will be compensated for a financial loss that occurs as the result of an accident.

Primitive Securities and Financial Derivatives

A custom agreement can better suit the needs of the parties involved; however, such instruments are extremely illiquid precisely because they are tailored to specific parties. Furthermore, such instruments would take time for anyone to completely understand the details, which would be necessary to assess the profit potential and risk. The solution to this illiquidity is to create financial instruments based on standardized contracts with standard terms and conditions.

Such financial instruments are called securities, which can be easily traded in financial markets, such as organized exchanges and in the over-the-counter market. Furthermore, they are more easily stored in an electronic book-entry system, which saves the cost of storing and transporting the instruments for clearing and settlement. Examples of securities include stocks, bonds, options, and futures.

Securities are classified as to whether they are based on real assets or on other securities or some other benchmark. Primitive securities are based on real assets or on the promise or performance of the issuer. For example, bonds are based on the issuer's ability to pay interest and principal and stocks depend on the performance of the company that issued the stock. Financial derivatives are based on the underlying asset which consists of other financial instruments or some benchmark, such as stock indexes, interest rates, or credit events. For example, the value of stock options depends on the price of the underlying stock, and mortgage-backed securities depend on an underlying pool of mortgages.

Valuation of Financial Instruments

The value of any financial instrument depends on how much it is expected to pay, the likelihood of payment, and the present value of the payment. Obviously, the greater the expected return of the instrument, the greater its value. This is why the stock of a fast-growing company is highly valued, for instance.

A financial instrument that has less risk will have a higher value than a similar instrument that has more risk—the greater the risk, the more it lowers the value of the security because risk requires compensation.

Financial Services

Financial services can be defined as the products and services offered by institutions like banks of various kinds for the facilitation of various financial transactions and other related activities in the world of finance like loans, insurance, credit cards, investment opportunities and money management as well as providing information on the stock market and other issues like market trends.

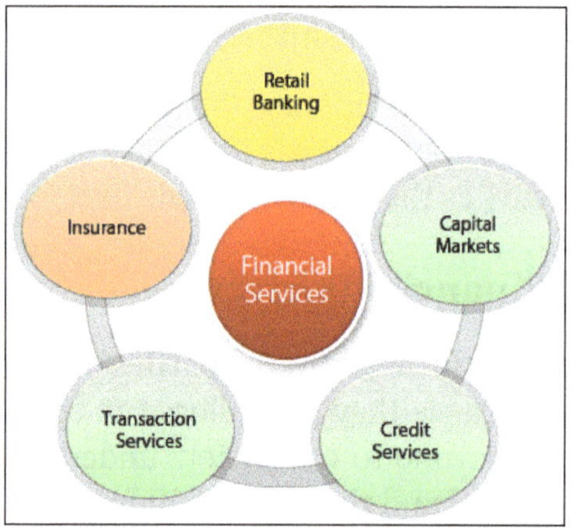

The finance industry encompasses a broad range of organizations that deal with the management of money. Among these organizations are banks, credit card companies, insurance companies, consumer finance companies, stock brokerages, investment funds and some government sponsored enterprises.

Functions of Financial Services

- Facilitating transactions (exchange of goods and services) in the economy.
- Mobilizing savings (for which the outlets would otherwise be much more limited).
- Allocating capital funds (notably to finance productive investment).
- Monitoring managers (so that the funds allocated will be spent as envisaged).
- Transforming risk (reducing it through aggregation and enabling it to be carried by those more willing to bear it).

Characteristics and Features of Financial Services

- Customer-Specific: Financial services are usually customer focused. The firms providing these services, study the needs of their customers in detail before deciding their financial strategy, giving due regard to costs, liquidity and maturity considerations. Financial services firms continuously remain in touch with their customers, so that they can design products which can cater to the specific needs of their customers. The providers of financial services constantly carry out market surveys, so they can offer new products much ahead of need and impending legislation. Newer technologies are being used to introduce innovative, customer friendly products and services which clearly indicate that the concentration of the providers of financial services is on generating firm/customer specific services.

- Intangibility: In a highly competitive global environment brand image is very crucial. Unless the financial institutions providing financial products and services have good image, enjoying the confidence of their clients, they may not be successful. Thus institutions have to focus on the quality and innovativeness of their services to build up their credibility.
- Concomitant: Production of financial services and supply of these services have to be concomitant. Both these functions i.e. production of new and innovative financial services and supplying of these services are to be performed simultaneously.
- Tendency to Perish: Unlike any other service, financial services do tend to perish and hence cannot be stored. They have to be supplied as required by the customers. Hence financial institutions have to ensure a proper synchronization of demand and supply.
- People Based Services: Marketing of financial services has to be people intensive and hence it's subjected to variability of performance or quality of service. The personnel in financial services organisation need to be selected on the basis of their suitability and trained properly, so that they can perform their activities efficiently and effectively.
- Market Dynamics: The market dynamics depends to a great extent, on socioeconomic changes such as disposable income, standard of living and educational changes related to the various classes of customers. Therefore financial services have to be constantly redefined and refined taking into consideration the market dynamics. The institutions providing financial services, while evolving new services could be proactive in visualizing in advance what the market wants, or being reactive to the needs and wants of their customers.

Scope of Financial Services

Financial services cover a wide range of activities. They can be broadly classified into two, namely:

Traditional Activities

Traditionally, the financial intermediaries have been rendering a wide range of services encompassing both capital and money market activities. They can be grouped under two heads, viz. Fund based activities and Non-fund based activities.

Fund based activities: The traditional services which come under fund based activities are the following:

- Underwriting or investment in shares, debentures, bonds, etc. of new issues (primary market activities).
- Dealing in secondary market activities.

- Participating in money market instruments like commercial papers, certificate of deposits, treasury bills, discounting of bills etc.
- Involving in equipment leasing, hire purchase, venture capital, seed capital etc.
- Dealing in foreign exchange market activities. Non fund based activities

Non fund based activities: Financial intermediaries provide services on the basis of non-fund activities also. This can be called 'fee based' activity. Today customers, whether individual or corporate, are not satisfied with mere provisions of finance. They expect more from financial services companies. Hence a wide variety of services, are being provided under this head. They include:

- Managing the capital issue i.e. management of pre-issue and post-issue activities relating to the capital issue in accordance with the SEBI guidelines and thus enabling the promoters to market their issue.
- Making arrangements for the placement of capital and debt instruments with investment institutions.
- Arrangement of funds from financial institutions for the clients project cost or his working capital requirements.
- Assisting in the process of getting all Government and other clearances.

Modern Activities

Beside the above traditional services, the financial intermediaries render innumerable services in recent times. Most of them are in the nature of non-fund based activity. In view of the importance, these activities have been in brief under the head 'New financial products and services'. However, some of the modern services provided by them are given in brief here under:

- Rendering project advisory services right from the preparation of the project report till the raising of funds for starting the project with necessary Government approvals.
- Planning for M&A and assisting for their smooth carry out.
- Guiding corporate customers in capital restructuring.
- Acting as trustees to the debenture holders.
- Recommending suitable changes in the management structure and management style with a view to achieving better results.
- Structuring the financial collaborations/joint ventures by identifying suitable joint venture partners and preparing joint venture agreements.
- Rehabilitating and restructuring sick companies through appropriate scheme of reconstruction and facilitating the implementation of the scheme.
- Hedging of risks due to exchange rate risk, interest rate risk, economic risk, and political risk by using swaps and other derivative products.

- Managing in-portfolio of large Public Sector Corporations.
- Undertaking risk management services like insurance services, buy-back options etc.
- Advising the clients on the questions of selecting the best source of funds taking into consideration the quantum of funds required, their cost, lending period etc.
- Guiding the clients in the minimization of the cost of debt and in the determination of the optimum debt-equity mix.
- Promoting credit rating agencies for the purpose of rating companies which want to go public by the issue of debt instrument.
- Undertaking services relating to the capital market, such as Clearing services, Registration and transfers, Safe custody of securities and Collection of income on securities.

Importance of Financial System

Promoting Investment

The presence of financial services creates more demand for products and the producer, in order to meet the demand from the consumer goes for more investment. At this stage, the financial services come to the rescue of the investor such as merchant banker through the new issue market, enabling the producer to raise capital.

The stock market helps in mobilizing more funds by the investor. Investments from abroad are attracted. Factoring and leasing companies, both domestic and foreign enable the producer not only to sell the products but also to acquire modern machinery/technology for further production.

Promoting Savings

Financial services such as mutual funds provide ample opportunity for different types of saving. In fact, different types of investment options are made available for the convenience of pensioners as well as aged people so that they can be assured of a reasonable return on investment without many risks.

For people interested in the growth of their savings, various reinvestment opportunities are provided. The laws enacted by the government regulate the working of various financial services in such a way that the interests of the public who save through these financial institutions are highly protected.

Minimizing the Risks

The risks of both financial services as well as producers are minimized by the presence of insurance companies. Various types of risks are covered which not only offer protection from the fluctuating business conditions but also from risks caused by natural calamities. Insurance is not only a source of finance but also a source of savings, besides minimizing the risks.

Maximizing the Returns

The presence of financial services enables businessmen to maximize their returns. This is possible due to the availability of credit at a reasonable rate. Producers can avail various types of credit facilities for acquiring assets. In certain cases, they can even go for leasing of certain assets of very high value.

Factoring companies enable the seller as well as producer to increase their turnover which also increases the profit. Even under stiff competition, the producers will be in a position to sell their products at a low margin. With a higher turnover of stocks, they are able to maximize their return.

Ensures Greater Yield

There is a subtle difference between return and yield. It is the yield which attracts more producers to enter the market and increase their production to meet the demands of the consumer. The financial services enable the producer to not only earn more profits but also maximize their wealth.

Financial services enhance their goodwill and induce them to go in for diversification. The stock market and the different types of derivative market provide ample opportunities to get a higher yield for the investor.

Economic Growth

The development of all the sectors is essential for the development of the economy. The financial services ensure equal distribution of funds to all the three sectors namely, primary, secondary and tertiary so that activities are spread over in a balanced manner in all the three sectors. This brings in a balanced growth of the economy as a result of which employment opportunities are improved.

The tertiary or service sector not only grows and this growth is an important sign of development of any economy. In a well-developed country, service sector plays a major role and it contributes more to the economy than the other two sectors.

Economic Development

Financial services enable the consumers to obtain different types of products and services by which they can improve their standard of living. Purchase of car, house and other essential as well as luxurious items are made possible through hire purchase, leasing and housing finance companies. Thus, the consumer is compelled to save while he enjoys the benefits of the assets which he has acquired with the help of financial services.

Benefit to Government

The presence of financial services enables the government to raise both short-term and long-term funds to meet both revenue and capital expenditure. Through the money market, government raises short term funds by the issue of Treasury Bills. These are purchased by commercial banks from out of their depositors' money.

In addition to this, the government is able to raise long-term funds by the sale of government securities in the securities market which forms apart of financial market. Even foreign exchange requirements of the government can be met in the foreign exchange market.

The most important benefit for any government is the raising of finance without offering any security. In this way, the financial services are a big boon to the government.

Expands Activities of Financial Institutions

The presence of financial services enables financial institutions to not only raise finance but also get an opportunity to disburse their funds in the most profitable manner. Mutual funds, factoring, credit cards, hire purchase finance are some of the services which get financed by financial institutions.

The financial institutions are in a position to expand their activities and thus diversify the use of their funds for various activities. This ensures economic dynamism.

Capital Market

One of the barometers of any economy is the presence of a vibrant capital market. If there is hectic activity in the capital market, then it is an indication of the presence of a positive economic condition. The financial services ensure that all the companies are able to acquire adequate funds to boost production and to reap more profits eventually.

In the absence of financial services, there will be paucity of funds which will adversely affect the working of companies and will only result in a negative growth of the capital market. When the capital market is more active, funds from foreign countries also flow in. Hence, the changes in capital market are mainly due to the availability of financial services.

Promotion of Domestic and Foreign Trade

Financial services ensure promotion of domestic as well as foreign trade. The presence of factoring and forfaiting companies ensures increasing sale of goods in the domestic market and export of goods in the foreign market. Banking and insurance services further contribute to step up such promotional activities.

Balanced Regional Development

The government monitors the growth of economy and regions that remain backward economically are given fiscal and monetary benefits through tax and cheaper credit by which more investment is promoted. This generates more production, employment, income, demand and ultimately increases in prices.

References

- Financial-system: investopedia.com, Retrieved 18 April, 2019
- Spot-market, business, reference: readyratios.com, Retrieved 27 May, 2019
- Concept-of-financial-market, financial-markets, business-studies, guides: toppr.com, Retrieved 24 March, 2019

- Spot-market, dictionary: investinganswers.com, Retrieved 1 June, 2019
- What-are-futures-definition-and-examples: thebalance.com, Retrieved 21 March, 2019
- Difference-between-spot-market-and-futures-market: knowledgiate.com, Retrieved 12 April, 2019
- Financial-instruments, banking, money: thismatter.com, Retrieved 23 June, 2019
- Definition-of-financial-services, business-finance: mbaknol.com, Retrieved 3 August, 2019
- Financial-services-meaning-importance: accountlearning.com, Retrieved 19 May, 2019

3

Financial Statements and Analysis

The formal records of the financial activities and position of entities such as a person or business are known as financial statements. The process of analyzing and reviewing a firm's financial statements for the purpose of making informed business decisions is termed as financial statement analysis. The topics elaborated in this chapter will help in gaining a better perspective about the different types of financial statements and their analysis.

A financial statement is the combination of the three major reports on a business. It will contain the cash flow statement, the income statement and the balance sheet of the business. All three together produce an overall picture of the health of the business.

Importance of Financial Statement

It is the complete report on the health of the business taking in cash flow, income and the balance sheet. The financial statement determines if a business has to ability to repay loans, if it has the cash flow to meet bills and purchase stock. It will also tell from where the business is generating cash and where the cash goes.

The financial statement tells if the business is profitable, if it will stay profitable and if there are any large problems looming, such as a continuous drop in sales over time. Reading the financial statement will give an overall view of the condition of the business and if there are any warnings signs of possible future problems. A bank or other such institution will look to the financial statement as the first indicator of how the business is performing and if there is a need for further investigation.

Prerequisites for a Company to Prepare Financial Statement

Every business will ready a financial statement to go with their end of year results, to give interested parties the overview of how the business is functioning. If a business is looking to increase credit facilities with a bank or trying to raise capital for an expansion, it will produce a financial statement for the end of a fiscal quarter or the most recent month. When preparing a financial statement for such purposes the best practice is to use general accountancy language, understood by all parties. A financial statement that may accompany an end of year report and read just by employees is often in terms familiar to just those involved.

Often a government body may request a financial statement for tax purposes and the company will need to produce one of high quality using generally accepted guidelines. A bank or investors may also request a financial statement without warning, if they are concerned about the profitability or otherwise of the company. For these reason alone it is vital for any business to keep good and current records so that a financial statement is easy and quick to produce.

Income Statement

The income statement, also called the profit and loss statement, is a report that shows the income, expenses, and resulting profits or losses of a company during a specific time period. The income statement is the first financial statement typically prepared during the accounting cycle because the net income or loss must be calculated and carried over to the statement of owner's equity before other financial statements can be prepared.

The income statement calculates the net income of a company by subtracting total expenses from total income. This calculation shows investors and creditors the overall profitability of the company as well as how efficiently the company is at generating profits from total revenues.

The income and expense accounts can also be subdivided to calculate gross profit and the income or loss from operations. These two calculations are best shown on a multi-step income statement. Gross profit is calculated by subtracting cost of goods sold from net sales. Operating income is calculated by subtracting operating expenses from the gross profit.

Unlike the balance sheet, the income statement calculates net income or loss over a range of time. For example annual statements use revenues and expenses over a 12-month period, while quarterly statements focus on revenues and expenses incurred during a 3-month period.

Purpose of Income Statement

What is an Income Statement used for?

There are several different types of income statements that are created for different reasons. For example, the year-end statement that is prepared annually for stockholders and potential investors don't do much good for management while they are trying to run the company throughout the year. Thus, interim financial statements are prepared for management to check the status of operations during the year. Management also typically prepares departmental statements that break down revenue and expense numbers by business segment.

In the end, the main purpose of all profit and loss statements is to communicate the profitability and business activities of the company with end users. Each one of these end users has their own use for this information. Let's look at who uses the P&L and what they use it for.

Who uses an Income Statement?

There are two different groups of people who use this financial statement: internal users and external users.

Internal users like company management and the board of directors use this statement to analyze the business as a whole and make decisions on how it is run. For example, they use performance numbers to gauge whether they should open new branch, close a department, or increase production of a product.

External users like investors and creditors, on the other hand, are people outside of the company who have no source of financial information about the company except published reports. Investors want to know how profitable a company is and whether it will grow and become more profitable in the future. They are mainly concerned with whether or not investing their money is the company with yield them a positive return.

Creditors, on the other hand, aren't as concerned about profitability as investors are. Creditors are more concerned with a company's cash flow and if they are generating enough income to pay back their loans.

Competitors are also external users of financial statements. They use competitors' P&L to gauge how well other companies are doing in their space and whether or not they should enter new markets and try to compete with other companies.

Format of Income Statement

There are two income statement formats that are generally prepared:

- Single-step income statement: The single step statement only shows one category of income and one category of expenses. This format is less useful of external users because they can't calculate many efficiency and profitability ratios with this limited data.
- Multi-step income statement: The multi-step statement separates expense accounts into more relevant and usable accounts based on their function. Cost of goods sold, operating and non-operating expenses are separated out and used to calculate gross profit, operating income, and net income.

In both income statement formats, revenues are always presented before expenses. Expenses can be listed alphabetically or by total dollar amount. Either presentation is acceptable. P&L expenses can also be formatted by the nature and the function of the expense.

All income statements have a heading that display's the company name, title of the statement and the time period of the report. For example, an annual income statement issued by ABC Inc. would have the following heading:

- ABC Inc,
- Income Statement,
- For the Year Ended December 31, 2015.

Income Statement Example

Single Step Income Statement

This example income statement is a single-step statement because it only lists expenses in one main category. Although this statement might not be extremely useful for investors looking for detailed information, it does accurately calculate the net income for the year.

ABC Inc. Income Statement For the Year Ended December XXX			
Revenues			
	Merchandise Sales	$ 24,800	
	Music Lesson Income	3,000	
	Total Revenues		$ 27,800
Expenses			
	Cost of Goods Sold	10,200	
	Depreciation expense	2,000	
	Wage expense	750	
	Rent expense	500	
	Interest expense	500	
	Supplies expense	500	
	Utilities expense	400	
	Total Expenses		14,850
Net Income			$ 12,950

Components of an Income Statement

The income statement may have minor variations between different companies, as expenses and income will be dependent on the type of operations or business conducted. However, there are several generic line items that are commonly seen in any income statement. The most common income statement items include:

Revenue/Sales

Sales Revenue is the company's revenue from sales or services, displayed at the very top of the statement. This value will be the gross of the costs associated with creating the goods sold or in providing services. Some companies have multiple revenue streams that add to a total revenue line.

Cost of Goods Sold (COGS)

Cost of Goods Sold (COGS) is a line-item that aggregates the direct costs associated with selling products to generate revenue. This line item can also be called Cost of Sales if the company is a service business. Direct costs can include labor, parts, materials, and an allocation of other expenses such as depreciation.

Gross Profit

Gross Profit Gross profit is calculated by subtracting Cost of Goods Sold (or Cost of Sales) from Sales Revenue.

Marketing, Advertising and Promotion Expenses

Most businesses have some expenses related to selling goods and/or services. Marketing, advertising, and promotion expenses are often grouped together as they are similar expenses, all related to selling.

General and Administrative Expenses

SG&A Expenses include the selling, general, and the administrative section that contains all other indirect costs associated with running the business. This includes salaries and wages, rent and office expenses, insurance, travel expenses, and sometimes depreciation and amortization, along with other operational expenses. Entities may, however, elect to separate out depreciation and amortization in its own section.

EBITDA

EBITDA, while not present in all income statements, stands for Earnings Before Interest, Tax, Depreciation, and Amortization. It is calculated by subtracting SG&A expenses (excluding amortization and depreciation) from gross profit.

Depreciation and Amortization Expense

Depreciation and amortization are non-cash expenses that are created by accountants to spread out the cost of capital assets such as Property, Plant, and Equipment (PP&E).

Operating Income (or EBIT)

Operating Income represents what's earned from regular business operations. In other words, it's the profit before any non-operating income, non-operating expenses, interest, or taxes are subtracted from revenues. EBIT is a term commonly used in finance and stands for Earnings Before Interest and Taxes.

Interest

Interest Expense: It is common for companies to split out interest expense and interest income as a separate line item in the income statement. This is done in order to reconcile the difference between EBIT and EBT. Interest expense is determined by the debt schedule.

Other Expenses

Businesses often have other expenses that are unique to their industry. Other expenses may include things such as fulfilment, technology, research and development (R&D), stock-based compensation (SBC), impairment charges, gains/losses on the sale of investments, foreign exchange impacts, and many other expenses that are industry or company-specific.

EBT (Pre-Tax Income)

EBT stands for Earnings Before Tax, also known as pre-tax income, and is found by subtracting interest expense from Operating Income. This is the final subtotal before arriving at net income.

Income Taxes

Income Taxes refer to the relevant taxes charged on pre-tax income. The total tax expense can consist of both current taxes and future taxes.

Net Income

Net Income is calculated by deducting income taxes from pre-tax income. This is the amount that flows into retained earnings on the balance sheet, after deductions for any dividends.

A Real Example of an Income Statement

Below is an example of Amazon's consolidated statement of operations, or income statement, for the years ended December 31, 2015 – 2017. Take a look at the P&L and then read a breakdown of it below.

XYZ.COM, INC. Consolidated Statements of Operations (in millions, except per share data)			
	Year Ended December 31,		
	2015	2016	2017
Net product sales	$ 79,268	$ 94,665	$ 118,573
Net service sales	27,738	41,322	59,293
Total net sales	107,006	135,987	177,866
Operating expenses:			
Cost of sales	71,651	88,265	111,934
Fulfilment	13,410	17,619	25,249
Marketing	5,254	7,233	10,069
Technology and content	12,540	16,085	22,620
General and administrative	1,747	2,432	3,674
Other operating expenses, net	171	167	214
Total operating expenses	104,773	131,801	173,760
Operating income	2,233	4,186	4,106
Interest income	50	100	202
Interest expense	(459)	(484)	(848)
Other income (expense), net	(256)	90	346
Total non-operating income (expense)	(665)	(294)	(300)
Income before income taxes	1,568	3,892	3,806
Provision for income taxes	(950)	(1,425)	(769)
Equity-method investment activity, net of tax	(22)	(96)	(4)
Net income	$ 596	$ 2,371	$ 3,033
Basic earnings per share	$ 1.28	$ 5.01	$ 6.32
Diluted earnings per share	$ 1.25	$ 4.90	$ 6.15
Weight-average shares used in computation of earnings per share:			
Basic	467	474	480
Diluted	477	484	493

Starting at the top we see that Amazon has two different revenue streams – products and services – which combine to form total revenue.

There is no gross profit subtotal, as the cost of sales is grouped with all other expenses, which include fulfillment, marketing, technology, content, general and administration (G&A), and other expenses.

After deducting all the above expenses we finally arrive at the first subtotal on the income statement, Operating Income (also known as EBIT or Earnings Before Interest and Taxes).

Everything below Operating Income is not related to the ongoing operation of the business – such as non-operating expenses, provision for income taxes (i.e., future taxes), and equity-method investment activity (profits or losses from minority investments), net of tax.

Finally, we arrive at the net income (or net loss), which is then divided by the weighted average shares outstanding to determine the Earnings Per Share (EPS).

Recognition Principle

The revenue recognition principle provides guidelines for reporting revenue in the income statement. The principle generally requires that revenue be recognized in the financial statements when: (1) realized or realizable and (2) earned. Revenues are realized when products or services are exchanged or performed for cash or claims to cash. Revenues also are realizable when a company's things of monetary value (assets), such as products and debts owed to the company, are readily convertible into cash. Revenues are considered earned when a business has substantially accomplished what it must do to be entitled to the benefits represented by the revenues. Recognition through sales or the providing (performance) of services provides a uniform and reasonable test of realization. Limited exceptions to the basic revenue principle include recognizing revenue during production (on long-term construction contracts), at the completion of production (for many commodities), and subsequent to the sale at the time of cash collection (on installment sales).

In recognizing expenses, accountants rely on the matching principle because it requires that efforts (expenses) be matched with accomplishments (revenues) whenever it is reasonable and practical to do so. For example, matching (associating) the cost of goods sold with revenues from the interrelated sales that resulted directly and jointly from the same transaction as the expense is reasonable and practical. To recognize costs for which it is difficult to adopt some association with revenues, accountants use a rational and systematic allocation policy that assigns expenses to the periods during which the related assets are expected to provide benefits, such as depreciation, amortization, and insurance. Some costs are charged to the current period as expenses (or losses) merely because no future benefit is anticipated, no connection with revenue is apparent, or no allocation is rational and systematic under the circumstances, i.e., under an immediate recognition principle.

The current operating concept of income includes only those value changes and events that are controllable by management and that are incurred in the current period from ordinary, normal, and recurring operations. Any unusual and nonrecurring items of income or loss would be recognized directly in the statement of retained earnings. Under this concept of income, investors are primarily interested in continuing income from operations.

In the late 1990s, however, the FASB moved closer to adopting all-inclusive or comprehensive income reporting. The all-inclusive concept of income includes the total changes in equity recognized during a specific period, except for dividend distributions and capital transactions. this concept requires companies to include unusual and nonrecurring income or loss items in their income statements for the appropriate accounting period.

Consolidated Income Statements

Accountants prepare consolidated income statements by combining the revenues, gains, expenses, and losses of a parent company's accounts the accounts of its subsidiary operations. A subsidiary is a company with more than 50 percent of its voting stock owned by a parent company. Revenues and expenses that result from transactions between parent and subsidiary companies—intercompany transactions—are not included or are eliminated because they do not affect the assets of the overall company, when viewed as a consolidted operation. Intercompany transactions include sales between parent and subsidiary companies and rent received from or paid by affiliated companies to each other.

Advantages of Income Statements

- Information about revenue: Income statement provides thorough information about normal costs such as COGS and expenses associated with managing operations. It also accounts for additional costs including statutory taxes which are applied to gross revenue to arrive at net profit. Revenue also includes income from indirect sources such as interest income from business investments.
- Providing for Investor Analysis: Income Statement is an important document to provide information to prospective investors looking to buy stake in the business. Income statement makes it easier for calculation of earnings per share using the net profit. The higher the earnings per share, the better the prospect of business is going forward. Income statement is therefore an important checklist for the investors to gain stake in the business.
- Tracking the performance of business: Performance means profit and income statement, it is both gross profit and net profit. Performance growth is bottom line growth which needs to be tracked on regular basis. While analyzing revenue over various accounting periods, overall performance of the business must be reviewed and opined on. This helps the user to spot the trend early as possible and eliminate one-time charges that may affect the data.
- Means for Effective forecasting: Financial modelling requires the effective forecast of future accounting periods. Generally, the forecasts are prepared to sketch the future over 3 and 5 years. Income statements perfectly anticipate problems that may arise in the future.
- Overview of Cash Flows: Although cash flow statement is prepared specially for the movement of cash, the income statement can show eagle eye view of the movement of cash along with accruals and receivables on one accounting statement. This helps in making adjustments, following the cash trail and ultimately saving cash access for the future.
- Operating and Non-operating Income: Income Statement segregates into operating income and non-operating income. This helps the business owner to analyze how much

of the revenue is derived from operating i.e. regular business activities and how much income is from non-business activities. Robust operating income with growth thereon is a good sign for healthy businesses. It is also needed to be understood that operating income forms at least 80 % of the total revenue of the business. Non-operating income is very irregular income or one-off income that does not impact the financial viability of the business.

Limitations of Income Statement

Income statement is of vital importance for the users of the financial statements. However, it suffers from the following limitations:

- The accounting process is based on various assumptions and estimates. Therefore, the net income (or loss) measured by preparing an income statement is not absolutely accurate. An example of estimates used in the accounting process is the depreciation which is computed on the basis of estimated useful life of assets such as building, plants and equipment etc.
- The use of judgments and estimates in the accounting process enables management to use such figures that would generate desired net income or net loss figure for the period.
- A manipulation in net income is possible by using a particular inventory valuation method such as FIFO method, LIFO method and average costing method. The company may use such method that generates the desired result.
- While preparing income statement we take into account only those activities whose value can be objectively measured. For example, a sound customer's relation policy can develop a good customer base that can certainly be beneficial for a profitable business operation but its value cannot be objectively measured unless evidenced by an actual business transaction.

Gross Income

Gross income refers to the total income earned by an individual on a paycheck before taxes and other deductions. It comprises all incomes received by an individual from all sources – including wages, rental income, interest income, and dividends. For example, if the revenue earned by an individual for rendering consultancy services amounts to $300,000, the figure represents the gross income earned by that individual.

Gross income is referred to as gross profit when preparing financial statements for companies, and it equals the revenues from the sale of goods or services less the cost of goods sold. The revenue sources may comprise income from selling goods and services, intellectual properties, income from rental property, capital gains from investments, etc. The gross profit is a line item in the profit and loss statement.

Calculating Gross Income

The gross income of an individual is often a figure required by lenders when deciding whether or not to advance credit to an individual. The same applies to landlords when determining whether a potential tenant will be able to pay the rent on time. It is also the starting point when calculating taxes due to the government.

Gross Income for an Individual

The gross income for an individual is the amount of money earned before any deductions or taxes are taken out. An individual employed on a full-time basis has their annual salary or wages before tax as their gross income. However, a full-time employee may also have other sources of income that must be considered when calculating their income.

For example, any dividends on stocks held by an individual should be factored into the gross income. Other incomes that should be considered include income from rental property and interest income from investments and savings.

Example - Assume that John earns an annual income of $100,000 from his financial management consultancy work. John also earns $70,000 in rental income from his real estate properties, $10,000 in dividends from shares he owns at Company XYZ, and $5,000 in interest income from his savings account. John's income can be calculated as follows:

Gross Income = 100,000 + 70,000 + 10,000 + 5,000 = $185,000.

Gross Income for a Business

Gross profit is an item in the income statement of a business, and it is the company's profit for the year before deducting any expenses and taxes. It represents the revenue that a company earned from selling its goods or services after subtracting the direct costs incurred in producing the goods being sold.

Direct costs can include expenses such as labor costs, equipment used in the production process, supply costs, cost of raw materials, and costs of shipping. Taxes are not deducted since they are not directly related to the production and sale of the product.

The formula for calculating the gross income, or gross profit, of a business is as follows:

Gross Income = Gross Revenue – Cost of Goods Sold.

Example:

Assume that the gross revenue of ABC, a paint manufacturing company, totaled $1,300,000 and the expenses were as follows:

- Cost of raw materials: $150,000.
- Supply costs: $60,000.
- Cost of equipment: $340,000.
- Labor costs: $150,000.
- Packaging and shipping: $100,000.

The gross profit is calculated as follows:

Gross Income = (1,300,000) – (150,000 + 60,000 + 340,000 + 150,000 + 100,000)

= (1,300,000) – (800,000) = $500,000

Net Income

Net income, also called net profit, is a calculation that measures the amount of total revenues that exceed total expenses. It other words, it shows how much revenues are left over after all expenses have been paid. This is the amount of money that the company can save for a rainy day, use to pay off debt, invest in new projects, or distribute to shareholders. Many people refer to this measurement as the bottom line because it generally appears at the bottom of the income statement.

Investors, creditors, and company management tend to focus on the net income calculation because it is a good indicator of the company's financial position and ability to manage assets efficiently. Investors what to know that their investment will continue to appreciate and that the company will have enough cash to pay them a dividend. Creditors want to know the company if financially sound and able to pay off its debt with successful operations. Company management is typically concerned with both investor and credit concerns along with the company's ability to pay salaries and bonuses. So we've established that is an important measurement, but what is net income?

Formula

The net income formula is calculated by subtracting total expenses from total revenues. Many different textbooks break the expenses down into subcategories like cost of goods sold, operating expenses, interest, and taxes, but it doesn't matter. All revenues and all expenses are used in this formula.

Net Income

Net Income = Total Revenues – Total Expenses.

The net income equation is quite simple. It measures excess revenues over total expenses. This way investors, creditors, and management can see how efficient the company was a producing profit.

Example: Aaron owns a database and server technology company that he runs out of his house. He manages data, security, and servers for many different medical companies that require strict compliance with federal rules. As such, Aaron is able to make large amounts of revenue while keeping his expenses low. Here is a list of his income statement items for the year.

- Revenues $200,000.
- Computer expenses $10,000.
- Salaries $50,000.
- Utilities $5,000.
- Taxes $2,500.

Aaron would compute his annual net income by subtracting total expenses ($67,500) from total income.

Net Income

$ 132,500 = $ 200,000 – $ 67,500.

Since Aaron's revenues exceed his expenses, he will show $132,500 profit. If Aaron only made $50,000 of revenues for the year, he would not have negative earnings, however. Instead, he would have a net loss of $17,500. The net income definition goes against the concept of negative profits. If the company loses money, it is classified as a loss. If the company makes money, it is considered income or profits.

Analysis

A net profit is one of the most basic measurements in accounting and finance. Obviously, higher profits are almost always preferable to lower profits. Businesses can use higher profits to reinvest in new equipment, eliminate debt, and even make payments to shareholders, but higher profits aren't always favorable.

Since corporations pay taxes on their profits, it would make sense that management would try to minimize profits on a tax basis to reduce the taxable income. This is why many companies have a book to tax adjustment at the end of each year. They have to adjust their book income to reflect certain tax options that are being taken advantage of. For instance, some companies might use LIFO for tax purposes and FIFO for book purposes in order to reduce the income shown on the tax return. Accelerated depreciation is also used for the same reason.

Conversely, many companies are required to meet certain profits each year in order to maintain loan covenants with their lenders. These covenants present a problem. On one hand, management wants to show less profit to reduce taxes. On the other hand, they need to show more profit to meet lender's requirements. This is where earnings and net profit can get manipulated. Certain revenue recognition rules can be applied loosely in order to meet management's expectations. That is why it's important to read the financial statement footnotes and understand what measurements were used and how to find net income in the financial statements.

Income Tax

Income tax refers to annual taxes levied by the federal government and most state governments on individual and business income. By law, businesses and individuals must file federal and state income tax returns every year to determine whether they owe taxes. Governments use the taxes they collect to fund their activities.

Example: Income tax is applied to both earned income (wages, salaries and commission) and unearned income (dividends, interest and rents).

The U.S. and many other countries employ a progressive income tax system in which higher income earners pay a higher tax rate compared to their lower earning counterparts. The intent of progressive systems is to distribute wealth more evenly across a population.

Here's an example of how a progressive tax is structured: Assume you are single and report $80,000 in taxable income for the 2010 tax year (filing in 2011). In accordance with the federal tax rates defined for single filers in 2010, the first $8,350 of your income is taxed at 10%; the next $8,351 through $33,950 of earnings are taxed at 15%; and the remaining $33,951 through $80,000 of your earnings are taxed at 25%.

Importance of Income Tax

Income taxes reduce the amount of earnings that individuals and businesses are allowed to keep. There are a couple of strategies investors can use to retain more of their income. The first is investing in tax-advantaged assets like U.S. government bonds and municipal bonds.

The second is to open a retirement account that is tax-advantaged. An IRA, 401(k), SEP IRA and Roth IRA are all examples of tax-advantaged accounts. Investors can hold any asset they like within these accounts. The tax benefits of a retirement account don't depend on the investments you hold in the account.

The Balance Sheet

The balance sheet is one of the most important financial statements and is useful for doing accounting analysis and modeling. Balance Sheet is the "Snapshot" of a company's financial position at a given moment Balance Sheet reports the amount of a company's.

- Assets: Current assets/Long-term assets.
- Liabilities: Current Liabilities/Long-term liabilities.
- Stockholders' (or owner's) equity: Common stock/Retained earnings.

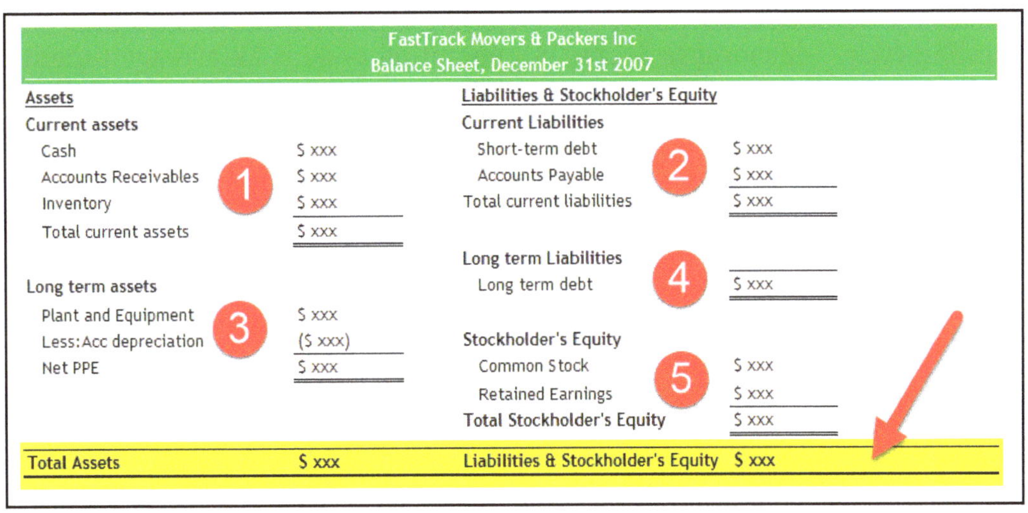

Remember the most important equation while forming the Balance Sheet:

Assets = Liabilities + Shareholders' Equity.

Unlike Income Statement, Balance Sheets are much less complicated (however, there are many items you need to include under few heads). And Balance Sheets portray the overall picture of a company's financial affair altogether.

Balance Sheets can't be formed without first setting up the income statement. Because we need to know the retained earnings from the income statement. Through Income Statement, we can ascertain the net profit. The portion of net profit that is not distributed among the shareholders is called "retained earnings".

Balance Sheet Structure

Assets are arranged on the left-hand side and the liabilities and shareholders' equity would be on the right-hand side. However, in most of the cases, companies put the assets first and then they set up liabilities and at the bottom shareholders' equity. The total assets should be equal to the total liabilities and total shareholders' equity.

Assets = Liabilities + Shareholders' Equity.

Balance Sheet Format is as follows:

- Current Assets,
- Current Liabilities,
- Long Term Assets,
- Long Term Liabilities,
- Shareholder's Equity.

Current Assets

Current assets are expected to be consumed, sold, or converted into cash either in one year or in the operating cycle, whichever is longer. An operating cycle is an average time it takes to convert an investment in inventory back into cash. Current assets are presented in order of liquidity.

	Schedule No.	Figures at the end of current financial year	Figures as at the end of previous financial year
1. Sources of funds			
a) Shareholders funds			
i) Capital			
ii) Reserves and surpluses			
b) Loan Funds			
i) Secured loans			
ii) Unsecured loans			
Total			

b) Investments c) Current Assets, loans and advances i) Inventories ii) Sundry debtors iii) Cash and bank balances iv) Loan and advances Less : Current Liabilities i) Liabilities ii) Provisions Net Current Assets d) Miscellaneous Expenditure to extent not written off or adjusted e) Profit and loss a/c (Debit) Total			

Assets are arranged on the basis of how quickly they can be converted into cash (means how liquid they are). That means, in the balance sheet, the first things we will put in are current assets. Under current assets, these are the items you can consider:

- Cash and Cash Equivalents: Cash could also include an amount required to be held for deposit to satisfy the terms of a lending agreement. Cash equivalents are securities (e.g. US Treasury bills) that have term of less than or equal to 90 days.
- Short-term investments: Short Term Marketable Securities primarily includes Bond Investments and Capital Stock Investments. Short-Term Marketable Securities are not as ready as money in your account, but they provided added cushion if some immediate need were to arise.
- Inventories: Inventory consists of merchandise a business owns but has not sold. Classified as current assets because investor assumes that inventory can be sold in the near future, turning it into cash.
- Trade and other Receivables: Money that is owed to the company by the customers.
- Prepayments and Accrued Income: Sometimes a business will have to pay for goods or services before they actually receive the product. Expenses that have been paid in the current fiscal period but that will not be subtracted from revenue until a subsequent fiscal period.

Other current assets also include Derivative Assets, Current Income Tax Assets, Assets Held for Sale etc. Current Assets will look like following:

	X (in US $)	Y (in US $)
Cash	10000	3000
Cash Equivalent	1000	500
Accounts Receivable	1000	5000
Inventories	500	6000
Total Current Assets	12500	14500

Current Liabilities

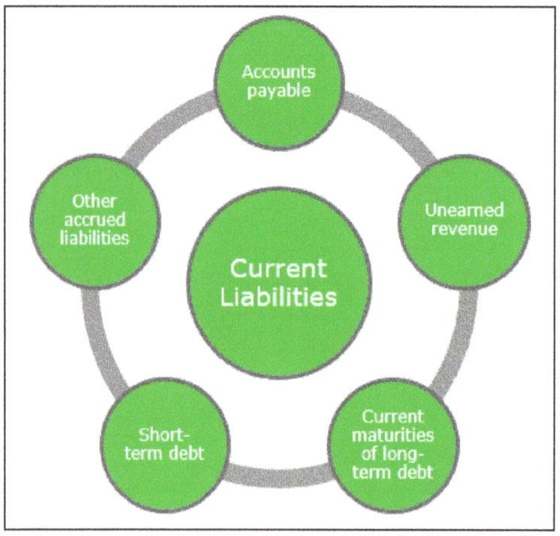

Current Liabilities are probable future payments of assets or services that a firm is obligated to make as a result of previous operations. These obligations are expected to require the use of existing current assets or the creation of other current liabilities.

"Current Liabilities" generally include the following:

- Accounts Payable: Amounts owed to suppliers for goods and services that have been purchased on credit. Accounts payable are debts that must be paid off within a given period of time in order to avoid default.
- Short Term Debt: Short Term Debt is also referred to as Notes Payable. Sometimes when the demand is high, a company may raise short-term loans to stock up the inventory (Utilizing leverage).
- Current Maturities of Long-Term Debt: Any portion of long-term debt that is to be repaid within a year of the balance sheet date is reclassified from the noncurrent liability section to the current liability section of the title, current maturities of long-term debt.
- Unearned Revenues: Unearned revenue is created when customers pay for services or products before delivery.
- Other Accrued Liabilities: This could include Money owed to employees as salary and bonus that the company has not yet paid.

Other than that, current liabilities also include accounts payable, sales taxes payable, income taxes payable, interest payable, bank overdrafts, payroll taxes payable, customer deposits in advance, accrued expenses, short-term loans, current maturities of long-term debt etc.

	X (in US $)	Y (in US $)
Accounts Payable	4000	3000
Current Taxes Payable	5000	6000
Current Long-term Liabilities	11000	9000
Total Current Liabilities	20000	18000

Long Term Assets

Long term assets are typically physical assets that the company own and are employed in the production process of the firm and have a useful life greater than one year. Long term assets are not for sale to the firm's customers (they are not inventory).

Long-term assets can be classified into three main categories:

- Tangible Assets: These assets have physical existence. Assets like Real Estate, Buildings, Offices, Machinery, Furniture, and Telephone belong to this category. The process of allocating the cost of tangible assets over the useful life is called "depreciation".
- Natural Resources: These assets have an economic value derived from Earth and used up over time. Examples include Oil fields, mines etc.
- Intangible Assets: These assets have no physical existence and they cannot be felt or touched or seen. Examples include trademarks, copyrights, patents, franchise, and goodwill. The cost of intangible assets is allocated to periods over which it provides benefits through a process called amortization.

Long term assets are generally reported at their carrying value or book value. If the asset has lost its revenue generating ability, it may be written down (asset impairment, amount of written down is recorded as loss).

Long Term Liabilities

Long-Term Liabilities are obligations that are not expected to require the use of current assets or not expected to create current liabilities within one year or the normal operating cycle (whichever is longer).

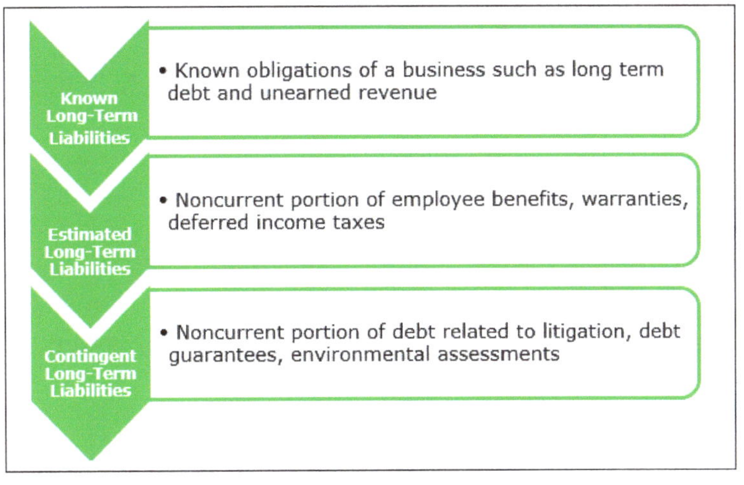

- In most cases, it contains long-term debt. Long-term debt is subject to various covenants or restrictions. Long-term debt can be obtained from many sources and may differ in the structure of interest and principal payments and the claims creditors have on the assets of the firm.
- Bonds are contracted between the borrowers and the lender that obligates the bond issuer to make payments to the bondholder over the life of the bond.

- Creditors' claims could be subdivided into two types:
    - Senior.
    - Subordinate.

Shareholder's Equity

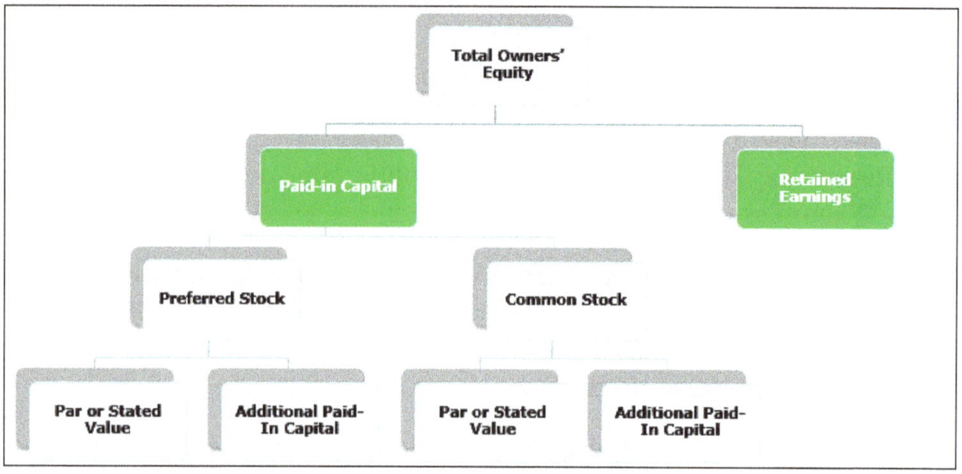

Stockholders' Equity is the residual interest of the stockholders in the assets of the corporation. There are two primary sources of Equity – Paid-in Capital and Retained Earnings.

Each share of common stock conveys certain rights to the:

- Attend stockholders' meetings.
- Elect directors and vote on other matters.
- Receive dividends as declared by the board of directors.
- Preemptive right: The preemptive right is a shareholder's right to purchase a proportionate amount of any new stock issued at a later date.

Shareholder's Accounts need to be maintained for:

- Par Value (Par value has no economic significance).
- Additional Paid-in Capital.

Preferred stock has certain preferences or features not possessed by common stock.

Method to Read the Balance Sheet

Balance Sheet provides useful information about company's financial affairs. As an investor, you need to know how to read the Balance Sheet to be able to extract the most of it.

These are the steps that can help you read Balance Sheets:

- The first thing is really the first thing. You need to know the balance sheet equation. You need to see whether the total assets and total liabilities & total shareholders' equity are equal. Assets = Liabilities + Equity.

- Then you will look at the current assets. These assets will give ideas about the liquidity of the company and where the company expects to liquidate the assets from. These assets can easily be converted into cash.
- Then you should follow the non-current assets which include fixed assets and intangible assets (like patents etc.) as well. You need to find out the wear and tear (depreciation) and other expenses and whether they have been taken into account or not. Match it up with the income statement and cash flow statement to understand whether there is any loophole or not.
- Then you need to learn about the liabilities of the company. They can be both current and non-current. Current liabilities are items which can be dealt quickly and the keyword for it is "short term". In the case of non-current liabilities, it takes longer for the firm to pay off which includes long-term loan and other payables.
- The last step is to look through the shareholders' equity. Check out the retained earnings and compare it with a net profit. And you will get an idea about how much dividend is being paid (if any).
- It is important for you to know that you shouldn't skip any step mentioned above. Don't look at shareholders' equity until you have completed looking at all other items in the balance sheet. The best way is to keep a pen and paper and take notes while looking through the items and matching them up with the other financial statements.

Balance Sheet Example – Vertical Analysis

For understanding Colgate's Balance sheet trends over the period of time, we can perform Vertical Analysis. Vertical Analysis on the Balance Sheet normalizes the Balance Sheet and expresses each item in the percentage of total assets/liabilities. It helps us to understand how each item of the balance sheet has moved over the years.

- For each year, Balance Sheet line items are divided by its respective year's Top Assets (or Total Liabilities) number.
- For example, for Accounts Receivables, we calculate as Receivables / Total Assets. Likewise for other balance sheet items.

	Dec-07	Dec-08	Dec-09	Dec-10	Dec-11	Dec-12	Dec-13	Dec-14	Dec-15
Assets									
Current Assets									
Cash and cash equivalents	4.2%	5.6%	5.4%	4.4%	6.9%	6.6%	6.9%	8.1%	8.1%
Receivables	16.6%	16.0%	14.6%	14.4%	13.2%	12.5%	11.8%	11.5%	11.9%
Inventories	11.6%	12.0%	10.9%	10.9%	10.4%	10.2%	10.3%	10.3%	9.9%
Other current assets	3.3%	3.7%	3.4%	3.7%	4.1%	4.8%	5.8%	6.2%	6.7%
Total current assets	35.8%	37.2%	34.2%	33.4%	34.6%	34.0%	34.8%	36.1%	36.7%
Property, plant and equipment, net	29.8%	31.3%	31.6%	33.1%	28.[illegible]	28.7%	29.4%	30.3%	31.7%
Goodwill, net	22.5%	21.6%	20.7%	21.1%	19.6%	18.7%	17.8%	17.1%	17.6%
Other intangible assets, net	8.4%	8.4%	7.4%	7.4%	11.8%	11.2%	10.8%	10.5%	11.3%
Deferred income taxes	0.0%	0.0%	0.0%	0.8%	0.9%	0.7%	0.6%	0.6%	0.6%
Other assets	3.6%	1.6%	6.2%	4.2%	4.3%	6.8%	6.7%	5.3%	2.2%
Total assets	100.0%	100.0%	100.0%	100.0%	100.0%	100.0%	100.0%	100.0%	100.0%

- Cash and Cash equivalents have increased from 4.2% in 2007 and are currently standing at 8.1% of the total assets.
- Receivables have decreased from 16.6% in 2007 to 11.9% in 2015.

- Inventories have decreased too from 11.6% to 9.9% overall.
- What is included in “other current assets”? It shows a steady increase from 3.3% to 6.7% of the total assets over the last 9 years.

Liabilities and Shareholders' Equity	Dec-07	Dec-08	Dec-09	Dec-10	Dec-11	Dec-12	Dec-13	Dec-14	Dec-15
Current Liabilities									
Notes and loans payable	1.5%	1.1%	0.3%	0.4%	0.3%	0.4%	0.1%	0.1%	0.0%
Current portion of long-term debt	1.4%	0.9%	2.9%	5.0%	2.7%	1.9%	6.4%	3.6%	2.5%
Accounts payable	10.6%	10.6%	10.5%	10.4%	9.8%	9.6%	9.7%	9.1%	9.3%
Accrued income taxes	2.6%	2.7%	3.5%	2.4%	3.1%	1.9%	1.7%	2.2%	2.3%
Other accruals	15.2%	14.2%	15.1%	15.1%	13.4%	[illegible]	14.3%	14.2%	15.4%
Total current liabilities	31.3%	29.6%	32.3%	33.4%	29.2%	[illegible]	32.2%	29.3%	29.6%
Long-term debt	31.9%	35.9%	25.3%	25.2%	[illegible]	36.8%	34.2%	41.9%	52.4%
Deferred income taxes	2.6%	0.8%	0.7%	1.0%	2.0%	[illegible]	3.2%	1.9%	1.9%
Other liabilities	10.6%	13.2%	12.3%	[illegible]	[illegible]	[illegible]	12.1%	16.5%	16.4%
Total liabilities	76.3%	79.5%	70.7%	[illegible]	[illegible]	82.2%	81.7%	89.7%	100.4%
Commitments and contingent liabilities									
Shareholders' Equity									
Preference stock	2.0%	1.8%	1.5%	[illegible]	0.0%	0.0%	0.0%	0.0%	0.0%
Common stock	7.2%	7.3%	6.6%	[illegible]	5.8%	10.9%	10.6%	10.9%	12.3%
Additional paid-in capital	15.0%	16.1%	15.8%	10.1%	10.5%	6.1%	7.2%	9.2%	12.0%
Retained earnings	105.1%	117.8%	118.2%	128.3%	123.0%	126.6%	129.4%	139.9%	157.7%
Accumulated other comprehensive income (los	-16.5%	-24.8%	-18.8%	-18.9%	[illegible]	-19.6%	-17.7%	-26.1%	-33.0%
Unearned compensation	-2.2%	-1.9%	-1.2%	-0.9%	[illegible]	-0.3%	-0.2%	-0.1%	-0.1%
Treasury stock, at cost	-88.1%	-97.2%	-94.1%	-101.2%	[illegible]	-107.4%	-112.7%	-125.3%	-151.4%
Total Colgate-Palmolive Company shareholders' equity	22.6%	19.3%	28.0%	23.9%	18.7%	16.3%	16.6%	8.5%	-2.5%
Noncontrolling interests	1.1%	1.2%	1.3%	1.3%	1.3%	1.5%	1.7%	1.8%	2.1%
Total shareholders' equity	23.7%	20.5%	29.3%	25.2%	20.0%	17.8%	18.3%	10.3%	-0.4%
Total liabilities and shareholders' equity	100.0%	100.0%	100.0%	100.0%	100.0%	100.0%	100.0%	100.0%	100.0%

- On the liabilities side, there can be many observations we can highlight. Accounts payable decreased continuously over the past 9 years and currently stands at 9.3% of the total assets.
- There has been a significant jump in the Long-Term Debt to 52,4% in 2015. For this, we need to investigate its SEC Filings further.
- Non-controlling interests have also increased over the period of 9 years and is now at 2.1%.

Example of the Balance Sheet

Most accounting balance sheets classify a company's assets and liabilities into distinctive groupings such as Current Assets; Property, Plant, and Equipment; Current Liabilities; etc. These classifications make the balance sheet more useful. The following balance sheet example is a classified balance sheet.

<table>
<tr><th colspan="4">Example Company Balance Sheet
December XXX</th></tr>
<tr><td colspan="2">Assets</td><td colspan="2">Liabilities</td></tr>
<tr><td colspan="2">Current assets</td><td colspan="2">Current liabilities</td></tr>
<tr><td>Cash</td><td>$ 2,100</td><td>Notes payable</td><td>$ 5,000</td></tr>
<tr><td>Petty cash</td><td>100</td><td>Account payable</td><td>35,900</td></tr>
<tr><td>Temporary investments</td><td>10,000</td><td>Wages payable</td><td>8,500</td></tr>
<tr><td>Account receivable – net</td><td>40,500</td><td>Interest payable</td><td>2,900</td></tr>
<tr><td>Inventory</td><td>31,000</td><td>Taxes payable</td><td>6,100</td></tr>
<tr><td>Supplies</td><td>3,800</td><td>Warranty liability</td><td>1,100</td></tr>
</table>

Prepaid insurance	1,500	Unearned revenues	1,500
Total current assets	89,000	Total current liabilities	61,000
Investment	36,000	Long-term liabilities	
		Notes payable	20,000
Property, plant & equipment		Bonds payable	400,000
Land	5,500	Total long-term liabilities	420,000
Land improvements	6,500		
Buildings	180,000		
Equipment	201,000	Total liabilities	481,000
Less: Accum depreciation	(56,000)		
Prop, plant and equip - net	337,000		
Intangible assets		Stockholders' Equity	
Goodwill	105,000	Common stock	110,000
Trade names	200,000	Retained earnings	220,000
Total intangible assets	305,000	Accum other comprehensive income	9,000
		Less: Treasury stock	(50,000)
Other assets	3,000	Total stockholders' equity	289,000
Total assets	$ 770,000	Total liabilities and stockholders' equity	$ 770,000

Cash Flow

Cash Flow (CF) is the increase or decrease in the amount of money a business, institution, or individual has. In finance, the term is used to describe the amount of cash (currency) that is generated or consumed in a given time period. There are many types of CF, with various important uses for running a business and performing financial analysis.

Types of Cash Flow

- Cash from Operating Activities: Cash that is generated by a company's core business activities does not include cash flow from investing. This is found on the company's Statement of cash flows.
- Free Cash Flow to Equity (FCFE): FCFE represents the cash that's available after reinvestment back into the business (capital expenditures). Read more about FCFE.
- Free Cash Flow to the Firm (FCFF): This is a measure that assumes a company has no leverage (debt). It is used in financial modeling and valuation. Read more about FCFF.
- Net Change in Cash: The change in the amount of cash flow from one accounting period to the next. This is found at the bottom of the cash flow statement.

Uses of Cash Flow

Cash Flow has many uses in both operating a business and in performing financial analysis. In fact, it's one of the most important metrics in all of finance and accounting.

The most common cash metrics and uses of cash flow are the following:

- Net Present Value: Calculating the value of a business by building a DCF Model and calculating the net present value (NPV).
- Internal Rate of Return: Determining the IRR an investor achieves for making an investment.
- Liquidity: Assessing how well a company can meet its short-term financial obligations.
- Cash Flow Yield: Measuring how much cash a business generates per share, relative to its share price, expressed as a percentage.
- Cash Flow Per Share (CFPS): Cash from operating activities divided by the number of shares outstanding.
- P/CF Ratio: The price of a stock divided by the CFPS, sometimes used as an alternative to the Price-Earnings or P/E ratio.
- Cash Conversion Ratio: The amount of time between when a business pays for its inventory (cost of goods sold) and receives payment from its customers is the cash conversion ratio
- Funding Gap: A measure of the shortfall a company has to overcome (how much more cash it needs).
- Dividend Payments: CF can be used to fund dividend payments to investors.
- Capital Expenditures: CF can also be used to fund reinvestment and growth in the business.

Cash Flow vs. Income

Investors and business operators care deeply about CF because it's the lifeblood of a company. Income and profit are based on accrual accounting principles, which smooth's-out expenditures and matches revenues to the timing of when products/services are delivered. Due to revenue recognition policies and the matching principle, a company's net income or net earning can actually be materially different from its Cash Flow.

Companies pay close attention to their cash flow and seek to manage it as carefully as possible. Professionals working in the finance, accounting, and financial planning & analysis (FP&A) functions at a company spend significant time evaluating the flow of funds in the business and identifying potential problems.

Cash Flow Generation Strategies

Since CF matters so much, it's only natural that managers of businesses do everything in their power to increase it. Below is an info graphic that demonstrates how CF can be increased using different strategies.

Managers of business can increase CF using any of the levers listed above. The strategies for improving CF fall into one of three categories: revenue growth, operating margins, and capital efficiency. Each of those can then be broken down into higher volume, higher prices, lower cost of goods sold, lower SG&A, more efficient property plant & equipment (PP&E), and more efficient inventory management.

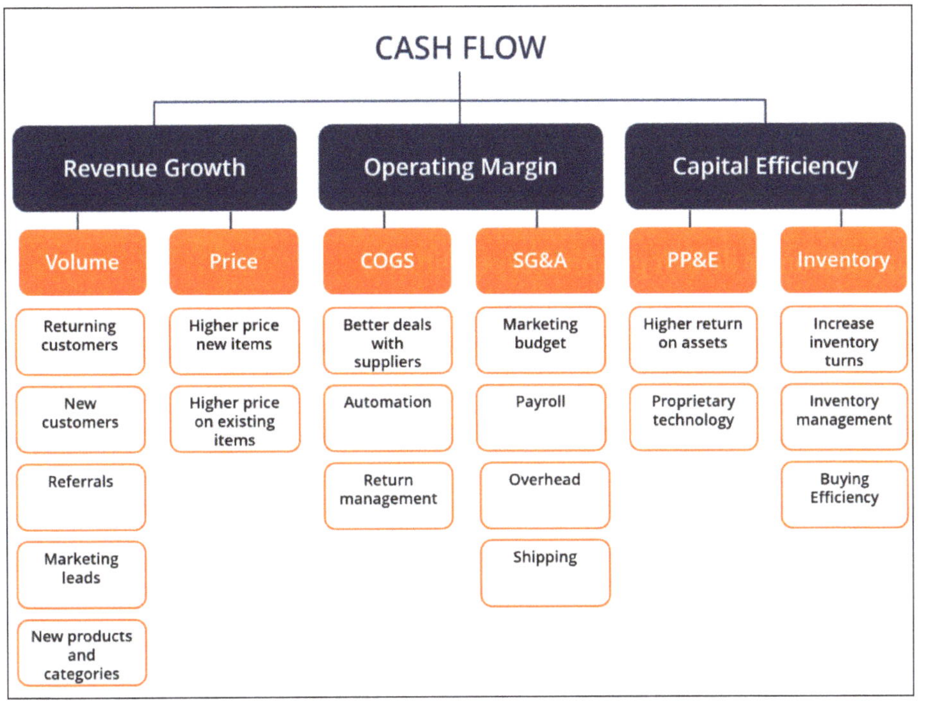

Free Cash Flow

Free cash flow is the net change in cash generated by the operations of a business during a reporting period, minus cash outlays for working capital, capital expenditures, and dividends during the same period. This is a strong indicator of the ability of an entity to remain in business, since these cash flows are needed to support operations and pay for ongoing capital expenditures.

How to Calculate Free Cash Flow

The free cash flow formula is:

> Free cash flow = Operating cash flow - Working capital changes - Capital expenditures – Dividends.

The calculation of free cash flow for a nonprofit entity is somewhat different, since a nonprofit does not issue dividends. In this situation, the revised formula is:

> Nonprofit free cash flow = Operating cash flow - Working capital changes - Capital expenditures.

The "operating cash flow" component of the equation is calculated as:

> Operating cash flow = Net income + Depreciation + Amortization.

Importance of Free Cash Flow

The free cash flow model is important because it is an indicator of the financial health of a business, and particularly of its ability to invest in new business opportunities. The model is also used by investors to estimate the amount of cash flow that may be available for distribution to them in the form of dividends. However, there can be a variety of situations in which a company can report positive free cash flow, and which are due to circumstances not necessarily related to a healthy long-term situation. For example, positive free cash flow can be caused by:

- Selling off major corporate assets.
- Cutting back on or delaying capital expenditures.
- Delaying the payment of accounts payable.
- Accelerating receivable receipts with high-cost early payment discounts.
- Foregoing a dividend.
- Cutting back on key maintenance expenditures.
- Reducing marketing expenditures.
- Curtailing scheduled pay increases.
- The receipt of a large advance payment from a customer.
- Entering into sale and leaseback arrangements for key assets.

In these examples, management has taken steps to reduce the long-term viability of a business in order to improve its short-term free cash flows. Other actions, such as accelerating the collection of accounts receivable through changes in payment terms or switching to just-in-time production systems, can be beneficial to a business while still reducing its outgoing cash flows.

Free cash flow can also be impacted by the growth rate of a business. If a company is growing rapidly, then it requires a significant investment in accounts receivable and inventory, which increases its working capital investment and therefore decreases the amount of free cash flow. Conversely, if a business is shrinking, it is converting some of its working capital back into cash as receivables are paid off and inventory liquidated, resulting in an increasing amount of free cash flow.

An additional consideration is the ability of a business to repatriate cash from a subsidiary. If a subsidiary is spinning off enormous amounts of cash, it makes little difference to the corporate parent if it cannot access the cash, due to stringent controls over cash repatriation by the applicable government.

Free Cash Flow (FCF) in Company Analysis

Because FCF accounts for changes in working capital, it can provide important insights into the value of a company and the health of its fundamental trends. For example, a decrease in accounts payable (outflow) could mean that vendors are requiring faster payment. A decrease in accounts receivable (inflow) means the company is collecting from its clients more quickly. An increase in inventory (outflow) could indicate a building stockpile of unsold products. Including working capital in a measure of profitability provides an insight that is missing from the income statement.

For example, assume that a company had made $50,000,000 per year in net income each year for the last decade. On the surface, that seems stable but what if FCF has been dropping over the last two years as inventories were rising (outflow), customers started to delay payments (outflow) and vendors began demanding faster payments (outflow) from the firm? In this situation, FCF would reveal a serious financial weakness that wouldn't have been apparent from an examination of the income statement alone.

FCF is also helpful as the starting place for potential shareholders or lenders to evaluate how likely the company will be able to pay their expected dividends or interest. If the company's debt payments are deducted from FCF (Free Cash Flow to the Firm), a lender would have a better idea for the quality of cash flows available for additional borrowings. Similarly, shareholders can use FCF-interest payments to think about the expected stability of future dividend payments.

Financial Statement Analysis

Financial statement analysis involves gaining an understanding of an organization's financial situation by reviewing its financial reports. The results can be used to make investment and lending decisions. This review involves identifying the following items for a company's financial statements over a series of reporting periods:

- Trends: Create trend lines for key items in the financial statements over multiple time periods, to see how the company is performing. Typical trend lines are for revenue, the gross margin, net profits, cash, accounts receivable, and debt.
- Proportion analysis: An array of ratios are available for discerning the relationship between the size of various accounts in the financial statements. For example, one can calculate a company's quick ratio to estimate its ability to pay its immediate liabilities, or its debt to equity ratio to see if it has taken on too much debt. These analyses are frequently between the revenues and expenses listed on the income statement and the assets, liabilities, and equity accounts listed on the balance sheet.

Financial statement analysis is an exceptionally powerful tool for a variety of users of financial statements, each having different objectives in learning about the financial circumstances of the entity.

Users of Financial Statement Analysis

There are a number of users of financial statement analysis. They are:

- Creditors: Anyone who has lent funds to a company is interested in its ability to pay back the debt, and so will focus on various cash flow measures.

- Investors: Both current and prospective investors examine financial statements to learn about a company's ability to continue issuing dividends, or to generate cash flow, or to continue growing at its historical rate (depending upon their investment philosophies).
- Management: The company controller prepares an ongoing analysis of the company's financial results, particularly in relation to a number of operational metrics that are not seen by outside entities (such as the cost per delivery, cost per distribution channel, profit by product, and so forth).
- Regulatory authorities: If a company is publicly held, its financial statements are examined by the Securities and Exchange Commission (if the company files in the United States) to see if its statements conform to the various accounting standards and the rules of the SEC.

Methods of Financial Statement Analysis

There are two key methods for analyzing financial statements. The first method is the use of horizontal and vertical analysis. Horizontal analysis is the comparison of financial information over a series of reporting periods, while vertical analysis is the proportional analysis of a financial statement, where each line item on a financial statement is listed as a percentage of another item. Typically, this means that every line item on an income statement is stated as a percentage of gross sales, while every line item on a balance sheet is stated as a percentage of total assets. Thus, horizontal analysis is the review of the results of multiple time periods, while vertical analysis is the review of the proportion of accounts to each other within a single period.

The second method for analyzing financial statements is the use of many kinds of ratios. Ratios are used to calculate the relative size of one number in relation to another. After a ratio is calculated, you can then compare it to the same ratio calculated for a prior period, or that is based on an industry average, to see if the company is performing in accordance with expectations. In a typical financial statement analysis, most ratios will be within expectations, while a small number will flag potential problems that will attract the attention of the reviewer. There are several general categories of ratios, each designed to examine a different aspect of a company's performance. The general groups of ratios are:

- Liquidity ratios: This is the most fundamentally important set of ratios, because they measure the ability of a company to remain in business.
    - Cash coverage ratio: Shows the amount of cash available to pay interest.
    - Current ratio: Measures the amount of liquidity available to pay for current liabilities.
    - Quick ratio: The same as the current ratio, but does not include inventory.
    - Liquidity index. Measures the amount of time required to convert assets into cash.
- Activity ratios: These ratios are a strong indicator of the quality of management, since they reveal how well management is utilizing company resources.
    - Accounts payable turnover ratio: Measures the speed with which a company pays its suppliers.

- Accounts receivable turnover ratio: Measures a company's ability to collect accounts receivable.
- Fixed asset turnover ratio: Measures a company's ability to generate sales from a certain base of fixed assets.
- Inventory turnover ratio: Measures the amount of inventory needed to support a given level of sales.
- Sales to working capital ratio: Shows the amount of working capital required to support a given amount of sales.
- Working capital turnover ratio: Measures a company's ability to generate sales from a certain base of working capital.

- Leverage ratios: These ratios reveal the extent to which a company is relying upon debt to fund its operations, and its ability to pay back the debt.
    - Debt to equity ratio: Shows the extent to which management is willing to fund operations with debt, rather than equity.
    - Debt service coverage ratio: Reveals the ability of a company to pay its debt obligations.
    - Fixed charge coverage: Shows the ability of a company to pay for its fixed costs.
- Profitability ratios: These ratios measure how well a company performs in generating a profit.
    - Breakeven point: Reveals the sales level at which a company breaks even.
    - Contribution margin ratio: Shows the profits left after variable costs are subtracted from sales.
    - Gross profit ratio: Shows revenues minus the cost of goods sold, as a proportion of sales.
    - Margin of safety: Calculates the amount by which sales must drop before a company reaches its breakeven point.
    - Net profit ratio. Calculates the amount of profit after taxes and all expenses have been deducted from net sales.
    - Return on equity: Shows company profit as a percentage of equity.
    - Return on net assets: Shows company profits as a percentage of fixed assets and working capital.
    - Return on operating assets: Shows company profit as percentage of assets utilized.

Problems with Financial Statement Analysis

While financial statement analysis is an excellent tool, there are several issues to be aware of that can interfere with the interpretation of the analysis results. These issues are:

- Comparability between periods: The Company preparing the financial statements may have changed the accounts in which it stores financial information, so that results may differ from period to period. For example, an expense may appear in the cost of goods sold in one period, and in administrative expenses in another period.

- Comparability between companies: An analyst frequently compares the financial ratios of different companies in order to see how they match up against each other. However, each company may aggregate financial information differently, so that the results of their ratios are not really comparable. This can lead an analyst to draw incorrect conclusions about the results of a company in comparison to its competitors.
- Operational information: Financial analysis only reviews a company's financial information, not its operational information, so you cannot see a variety of key indicators of future performance, such as the size of the order backlog, or changes in warranty claims. Thus, financial analysis only presents part of the total picture.

Financial Ratios

Financial ratios are created with the use of numerical values taken from financial statements to gain meaningful information about a company. The numbers found on a company's financial statements – balance sheet, income statement, and cash flow statement are used to perform quantitative analysis and assess a company's liquidity, leverage, growth, margins, profitability, rates of return, valuation, and more.

Financial ratios are grouped into the following categories:

- Liquidity ratios,
- Leverage ratios,
- Efficiency ratios,
- Profitability ratios,
- Market value ratios.

Uses and Users of Financial Ratio Analysis

Analysis of financial ratios serves two main purposes:

- Track company performance: Determining individual financial ratios per period and tracking the change in their values over time is done to spot trends that may be developing in a company. For example, an increasing debt-to-asset ratio may indicate that a company is overburdened with debt and may eventually be facing default risk.
- Make comparative judgments regarding company performance: Comparing financial ratios with that of major competitors is done to identify whether the company is performing better or worse than the industry average. For example, comparing the return on assets

between companies helps an analyst or investor to determine which of the company's assets are being used most efficiently.

Users of financial ratios include parties external and internal to the company:

- External users: Financial analysts, retail investors, creditors, competitors, tax authorities, regulatory authorities, and industry observers.
- Internal users: Management team, employees, and owners.

Liquidity Ratios

Liquidity ratios are financial ratios that measure a company's ability to repay both short- and long-term obligations. Common liquidity ratios include the following:

The current ratio measures a company's ability to pay off short-term liabilities with current assets:

Current ratio = Current assets/Current liabilities.

The acid-test ratio measures a company's ability to pay off short-term liabilities with quick assets:

Acid-test ratio = Current assets – Inventories/Current liabilities.

The cash ratio measures a company's ability to pay off short-term liabilities with cash and cash equivalents:

Cash ratio = Cash and Cash equivalents/Current Liabilities.

The operating cash flow ratio is a measure of the number of times a company can pay off current liabilities with the cash generated in a given period:

Operating cash flow ratio = Operating cash flow/Current liabilities.

Leverage Financial Ratios

Leverage ratios measure the amount of capital that comes from debt. In other words, leverage financial ratios are used to evaluate a company's debt levels. Common leverage ratios include the following:

The debt ratio measures the relative amount of a company's assets that are provided from debt:

Debt ratio = Total liabilities/Total assets.

The debt to equity ratio calculates the weight of total debt and financial liabilities against shareholders' equity:

Debt to equity ratio = Total liabilities/Shareholder's equity.

The interest coverage ratio determines how easily a company can pay its interest expenses:

Interest coverage ratio = Operating income/Interest expenses.

The debt service coverage ratio determines how easily a company can pay its debt obligations:

Debt service coverage ratio = Operating income/Total debt service.

Efficiency Ratios

Efficiency ratios, also known as activity financial ratios, are used to measure how well a company is utilizing its assets and resources. Common efficiency ratios include:

The asset turnover ratio measures a company's ability to generate sales from assets:

Asset turnover ratio = Net sales/Total assets.

The inventory turnover ratio measures how many times a company's inventory is sold and replaced over a given period:

Inventory turnover ratio = Cost of goods sold/Average inventory.

The accounts receivable turnover ratio measures how many times a company can turn receivables into cash over a given period:

Receivables turnover ratio = Net credit sales/Average accounts receivable.

The days sales in inventory ratio measures the average number of days that a company holds onto its inventory before selling it to customers:

Days sales in inventory ratio = 365 days/Inventory turnover ratio.

Profitability Ratios

Profitability ratios measure a company's ability to generate income relative to revenue, balance sheet assets, operating costs, and equity. Common profitability financial ratios include the following:

The gross margin ratio compares the gross profit of a company to its net sales to show how much profit a company makes after paying off its cost of goods sold:

Gross margin ratio = Gross profit/Net sales.

The operating margin ratio compares the operating income of a company to its net sales to determine operating efficiency:

Operating margin ratio = Operating income/Net sales.

The return on assets ratio measures how efficiently a company is using its assets to generate profit:

Return on assets ratio = Net income/Total assets.

The return on equity ratio measures how efficiently a company is using its equity to generate profit:

Return on equity ratio = Net income/Shareholder's equity.

Market Value Ratios

Market value ratios are used to evaluate the share price of a company's stock. Common market value ratios include the following:

The book value per share ratio calculates the per-share value of a company based on equity available to shareholders:

Book value per share ratio = Shareholder's equity/Total shares outstanding.

The dividend yield ratio measures the amount of dividends attributed to shareholders relative to the market value per share:

Dividend yield ratio = Dividend per share/Share price.

The earnings per share ratio measures the amount of net income earned for each share outstanding:

Earnings per share ratio = Net earnings/Total shares outstanding.

The price-earnings ratio compares a company's share price to the earnings per share:

Price-earnings ratio = Share price/Earnings per share.

Return on Equity (ROE)

Return on Equity (ROE) is the measure of a company's annual return (net income) divided by the value of its total shareholders' equity, expressed as a percentage (e.g., 12%). Alternatively, ROE can also be derived by dividing the firm's dividend growth rate by its earnings retention rate (1 – dividend payout ratio).

Return on Equity is a two-part ratio in its derivation because it brings together the income statement and the balance sheet, where net income or profit is compared to the shareholders' equity. The number represents the total return on equity capital and shows the firm's ability to turn assets into profits. To put it another way, it measures the profits made for each dollar from shareholders' equity.

Return on Equity

$$\text{ROE} = \frac{\text{Net Income (annual)}}{\text{Shareholders' Equity}}$$

Return on Equity Formula

The following is the ROE equation:

ROE = Net Income/Shareholders' Equity.

ROE provides a simple metric for evaluating returns. By comparing a company's ROE to the industry's average, something may be pinpointed about the company's competitive advantage. ROE may also provide insight into how the company management is using the financing from equity to grow the business.

A sustainable and increasing ROE over time can mean a company is good at generating shareholder value because it knows how to reinvest its earnings wisely, so as to increase productivity and profits. In contrast, a declining ROE can mean that management is making poor decisions on reinvesting capital in unproductive assets.

ROE Formula Drivers

While the simple return on equity formula is net income divided by shareholder's equity, we can break it down further into additional drivers.

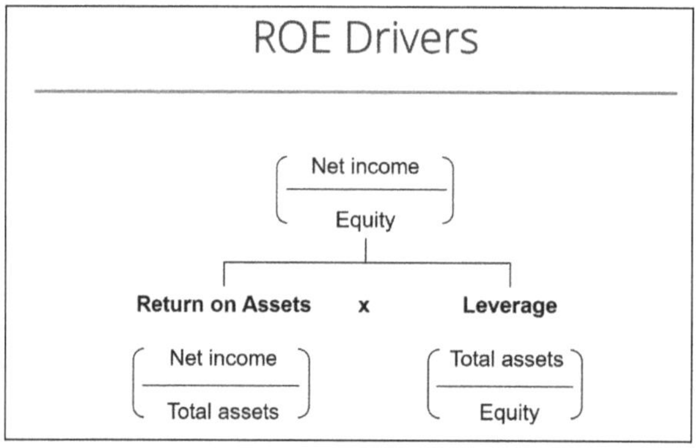

Importance of ROE

With net income in the numerator, Return on Equity (ROE) looks at the firm's bottom line to gauge overall profitability for the firm's owners and investors. Stockholders are at the bottom of the pecking order of a firm's capital structure, and the income returned to them is a useful measure that represents excess profits that remain after paying mandatory obligations and reinvesting in the business.

Shareholders' Equity (Beginning)

+ Net Income

– Dividends

Shareholders' Equity (Ending)

Use of Return on Equity Matric

Simply put, with ROE, investors can see if they're getting a good return on their money, while a company can evaluate how efficiently they're utilizing the firm's equity. ROE must be compared to the historical ROEs of the company and to the industry's ROE average – it means little if merely looked at in isolation. Other financial ratios can be looked at to get a more complete and informed picture of the company for evaluation purposes.

In order to satisfy investors, a company should be able to generate a higher ROE than the return available from a lower risk investment.

Effect of Leverage

A high ROE could mean a company is more successful in generating profit internally. However, it doesn't fully show the risk associated with that return. A company may rely heavily on debt to generate a higher net profit, thereby boosting the ROE higher.

The image below from CFI's Financial Analysis Course shows how leverage increases equity returns.

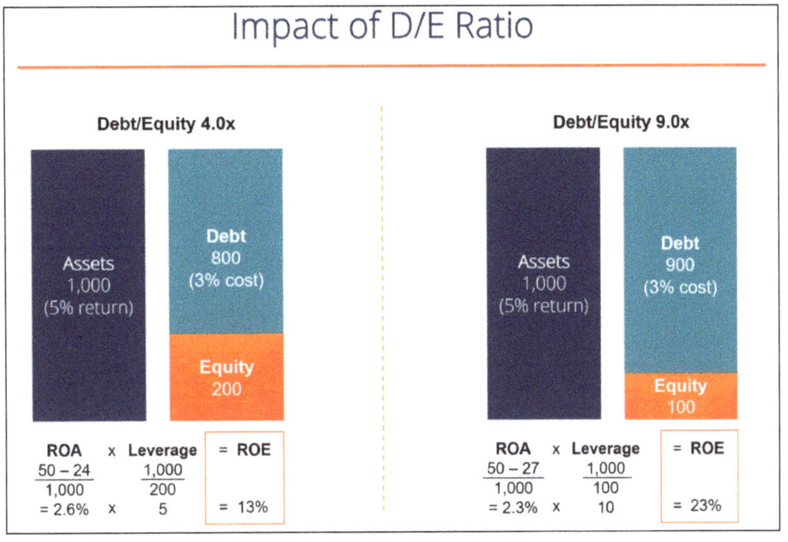

As an example, if a company has $150,000 in equity and $850,000 in debt, then the total capital employed is $1,000,000. This is the same number of total assets employed. At 5%, it will cost $42,000 to service that debt, annually. If the company manages to increase its profits before interest to a 12% return on capital employed (ROCE), the remaining profit after paying the interest is $78,000, which will increase equity by more than 50%, assuming the profit generated gets reinvested back. As we can see, the effect of debt is to magnify the return on equity.

Drawbacks of ROE

The return on equity ratio can also be skewed by share buybacks. When management repurchases its shares from the marketplace, this reduces the number of outstanding shares. Thus, ROE increases as the denominator shrinks.

Another weakness is that some ROE ratios may exclude intangible assets from shareholders' equity. Intangible assets are non-monetary items such as goodwill, trademarks, copyrights, and patents. This can make calculations misleading and difficult to compare to other firms that have chosen to include intangible assets.

Finally, the ratio includes some variations on its composition, and there may be some disagreements between analysts. For example, the shareholders' equity can either be the beginning number, ending number, or the average of the two, while Net Income may be substituted for EBITDA and EBIT, and can be adjusted or not for non-recurring items.

Return on Assets (ROA)

Return on Assets (ROA) is a type of return on investment (ROI) metric that measures the profitability of a business in relation to its total assets. This ratio indicates how well a company is performing by comparing the profit (net income) it's generating to the capital it's invested in assets. The higher the return, the more productive and efficient management is in utilizing economic resources.

	Company #1	Company #2
Net Income	$ 50,000,000	$ 10,000,000
Start of Period Assets	$ 505,000,000	$ 14, 000,000
End of Period Assets	$ 495,000,000	$ 16,000,000
Average Assets	$ 500,000,000	$ 15,000,000
ROA	10.0%	66.7%

ROA Formula

The ROA formula is:

ROA = Net Income/Average Assets.

or

ROA = Net Income/End of Period Assets.

Where: Net Income is equal to net earnings or net income in the year (annual period).

Average Assets is equal to ending assets minus beginning assets divided by 2.

	Company #1	Company #2
Net Income	$ 50,000,000	$ 10,000,000
Start of Period Assets	$ 505,000,000	$ 14,000,000
End of Period Assets	$ 495,000,000	$ 16,000,000
Average Assets	$ 500,000,000	$ 15,000,000
ROA	10.0%	= D3/D7

Example of ROA Calculation

If a business posts a net income of $10 million in current operations, and owns $50 million worth of assets as per the balance sheet, what is its return on assets?

Solution: $10 million divided by $50 million is 0.2, therefore the business's ROA is 20%. For every dollar of debt and equity the business takes on, it can return 20 cents in net profit (after all deductions). For every dollar of assets the company invests in, it returns 20 cents in net profit per year.

Importance of Return on Assets

The ROA formula is an important ratio in analyzing a company's profitability. The ratio is typically used when comparing a company's performance between periods, or when comparing two different companies of similar size and industry. Note that it is very important to consider the scale of a business and the operations performed when comparing two different firms using ROA.

Typically different industries have different ROA's. Industries that are capital-intensive and require a high value of fixed assets for operations will generally have a lower ROA, as their large asset base will increase the denominator of the formula. Naturally, a company with a large asset base can have a large ROA, if their income is high enough.

The DuPont Equation

The DuPont equation is an expression which breaks return on equity down into three parts. The name comes from the DuPont Corporation, which created and implemented this formula into their business operations in the 1920s. This formula is known by many other names, including DuPont analysis, DuPont identity, the DuPont model, the DuPont method, or the strategic profit model.

$$\text{ROE} = \frac{\text{Net income}}{\text{Sales}} \times \frac{\text{Sales}}{\text{Total Assets}} \times \frac{\text{Total Assets}}{\text{Average Shareholder Equity}}$$

The DuPont Equation: In the DuPont equation, ROE is equal to profit margin multiplied by asset turnover multiplied by financial leverage.

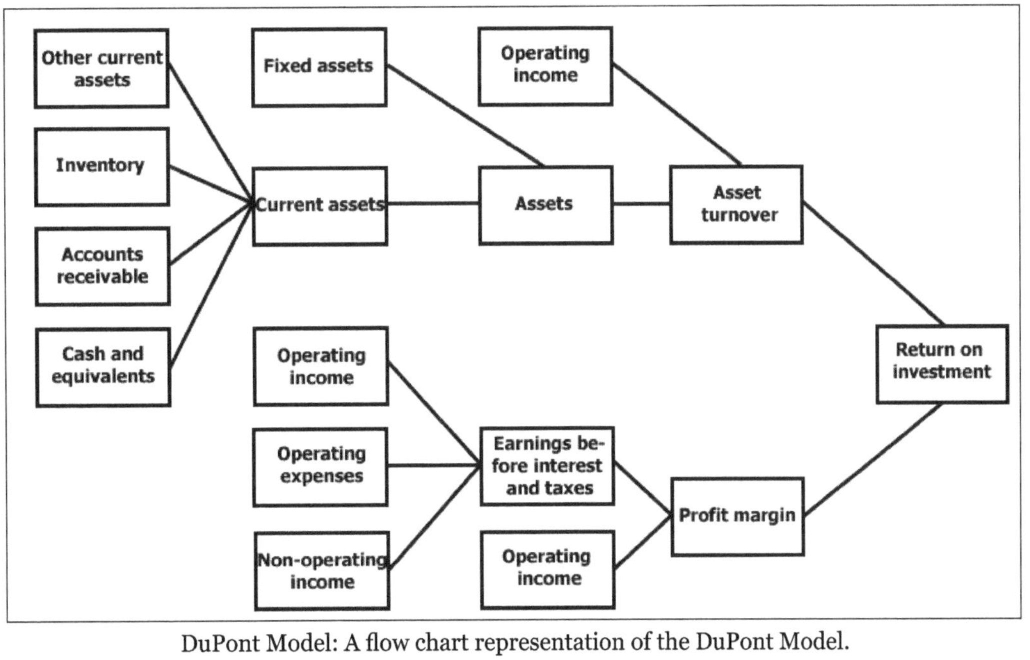

DuPont Model: A flow chart representation of the DuPont Model.

Under DuPont analysis, return on equity is equal to the profit margin multiplied by asset turnover multiplied by financial leverage. By splitting ROE (return on equity) into three parts, companies can more easily understand changes in their ROE over time.

Components of the DuPont Equation

Profit Margin

Profit margin is a measure of profitability. It is an indicator of a company's pricing strategies and how well the company controls costs. Profit margin is calculated by finding the net profit as a percentage of the total revenue. As one feature of the DuPont equation, if the profit margin of a company increases, every sale will bring more money to a company's bottom line, resulting in a higher overall return on equity.

Asset Turnover

Asset turnover is a financial ratio that measures how efficiently a company uses its assets to generate sales revenue or sales income for the company. Companies with low profit margins tend to have high asset turnover, while those with high profit margins tend to have low asset turnover. Similar to profit margin, if asset turnover increases, a company will generate more sales per asset owned, once again resulting in a higher overall return on equity.

Financial Leverage

Financial leverage refers to the amount of debt that a company utilizes to finance its operations, as compared with the amount of equity that the company utilizes. As was the case with asset turnover and profit margin, increased financial leverage will also lead to an increase in return on equity. This is because the increased use of debt as financing will cause a company to have higher interest payments, which are tax deductible. Because dividend payments are not tax deductible, maintaining a high proportion of debt in a company's capital structure leads to a higher return on equity.

The DuPont Equation in Relation to Industries

The DuPont equation is less useful for some industries, that do not use certain concepts or for which the concepts are less meaningful. On the other hand, some industries may rely on a single factor of the DuPont equation more than others. Thus, the equation allows analysts to determine which of the factors is dominant in relation to a company's return on equity. For example, certain types of high turnover industries, such as retail stores, may have very low profit margins on sales and relatively low financial leverage. In industries such as these, the measure of asset turnover is much more important.

High margin industries, on the other hand, such as fashion, may derive a substantial portion of their competitive advantage from selling at a higher margin. For high end fashion and other luxury brands, increasing sales without sacrificing margin may be critical. Finally, some industries, such as those in the financial sector, chiefly rely on high leverage to generate an acceptable return on equity. While a high level of leverage could be seen as too risky from some perspectives, DuPont analysis enables third parties to compare that leverage with other financial elements that can determine a company's return on equity.

Assessing Internal Growth and Sustainability

Sustainable– as opposed to internal– growth gives a company a better idea of its growth rate while keeping in line with financial policy.

Internal Growth and Sustainability

The true benefit of a high return on equity arises when retained earnings are reinvested into the company's operations. Such reinvestment should, in turn, lead to a high rate of growth for the company. The internal growth rate is a formula for calculating maximum growth rate that a firm can achieve without resorting to external financing. It's essentially the growth that a firm can supply by reinvesting its earnings. This can be described as (retained earnings)/(total assets), or conceptually as the total amount of internal capital available compared to the current size of the organization.

We find the internal growth rate by dividing net income by the amount of total assets (or finding return on assets) and subtracting the rate of earnings retention. However, growth is not necessarily favorable. Expansion may strain managers' capacity to monitor and handle the company's operations. Therefore, a more commonly used measure is the sustainable growth rate.

Sustainable growth is defined as the annual percentage of increase in sales that is consistent with a defined financial policy, such as target debt to equity ratio, target dividend payout ratio, target profit margin, or target ratio of total assets to net sales.

We find the sustainable growth rate by dividing net income by shareholder equity (or finding return on equity) and subtracting the rate of earnings retention. While the internal growth rate assumes no financing, the sustainable growth rate assumes you will make some use of outside financing that will be consistent with whatever financial policy being followed. In fact, in order to achieve a higher growth rate, the company would have to invest more equity capital, increase its financial leverage, or increase the target profit margin.

Optimal Growth Rate

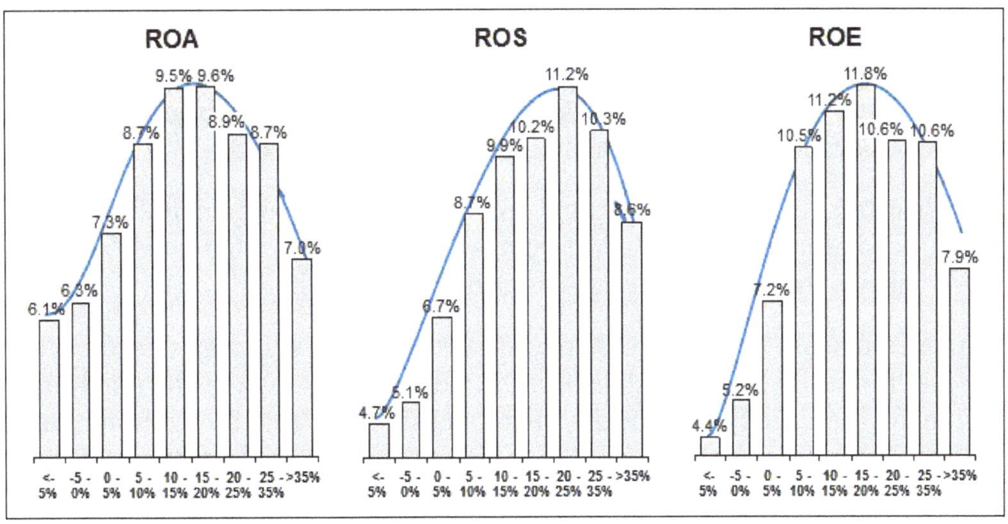

Revenue Growth and Profitability 1997-2009: ROA, ROS and ROE tend to rise with revenue growth to a certain extent.

Another measure of growth, the optimal growth rate, assesses sustainable growth from a total shareholder return creation and profitability perspective, independent of a given financial strategy. The concept of optimal growth rate was originally studied by Martin Handschuh, Hannes Lösch, and Björn Heyden. Their study was based on assessments on the performance of more than 3,500 stock-listed companies with initial revenue of greater than 250 million Euro globally, across industries, over a period of 12 years from 1997 to 2009.

Due to the span of time included in the study, the authors considered their findings to be, for the most part, independent of specific economic cycles. The study found that return on assets; return on sales and return on equity do in fact rise with increasing revenue growth of between 10% to 25%, and then fall with further increasing revenue growth rates. Furthermore, the authors attributed this profitability increase to the following facts:

- Companies with substantial profitability have the opportunity to invest more in additional growth, and
- Substantial growth may be a driver for additional profitability, whether by attracting high performing young professionals, providing motivation for current employees, attracting better business partners, or simply leading to more self-confidence.

However, according to the study, growth rates beyond the "profitability maximum" rate could bring about circumstances that reduce overall profitability because of the efforts necessary to handle additional growth (i.e., integrating new staff, controlling quality, etc).

Dividend Payments and Earnings Retention

The dividend payout and retention ratios offer insight into how much of a firm's profit is distributed to shareholders versus retained.

Dividends are payments made by a corporation to its shareholder members. It is the portion of corporate profits paid out to stockholders. On the other hand, retained earnings refer to the portion of net income which is retained by the corporation rather than distributed to its owners as dividends. Similarly, if the corporation takes a loss, then that loss is retained and called variously retained losses, accumulated losses or accumulated deficit. Retained earnings and losses are cumulative from year to year with losses offsetting earnings. Many corporations retain a portion of their earnings and pay the remainder as a dividend.

A dividend is allocated as a fixed amount per share. Therefore, a shareholder receives a dividend in proportion to their shareholding. Retained earnings are shown in the shareholder equity section in the company's balance sheet –the same as its issued share capital.

Public companies usually pay dividends on a fixed schedule, but may declare a dividend at any time, sometimes called a "special dividend" to distinguish it from the fixed schedule dividends. Dividends are usually paid in the form of cash, store credits (common among retail consumers' cooperatives), or shares in the company (either newly created shares or existing shares bought in the market). Further, many public companies offer dividend reinvestment plans, which automatically use the cash dividend to purchase additional shares for the shareholder.

Cash dividends (most common) are those paid out in currency, usually via electronic funds transfer or a printed paper check. Such dividends are a form of investment income and are usually taxable to the recipient in the year they are paid. This is the most common method of sharing corporate profits with the shareholders of the company. For each share owned, a declared amount of money is distributed. Thus, if a person owns 100 shares and the cash dividend is $0.50 per share, the holder of the stock will be paid $50. Dividends paid are not classified as an expense but rather a deduction of retained earnings. Dividends paid do not show up on an income statement but do appear on the balance sheet.

XYZ Company Balance Sheet As at 30 June XXX		
Current Assets		
Cash at bank	30,000	
Inventory	250,000	
Debtors	75,000	
Total Current assets		355,000
Non-Current Assets		
Buildings	550,000	
Plant & equipment	250,000	
Vehicles	120,000	
Total non-current assets		920,000
Total Assets		1,275,000
Current Liabilities		
Credit cards	15,000	
Creditors	110,000	
Tax payable	25,000	
Total Current liabilities		150,000
Non-current Liabilities		
Long term loans		700,000
Total Liabilities		850,000
Owners' Equity		
Capital	100,000	
Retained earnings	250,000	
Current earnings	75,000	
Total Owners Equity		425,000

Example Balance Sheet: Retained earnings can be found on the balance sheet, under the owners' (or shareholders') equity section.

Stock dividends are those paid out in the form of additional stock shares of the issuing corporation or another corporation (such as its subsidiary corporation). They are usually issued in proportion to shares owned (for example, for every 100 shares of stock owned, a 5% stock dividend will yield five extra shares). If the payment involves the issue of new shares, it is similar to a stock split in that it increases the total number of shares while lowering the price of each share without changing the market capitalization, or total value, of the shares held.

Dividend Payout and Retention Ratios

Dividend payout ratio is the fraction of net income a firm pays to its stockholders in dividends.

The part of the earnings not paid to investors is left for investment to provide for future earnings growth. These retained earnings can be expressed in the retention ratio. Retention ratio can be found by subtracting the dividend payout ratio from one or by dividing retained earnings by net income.

$$\text{Dividend payout ratio} = \frac{\text{Dividends}}{\text{Net Income for the same period}}$$

Dividend Payout Ratio: The dividend payout ratio is equal to dividend payments divided by net income for the same period.

ROA, ROE and Growth

In terms of growth rates, we use the value known as return on assets to determine a company's internal growth rate. This is the maximum growth rate a firm can achieve without resorting to external financing. We use the value for return on equity, however, in determining a company's sustainable growth rate, which is the maximum growth rate a firm can achieve without issuing new equity or changing its debt-to-equity ratio.

Capital Intensity and Growth

Return on assets gives us an indication of the capital intensity of the company. "Capital intensity" is the term for the amount of fixed or real capital present in relation to other factors of production, especially labor. The underlying concept here is how much output can be procured from a given input (assets!). The formula for capital intensity is below:

$$\text{Capital Intensity} = \frac{\text{Total Assets}}{\text{Sales}}$$

The use of tools and machinery makes labor more effective, so rising capital intensity pushes up the productivity of labor. While companies that require large initial investments will generally have lower return on assets, it is possible that increased productivity will provide a higher growth rate for the company. Capital intensity can be stated quantitatively as the ratio of the total money value of capital equipment to the total potential output. However, when we adjust capital intensity for real market situations, such as the discounting of future cash flows, we find that it is not independent of the distribution of income. In other words, changes in the retention or dividend payout ratios can lead to changes in measured capital intensity.

References

- Financial-statement, encyclopedia: shopify.in, Retrieved 28 April, 2019
- Income-statement, financial-statements: myaccountingcourse.com, Retrieved 8 August, 2019
- Income-statement, accounting, knowledge, resources: corporatefinanceinstitute.com, Retrieved 9 May, 2019

- Income-statement, encyclopedia: referenceforbusiness.com, Retrieved 31 March, 2019
- Advantages-of-income-statement: wikiaccounting.com, Retrieved 14 July, 2019
- Gross-income, accounting, knowledge, resources: corporatefinanceinstitute.com, Retrieved 17 May, 2019
- Explanation, balance-sheet: accountingcoach.com, Retrieved 19 April, 2019
- Cash-flow, finance, knowledge, resources: corporatefinanceinstitute.com, Retrieved 5 February, 2019
- What-is-free-cash-flow: accountingtools.com, Retrieved 26 July, 2019
- Return-on-assets-roa-formula, finance, knowledge, resources: corporatefinanceinstitute.com, Retrieved 21 May, 2019

4

Capital Structure and Management

The methods through which a company finances its assets by a combination of debt, equity or hybrid securities is known as capital structure. Some of the theories related to capital structure are net income approach, net operating income approach and Modigliani-Miller approach. This chapter discusses in detail these theories related to capital structure and its management.

Capital Structure

Capital Structure refers to the amount of debt and equity employed by a firm to fund its operations and finance its assets. The structure is typically expressed as a debt-to-equity or debt to capital ratio.

Debt and equity capital are used to fund a business' operations, capital expenditures, acquisitions, and other investments. There are tradeoffs firms have to make when they decide whether to raise debt or equity and managers will balance the two try and find the optimal capital structure.

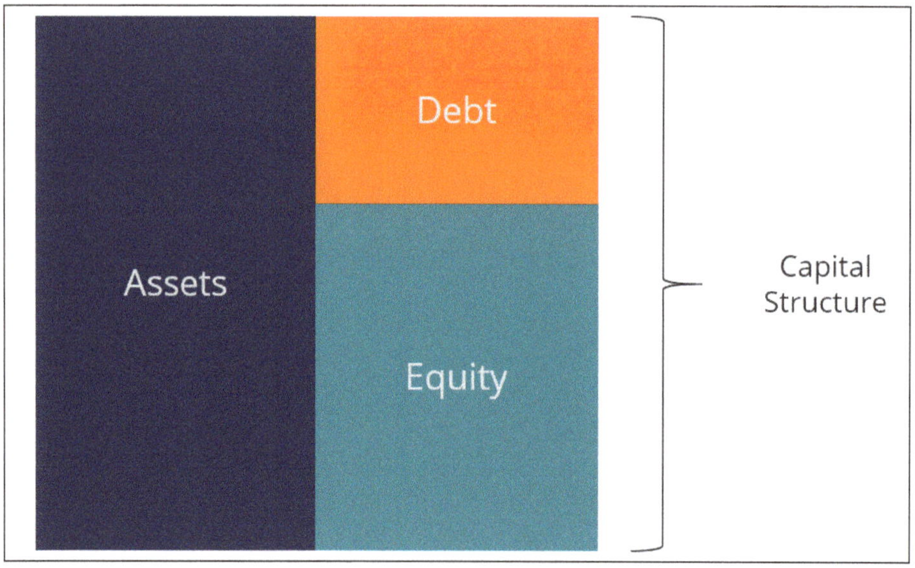

Optimal Capital Structure

The optimal capital structure of a firm is often defined as the proportion of debt and equity that result in the lowest weighted average cost of capital (WACC) for the firm. This technical definition is not always used in practice, and firms often have a strategic or philosophical view of what the structure should be.

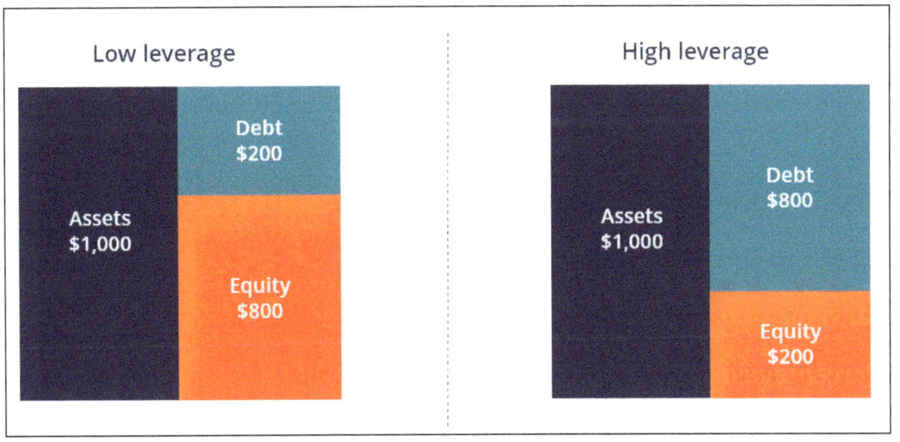

In order to optimize the structure, a firm will decide if it needs more debt or equity and can issue whichever it requires. The new capital that's issued may be used to invest in new assets or may be used to repurchase debt/equity that's currently outstanding as a form or recapitalization.

Dynamics of Debt and Equity

Below is a description of the dynamics between debt and equity from the view of investors and the firm.

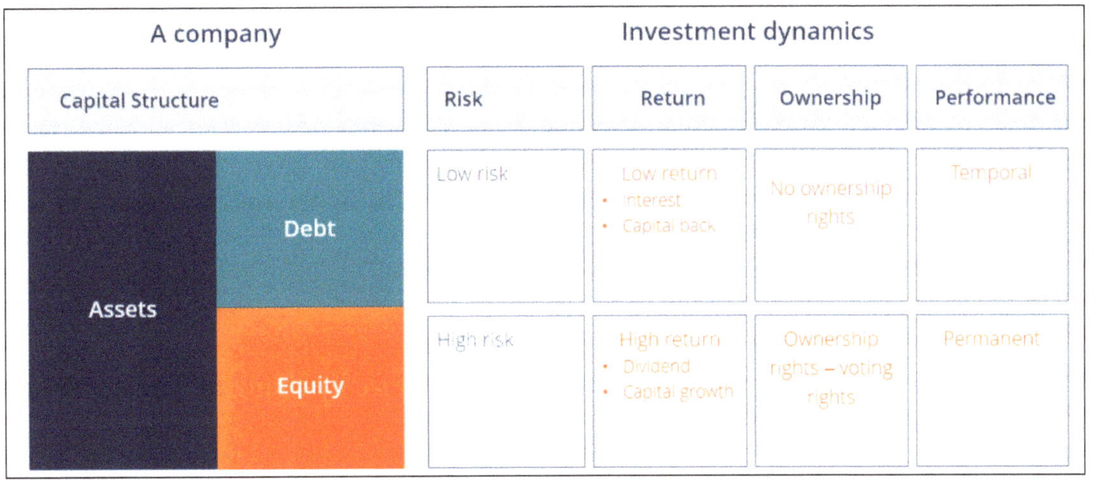

Debt investors take less risk because they have the first claim on the assets of the business in the event of bankruptcy. For this reason, they accept a lower rate of return, and thus the firm has a lower cost of capital when it issues debt compared to equity.

Equity investors take more risk as they only receive the residual value after debt investors have been repaid. In exchange for this risk equity investors expect a higher rate of return and therefore the implied cost of equity is greater than that of debt.

Cost of Capital

A firm's total cost of capital is a weighted average of the cost of equity and the cost of debt, known as the weighted average cost of capital (WACC).

The formula is equal to:

$$WACC = (E/V \times Re) + ((D/V \times Rd) \times (1 - T)).$$

Where:

E = Market value of the firm's equity (market cap).

D = Market value of the firm's debt.

V = Total value of capital (equity plus debt).

E/V = Percentage of capital that is equity.

D/V = Percentage of capital that is debt.

Re = Cost of equity (required rate of return).

Rd = Cost of debt (yield to maturity on existing debt).

T = Tax rate.

Capital Structure by Industry

Capital structures can vary significantly by industry. Cyclical industries like mining are often not suitable for debt, as their cash flow profiles can be unpredictable and there is too much uncertainty about their ability to repay the debt.

Other industries like banking and insurance use huge amounts of leverage and are their business models require large amounts of debt. Private companies may have a harder time using debt over equity, particularly small business which is required to have personal guarantees from their owners.

Recapitalizing a Business

A firm that decides they should optimize their capital structure by changing the mix of debt and equity has a few options to effect this change.

Methods of Recapitalization Include

- Issue debt and repurchase equity.
- Issue debt and pay a large dividend to equity investors.
- Issue equity and repay debt.

Each of these three methods can be an effective way of recapitalizing the business:

- In the first approach, the firm borrows money by issuing debt and then uses all that capital to repurchase shares from its equity investors. This has the effect of increasing the amount of debt and decreasing the amount of equity on the balance sheet.

- In the second approach, the firm will borrow money (i.e. issue debt) and use that money to pay a one-time special dividend, which has the effect of reducing the value of equity by the value of the divided. This is another method of increasing debt and reducing equity.
- In the third approach, the firm moves in the opposite direction and issues equity by selling new shares, then takes the money and uses it to repay debt. Since equity is costlier than debt, this approach is not desirable and often only done when a firm is overleveraged and desperately needs to reduce its debt.

Tradeoffs between Debt and Equity

There are many tradeoffs that owners and managers of firms have to consider when determining their capital structure. Below are some of the tradeoffs that should be considered.

Pros and cons of equity:

- No interest payments.
- No mandatory fixed payments (dividends are discretionary).
- No maturity dates (no capital repayment).
- Has ownership and control over the business.
- Has voting rights (typically).
- Has a high implied cost of capital.
- Expects a high rate of return (dividends and capital appreciation).
- Has last claim on the firm's assets in the event of liquidation.
- Provides maximum operational flexibility.

Pros and cons of debt:

- Has an interest payment (typically).
- Has a fixed repayment schedule.
- Has first claim on the firm's assets in the event of liquidation.
- Requires covenants and financial performance metrics that must be met.
- Contains restrictions on operational flexibility.
- Has a lower cost than equity.
- Expects a lower rate of return than equity.

Leveraged Buyouts

In a leveraged buyout (LBO) transaction a firm will take on significant leverage to finance the acquisition. This practice is commonly performed by private equity firms seeking to invest the smallest possible amount of equity and finance the balance with borrowed funds.

The image below demonstrates how the use of leverage can significantly increase equity returns as the debt is paid off over time.

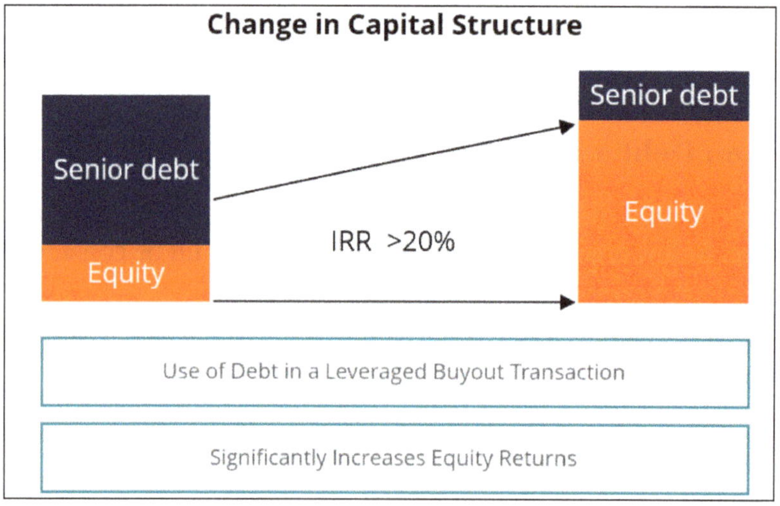

Importance of Capital Structure

- Increase in value of the firm: A sound capital structure of a company helps to increase the market price of shares and securities which, in turn, lead to increase in the value of the firm.

- Utilisation of available funds: A good capital structure enables a business enterprise to utilise the available funds fully. A properly designed capital structure ensures the determination of the financial requirements of the firm and raise the funds in such proportions from various sources for their best possible utilisation. A sound capital structure protects the business enterprise from over-capitalisation and under-capitalisation.

- Maximisation of return: A sound capital structure enables management to increase the profits of a company in the form of higher return to the equity shareholders i.e., increase in earnings per share. This can be done by the mechanism of trading on equity i.e., it refers to increase in the proportion of debt capital in the capital structure which is the cheapest source of capital. If the rate of return on capital employed (i.e., shareholders' fund + long-term borrowings) exceeds the fixed rate of interest paid to debt-holders, the company is said to be trading on equity.

- Minimisation of cost of capital: A sound capital structure of any business enterprise maximises shareholders' wealth through minimisation of the overall cost of capital. This can also be done by incorporating long-term debt capital in the capital structure as the cost of debt capital is lower than the cost of equity or preference share capital since the interest on debt is tax deductible.

- Solvency or liquidity position: A sound capital structure never allows a business enterprise to go for too much raising of debt capital because, at the time of poor earning, the solvency is disturbed for compulsory payment of interest to .the debt-supplier.

- Flexibility: A sound capital structure provides a room for expansion or reduction of debt capital so that, according to changing conditions, adjustment of capital can be made.
- Undisturbed controlling: A good capital structure does not allow the equity shareholders control on business to be diluted.
- Minimisation of financial risk: If debt component increases in the capital structure of a company, the financial risk (i.e., payment of fixed interest charges and repayment of principal amount of debt in time) will also increase. A sound capital structure protects a business enterprise from such financial risk through a judicious mix of debt and equity in the capital structure.

Factors Determining Capital Structure

The following factors influence the capital structure decisions:

- Risk of cash insolvency: Risk of cash insolvency arises due to failure to pay fixed interest liabilities. Generally, the higher proportion of debt in capital structure compels the company to pay higher rate of interest on debt irrespective of the fact that the fund is available or not. The non-payment of interest charges and principal amount in time call for liquidation of the company.

  The sudden withdrawal of debt funds from the company can cause cash insolvency. This risk factor has an important bearing in determining the capital structure of a company and it can be avoided if the project is financed by issues equity share capital.
- Risk in variation of earnings: The higher the debt content in the capital structure of a company, the higher will be the risk of variation in the expected earnings available to equity shareholders. If return on investment on total capital employed (i.e., shareholders' fund plus long-term debt) exceeds the interest rate, the shareholders get a higher return.

  On the other hand, if interest rate exceeds return on investment, the shareholders may not get any return at all.
- Cost of capital: Cost of capital means cost of raising the capital from different sources of funds. It is the price paid for using the capital. A business enterprise should generate enough revenue to meet its cost of capital and finance its future growth. The finance manager should consider the cost of each source of fund while designing the capital structure of a company.
- Control: The consideration of retaining control of the business is an important factor in capital structure decisions. If the existing equity shareholders do not like to dilute the control, they may prefer debt capital to equity capital, as former has no voting rights.
- Trading on equity: The use of fixed interest bearing securities along with owner's equity as sources of finance is known as trading on equity. It is an arrangement by which the company aims at increasing the return on equity shares by the use of fixed interest bearing securities (i.e., debenture, preference shares etc.).

If the existing capital structure of the company consists mainly of the equity shares, the return on equity shares can be increased by using borrowed capital. This is so because the interest paid on debentures is a deductible expenditure for income tax assessment and the after-tax cost of debenture becomes very low.

Any excess earnings over cost of debt will be added up to the equity shareholders. If the rate of return on total capital employed exceeds the rate of interest on debt capital or rate of dividend on preference share capital, the company is said to be trading on equity.

- Government policies: Capital structure is influenced by Government policies, rules and regulations of SEBI and lending policies of financial institutions which change the financial pattern of the company totally. Monetary and fiscal policies of the Government will also affect the capital structure decisions.
- Size of the company: Availability of funds is greatly influenced by the size of company. A small company finds it difficult to raise debt capital. The terms of debentures and long-term loans are less favourable to such enterprises. Small companies have to depend more on the equity shares and retained earnings.

  On the other hand, large companies issue various types of securities despite the fact that they pay less interest because investors consider large companies less risky.
- Needs of the investors: While deciding capital structure the financial conditions and psychology of different types of investors will have to be kept in mind. For example, a poor or middle class investor may only be able to invest in equity or preference shares which are usually of small denominations, only a financially sound investor can afford to invest in debentures of higher denominations.

  A cautious investor who wants his capital to grow will prefer equity shares.
- Flexibility: The capital structures of a company should be such that it can raise funds as and when required. Flexibility provides room for expansion, both in terms of lower impact on cost and with no significant rise in risk profile.
- Period of finance: The period for which finance is needed also influences the capital structure. When funds are needed for long-term (say 10 years), it should be raised by issuing debentures or preference shares. Funds should be raised by the issue of equity shares when it is needed permanently.
- Nature of business: It has great influence in the capital structure of the business, companies having stable and certain earnings prefer debentures or preference shares and companies having no assured income depends on internal resources.
- Legal requirements: The finance manager should comply with the legal provisions while designing the capital structure of a company.
- Purpose of financing: Capital structure of a company is also affected by the purpose of financing. If the funds are required for manufacturing purposes, the company may procure it from the issue of long- term sources. When the funds are required for non-manufacturing purposes i.e., welfare facilities to workers, like school, hospital etc. the company may procure it from internal sources.

- Corporate taxation: When corporate income is subject to taxes, debt financing is favourable. This is so because the dividend payable on equity share capital and preference share capital are not deductible for tax purposes, whereas interest paid on debt is deductible from income and reduces a firm's tax liabilities. The tax saving on interest charges reduces the cost of debt funds.

  Moreover, a company has to pay tax on the amount distributed as dividend to the equity shareholders. Due to this, total earnings available for both debt holders and stockholders is more when debt capital is used in capital structure. Therefore, if the corporate tax rate is high enough, it is prudent to raise capital by issuing debentures or taking long-term loans from financial institutions.

- Cash inflows: The selection of capital structure is also affected by the capacity of the business to generate cash inflows. It analyses solvency position and the ability of the company to meet its charges.

- Provision for future: The provision for future requirement of capital is also to be considered while planning the capital structure of a company.

- EBIT-EPS analysis: If the level of EBIT is low from HPS point of view, equity is preferable to debt. If the EBIT is high from EPS point of view, debt financing is preferable to equity. If ROI is less than the interest on debt, debt financing decreases ROE. When the ROI is more than the interest on debt, debt financing increases ROE.

Theories of Capital Structure

Net Income (NI) Approach

David Durand' suggested the two famous capital structure theories, viz, Net Income.

Approach and the Operating Income Approach

According to NI approach a firm may increase the total value of the firm by lowering its cost of capital. When cost of capital is lowest and the value of the firm is greatest, we call it the optimum capital structure for the firms and at this point, the market price per share is maximised.

The same is possible continuously by lowering its cost of capital by the use of debt capital. In other words, using more debt capital with a corresponding reduction in cost of capital, the value of the firm will increase.

The same is possible only when:

- Cost of Debt (K_d) is less then Cost of Equity (K_e);
- There are no taxes, and
- The use of debt does not change the risk perception of the investors since the degree of leverage is increased to that extent.

Since the amount of debt in the capital structure increases, weighted average cost of capital decreases which leads to increase the total value of the firm. So, the increased amount of debt with constant amount of cost of equity and cost of debt will highlight the earnings of the shareholders.

Workings

Average Cost of Capital is computed as under (under various financing plans). The value of the firm (V) will be increased if there is a proportionate increase in debt capital but there will be a reduction in overall cost of capital. So, Cost of Capital is increased and the value of the firm is maximum if a firm uses 100% debt capital.

The degree of leverage is plotted along with the X-axis whereas K_e K_w and K_d on the Y- axis. It reveals that when the cheaper debt capital in the capital structure is proportionally increased, the weighted average cost of capital K_w, decreases and consequently the cost of debt K_d. Thus, it is needless to say that the optimal capital structure is the minimum cost of capital, if financial leverage is one, in other words, the maximum application of debt capital.

The value of the firm (V) will also be the maximum at this point.

Net Operating Income Approach

Now we want to highlight the Net Operating Income (NOI) Approach which was advocated by David Durand based on certain assumptions.

They are:

- The overall capitalization rate of the firm K_w is constant for all degree of leverage;
- Net operating income is capitalized at an overall capitalisation rate in order to have the total market value of the firm.

  Thus, the value of the firm, V, is ascertained at overall cost of capital (K_w): $V = EBIT/\ K_w$ (Since both are constant and independent of leverage).
- The market value of the debt is then subtracted from the total market value in order to get the market value of equity.

  $S = V\text{-}T$
- As the Cost of Debt is constant, the cost of equity will be: $K_e = EBIT - I / S$.

Under this approach, the most significant assumption is that the K_u is constant irrespective of the degree of leverage. The segregation of debt and equity is not important here and the market capitalizes the value of the firm as a whole. Thus, an increase in the use of apparently cheaper debt funds is offset exactly by the corresponding increase in the equity-capitalisation rate.

So, the weighted average Cost of Capital K_w and K_d remain unchanged for all degrees of leverage. Needless to mention here that as the firm increases its degree of leverage it becomes more risky proposition and investors are to make some sacrifice by having a low P/E ratio.

Traditional Approach

It is accepted by all that the judicious use of debt will increase the value of the firm and reduce the cost of capital. So, the optimum capital structure is the point at which the value of the firm is highest and the cost of capital is at its lowest point. Practically, this approach encompasses all the ground between the net income approach and the net operating income approach i.e., it may be said as intermediate approach.

The traditional approach explains that up to a certain point, debt-equity mix will cause the market value of the firm to rise and the cost of capital to decline. But after attaining the optimum level, any additional debt will cause to decrease the market value and to increase the cost of capital.

In other words, after attaining the optimum level, any additional debt taken, will offset the use of cheaper debt capital since the average cost of capital will increase along with a corresponding increase in the average cost of debt capital.

Thus, the basic, proposition of this approach are enumerated below:

- The cost of debt capital, K_d, remains constant more or less up to a certain level and thereafter rises.
- The cost of equity Capital, K_e, remains constant more or less or rise gradually up to a certain level and thereafter increases rapidly.
- The average cost of capital, K_w, decreases up to a certain level, remains unchanged more or less and thereafter rises after attaining a certain level.

The traditional approach can graphically be represented in figure.

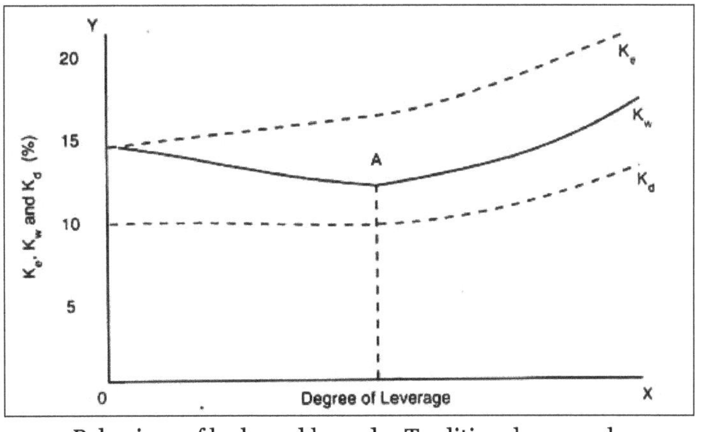

Behaviour of k_e, k_w and k_d under Traditional approach.

It is found from the above, the average cost curve is U-shaped. That is, at this stage the cost of capital would be minimum which is expressed by the letter 'A' in the graph. If we draw a perpendicular to the X-axis, the same will indicate the optimum capital structure for the firm.

Thus, the traditional position implies that the cost of capital is not independent of the capital structure of the firm and that there is an optimal capital structure. At that optimal structure, the marginal real cost of debt (explicit and implicit) is the same as the marginal Real cost of equity in equilibrium.

For degree of leverage before that point, the marginal real cost of debt is less than of equity, beyond that point the marginal real cost of debt excess that of equity.

Variations on the Traditional Theory

We know that this theory underlies between the Net Income Approach and the Net Operating Income Approach. Thus, there are some distinct variations in this theory. Some followers of the traditional school of thought suggest that K_e does not practically rise till some critical conditions arise.

After attaining that level only, the investors apprehend the increasing financial risk and penalize the market price of the shares. This variation expresses that a firm can have lower cost of capital with the initial use of leverage significantly.

This variation in Traditional Approach is depicted as under:

Other followers e.g., Solomon, are of opinion that K is as being saucer shaped along with a horizontal middle range. It explains that optimum capital structure has a range where the cost of capital is rather minimised and where the total value of the firm is maximised.

Under the circumstances, a change in leverage has, practically, no effect on the total firm's value. So, this approach grants some sorts of variation in the optimal capital structure for various firms under debt-equity mix.

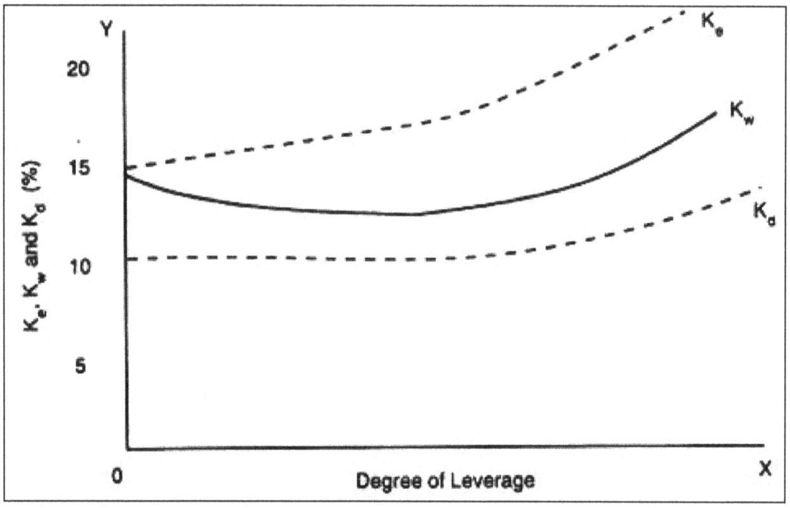

Behaviour if K_e, K_w and K_4 under Saucer- shaped K_w curve of traditional approach.

Modigliani-Miller Approach

Modigliani-Miller (MM) advocated that the relationship between the cost of capital, capital structure and the valuation of the firm, should be explained by NOI (Net Income Operating Approach) by making an attack on the Traditional Approach.

The Net Income Operating Approach, we know, supply proper justification for the irrelevance of the capital structure. In this context, MM support the NOI approach on the principle that the cost of capital is not dependent on the degree of leverage irrespective of the debt-equity mix.

In other words, according to their thesis, the total market value of the firm and the cost of capital are independent of the capital structure. They advocated that the weighted average cost of capital does not make any change with a proportionate change in debt-equity mix in the total capital structure of the firm.

The same can be shown with the help of the following diagram:

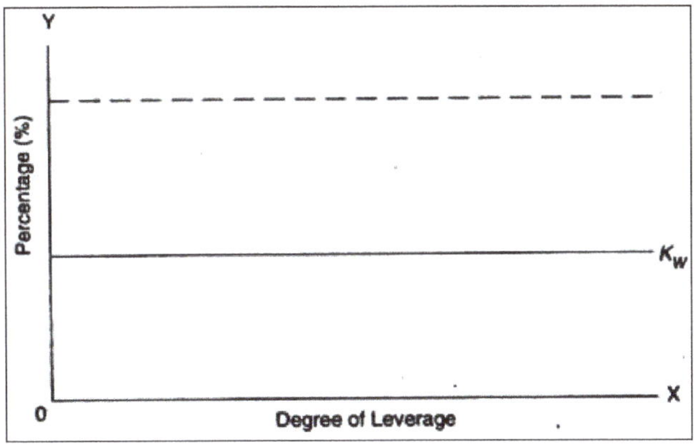

Shows that the weight average cost of does not make any change.

Trade-off Theory

The trade-off theory states that the optimal capital structure is a trade-off between interest tax shields and cost of financial distress:

Value of firm = Value if all-equity financed + PV(tax shield) - PV(cost of financial distress).

The trade-off theory can be summarized graphically. The starting point is the value of the all-equity financed firm illustrated by the black horizontal line in figure. The present value of tax shields is then added to form the red line. Note that PV(tax shield) initially increases as the firm borrows more, until additional borrowing increases the probability of financial distress rapidly. In addition, the firm cannot be sure to benefit from the full tax shield if it borrows excessively as it takes positive earnings to save corporate taxes. Cost of financial distress is assumed to increase with the debt level.

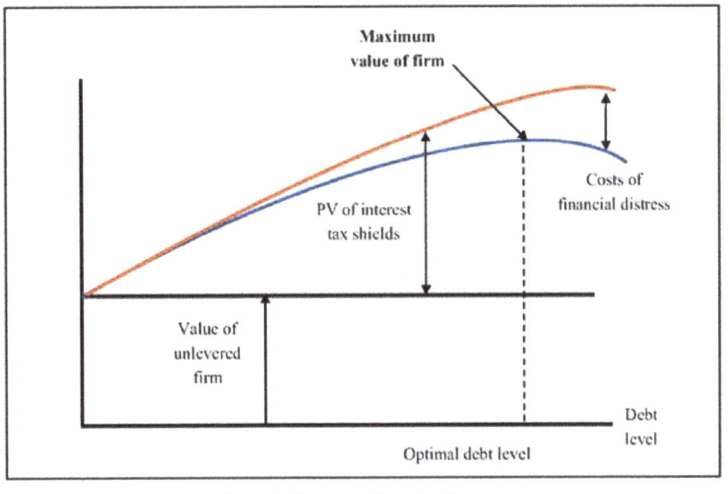

Trade-off theory of capital structure.

The cost of financial distress is illustrated in the diagram as the difference between the red and blue curve. Thus, the blue curve shows firm value as a function of the debt level. Moreover, as the graph suggest an optimal debt policy exists which maximized firm value.

The trade-off theory states that capital structure is based on a trade-off between tax savings and distress costs of debt. Firms with safe, tangible assets and plenty of taxable income to shield should have high target debt ratios. The theory is capable of explaining why capital structures differ between industries, whereas it cannot explain why profitable companies within the industry have lower debt ratios (trade-off theory predicts the opposite as profitable firms have a larger scope for tax shields and therefore subsequently should have higher debt levels).

Pecking Order Theory of Capital Structure

The pecking order theory has emerged as alternative theory to the trade-off theory. Rather than introducing corporate taxes and financial distress into the MM framework, the key assumption of the pecking order theory is asymmetric information. Asymmetric information captures that managers know more than investors and their actions therefore provides a signal to investors about the prospects of the firm.

The intuition behind the pecking order theory is derived from considering the following string of arguments:

- If the firm announces a stock issue it will drive down the stock price because investors believe managers are more likely to issue when shares are overpriced.
- Therefore firms prefer to issue debt as this will allow the firm to raise funds without sending adverse signals to the stock market. Moreover, even debt issues might create information problems if the probability of default is significant, since a pessimistic manager will issue debt just before bad news get out.

This leads to the following pecking order in the financing decision:

- Internal cash flow,
- Issue debt,
- Issue equity.

The pecking order theory states that internal financing is preferred over external financing, and if external finance is required, firms should issue debt first and equity as a last resort. Moreover, the pecking order seems to explain why profitable firms have low debt ratios: This happens not because they have low target debt ratios, but because they do not need to obtain external financing. Thus, unlike the trade-off theory the pecking order theory is capable of explaining differences in capital structures within industries.

Final Word on Weighted Average Cost of Capital

All variables in the weighted average cost of capital (WACC) formula refer to the firm as a whole.

$$WACC = r_D\left(1 - Tc\right)\left(\frac{D}{V}\right) + r_E\left(\frac{E}{V}\right),$$

where TC is the corporate tax rate.

The after-tax WACC can be used as the discount rate if;

- The project has the same business risk as the average project of the firm.
- The project is financed with the same amount of debt and equity.

If condition 1 is violated the right discount factor is the required rate of return on an equivalently risky investment, whereas if condition 2 is violated the WACC should be adjusted to the right financing mix. This adjustment can be carried out in three steps:

Step 1: Calculate the opportunity cost of capital.

Calculate the opportunity cost of capital without corporate taxation.

$$r = \frac{D}{V}r_D + \frac{E}{V}r_E.$$

Step 2: Estimate the cost of debt, rD, and cost of equity, rE, at the new debt level,

$$r_E = r + \left(r - r_D\right) + \frac{D}{E}.$$

Step 3: Recalculate WACC.

"Relever the WACC" by estimating the WACC with the new financing weights.

Example:

Consider a firm with a debt and equity ratio of 40% and 60%, respectively. The required rate of return on debt and equity is 7% and 12.5%, respectively. Assuming a 30% corporate tax rates the after-tax WACC of the firm is:

$$WACC = r_D\left(1 - Tc\right)\left(\frac{D}{V}\right) + r_E\left(\frac{E}{V}\right) = 7\% \cdot \left(1 - 0.3\right) \cdot 0.4 + 12.5\% \cdot 0.6 = 9.46\%.$$

The firm is considering investing in a new project with a perpetual stream of cash flows of $11.83 million per year pre-tax. The project has the same risk as the average project of the firm.

Given an initial investment of $125 million, which is financed with 20% debt, what is the value of the project?

The first insight is that although the business risk is identical, the project is financed with lower financial leverage. Thus, the WACC cannot be used as the discount rate for the project. Rather, the WACC should be adjusted using the three step procedure.

Step 1: Estimate opportunity cost of capital, i.e. estimate r using a 40% debt ratio, 60% equity ration as well as the firm's cost of debt and equity,

$$r=\frac{D}{V}r_D+\frac{E}{V}r_E=0.4\cdot 7\%+0.6\cdot 12.5\%=10.3\%.$$

Step 2: Estimate the expected rate of return on equity using the project's debt-equity ratio. As the debt ratio is equal to 20%, the debt-equity ratio equals 25%,

$$r_E=r+(r-r_D)\frac{D}{E}=10.3\%+(10.3\%-7\%)\cdot 0.25=11.1\%.$$

Step 3: Estimate the project's WACC,

$$WACC=r_D(1-Tc)\left(\frac{D}{V}\right)+r_E\left(\frac{E}{V}\right)=7\%\cdot(1-0.3)\cdot 0.2+11.1\%\cdot 0.8=9.86\%.$$

The adjusted WACC of 9.86% can be used as the discount rate for the new project as it reflects the underlying business risk and mix of financing. As the project requires an initial investment of $125 million and produced a constant cash flow of $11.83 per year for ever, the projects NPV is:

$$NPV=-125+\frac{11.83}{0.0986}=\cdot\$5.02\,\text{million}.$$

In comparison the NPV is equal to $5.03 if the company WACC is used as the discount rate. In this case we would have invested in a negative NPV project if we ignored that the project was financed with a different mix of debt and equity.

EBIT and EPS Analysis

EBIT-EPS analysis gives a scientific basis for comparison among various financial plans and shows ways to maximize EPS. Hence EBIT-EPS analysis may be defined as 'a tool of financial planning that evaluates various alternatives of financing a project under varying levels of EBIT and suggests the best alternative having highest EPS and determines the most profitable level of EBIT'.

Concept of EBIT-EPS Analysis

The EBIT-EBT analysis is the method that studies the leverage, i.e. comparing alternative methods of financing at different levels of EBIT. Simply put, EBIT-EPS analysis examines the effect of financial leverage on the EPS with varying levels of EBIT or under alternative financial plans.

It examines the effect of financial leverage on the behavior of EPS under different financing alternatives and with varying levels of EBIT. EBIT-EPS analysis is used for making the choice of the combination and of the various sources. It helps select the alternative that yields the highest EPS.

We know that a firm can finance its investment from various sources such as borrowed capital or equity capital. The proportion of various sources may also be different under various financial plans. In every financing plan the firm's objectives lie in maximizing EPS.

Advantages of EBIT-EPS Analysis

We have seen that EBIT-EPS analysis examines the effect of financial leverage on the behavior of EPS under various financing plans with varying levels of EBIT. It helps a firm in determining optimum financial planning having highest EPS.

Various advantages derived from EBIT-EPS analysis may be enumerated below:

- Financial Planning: Use of EBIT-EPS analysis is indispensable for determining sources of funds. In case of financial planning the objective of the firm lies in maximizing EPS. EBIT-EPS analysis evaluates the alternatives and finds the level of EBIT that maximizes EPS.
- Comparative Analysis: EBIT-EPS analysis is useful in evaluating the relative efficiency of departments, product lines and markets. It identifies the EBIT earned by these different departments, product lines and from various markets, which helps financial planners rank them according to profitability and also assess the risk associated with each.
- Performance Evaluation: This analysis is useful in comparative evaluation of performances of various sources of funds. It evaluates whether a fund obtained from a source is used in a project that produces a rate of return higher than its cost.
- Determining Optimum Mix: EBIT-EPS analysis is advantageous in selecting the optimum mix of debt and equity. By emphasizing on the relative value of EPS, this analysis determines the optimum mix of debt and equity in the capital structure. It helps determine the alternative that gives the highest value of EPS as the most profitable financing plan or the most profitable level of EBIT as the case may be.
- Limitations of EBIT-EPS Analysis: Finance managers are very much interested in knowing the sensitivity of the earnings per share with the changes in EBIT; this is clearly available with the help of EBIT-EPS analysis but this technique also suffers from certain limitations, as described below.
- No Consideration for Risk: Leverage increases the level of risk, but this technique ignores the risk factor. When a corporation, on its borrowed capital, earns more than the interest it has to pay on debt, any financial planning can be accepted irrespective of risk. But in times of poor business the reverse of this situation arises—which attracts high degree of risk. This aspect is not dealt in EBIT-EPS analysis.
- Contradictory Results: It gives a contradictory result where under different alternative financing plans new equity shares are not taken into consideration. Even the comparison becomes difficult if the number of alternatives increase and sometimes it also gives erroneous result under such situation.
- Over-capitalization: This analysis cannot determine the state of over-capitalization of a firm. Beyond a certain point, additional capital cannot be employed to produce a return in excess of the payments that must be made for its use. But this aspect is ignored in EBIT-EPS analysis.

Example: Ankim Ltd., has an EBIT of Rs 3, 20,000. Its capital structure is given as under.

	Rs
Equity share capital of Rs10 each	4,00,000
13 % preference share capital	1,00,000
9% Debentures	2,00,000

The company is in the tax bracket of 50%. You are required to calculate the earning per share.

Solution: Computation for EPS.

	Rs
EBIT	3,20,000
Less: interest $\left(2,00,000 \times \frac{9}{100}\right)$	18,000
EBT	3,02,000
Less: Tax @ 50%	1,51,000
EAT	1,51,000
Less: preference dividend $\left(1,00,000 \times \frac{13}{100}\right)$	13,000
Earnings available to equity shareholders	1,38,000

Number of equity shares = 40,000

$$\therefore \quad \text{Earnings per share} = \frac{\text{Earnings available to equity shareholders}}{\text{Number of equity shares}}$$

$$= \frac{\text{Rs}1,38,000}{40,000} = \text{Rs } 3.45.$$

Indifference Points

The indifference point, often called as a breakeven point, is highly important in financial planning because; at EBIT amounts in excess of the EBIT indifference level, the more heavily levered financing plan will generate a higher EPS. On the other hand, at EBIT amounts below the EBIT indifference points the financing plan involving less leverage will generate a higher EPS.

- Concept: Indifference points refer to the EBIT level at which the EPS is same for two alternative financial plans. According to J. C. Van Home, 'Indifference point refers to that EBIT level at which EPS remains the same irrespective of debt equity mix'. The management is indifferent in choosing any of the alternative financial plans at this level because all the financial plans are equally desirable. The indifference point is the cut-off level of EBIT below which financial leverage is disadvantageous. Beyond the indifference point level of EBIT the benefit of financial leverage with respect to EPS starts operating.

The indifference level of EBIT is significant because the financial planner may decide to take the debt advantage if the expected EBIT crosses this level. Beyond this level of EBIT the firm will be able to magnify the effect of increase in EBIT on the EPS.

In other words, financial leverage will be favorable beyond the indifference level of EBIT and will lead to an increase in the EPS. If the expected EBIT is less than the indifference point then the financial planners will opt for equity for financing projects, because below this level, EPS will be more for less levered firm.

- Computation: We have seen that indifference point refers to the level of EBIT at which EPS is the same for two different financial plans. So the level of that EBIT can easily be computed. There are two approaches to calculate indifference point: Mathematical approach and graphical approach.

Mathematical Approach

Under the mathematical approach, the indifference point may be obtained by solving equations. Let us present the income statement given in table with the following symbols in table. We are starting from EBIT only.

Table: Income statement presented with symbols.

EBIT	X
Less: Interest (I)	I
EBT	$(X-I)$
Less: Tax (at t% on EBT)	$(X-I)t$
EAT	$(X-I)(1-t)$
Less preference dividend	P_d
Earnings available to equity shareholder	$(X-I)(1-t)-P_d$
EPS = $\frac{(X-I)(1-t)P_d}{N}$	

where, N represents number of equity shares.

In case of financing, three types of sources may be opted: Equity, debt and preference shares. So we may have four possible combinations Equity, Equity-Debt, Equity- Preference Shares and Equity- Debt-Preference Shares.

So, EPS under various alternatives will be as follows:

$$\text{Equity – Dept: EPS } = \frac{(X-I)(1-t)}{N}$$

$$\text{Equity – Prefrence Shares : EPS } = \frac{X(1-t)P_d}{N}$$

Equity – Dept Prefrence Shares: EPS $=\frac{(X-I)(1-t)P_d}{N}$.

The symbols have their usual meaning. The indifference point between any two financial plans may be obtained by equalizing the respective equations of EPS and solving them to find the value of X.

Example: XYZ Co. Ltd., is planning an expansion programme. It requires Rs 20 lakhs of external financing for which it is considering two alternatives. The first alternative calls for issuing 15,000 equity shares of Rs 100 each and 5,000 10% Preference Shares of Rs 100 each; the second alternative requires 10,000 equity shares of Rs 100 each, 2,000 10% Preference Shares of Rs 100 each and Rs 8,00,000 Debentures carrying 9% interest. The company is in the tax bracket of 50%. You are required to calculate the indifference point for the plans and verify your answer by calculating the EPS.

Solution: Capital Structure.

	Plan I (Rs)	Plan II (Rs)
Equity share capital	15,00,000	10,00,000
10% preference share capital	5,00,000	2,00,000
9% debentures	-	8,00,000
Total	20,00,000	20,00,000
Number of equity shares	15,000	10,000

Let, at *X* level of EBIT, the EPS under both the plan will be same,

EPS under 1st alternative: $\frac{X(1-t)-P_d}{N_1}=\frac{X(1-0.5)-50,000}{15,000}$

Again, EPS under 2nd alternative: $\frac{(X-I)(1-t)-P_d}{N_2}=\frac{(X-72,000)(1-0.5)-20,000}{10,000}$

Now, equalizing both the EPS we get:

$$\Rightarrow \quad \frac{X(1-0.5)-50,000}{15,000}=\frac{(X-72,000)(1-0.5)-20,000}{10,000}$$

$$\Rightarrow \quad \frac{0.5X-50,000}{15,000}=\frac{0.5X-36,000-20,000}{10,000}$$

$$\Rightarrow \quad \frac{0.5X-50,000}{3}=\frac{0.5X-56,000}{2}$$

$$\Rightarrow \quad 1.5X-1,68,000=X-1,00,000$$

$$\therefore \quad X=\frac{68,000}{0.5}=\text{Rs}1,36,000$$

We may verify the result by calculating EPS under both the plans:

Table: Computation of EPS under different plans.

	Plan I	Plan II
EBIT	1,36,000	1,36,000
Less: Interest		72,000
EBT	1,36,000	64,000
Less: Tax	68,000	32,000
EAT	68,000	32,000
Less: Preference Dividend	50,000	20,000
Earnings available to equity shareholders	18,000	12,000
No. of equity shares	15,000	10,000
$\therefore \text{EPS} = \frac{\text{Earnings available to equity shareholders}}{\text{Number of equity shares}}$	$\frac{18,000}{15,000}$ = Rs 1.20	$\frac{12,000}{10,000}$ = Rs 1.20

Graphical Approach

The indifference point may also be obtained using a graphical approach. In figure we have measured EBIT along the horizontal axis and EPS along the vertical axis. Suppose we have two financial plans before us: Financing by equity only and financing by equity and debt. Different combinations of EBIT and EPS may be plotted against each plan. Under Plan-I the EPS will be zero when EBIT is nil so it will start from the origin.

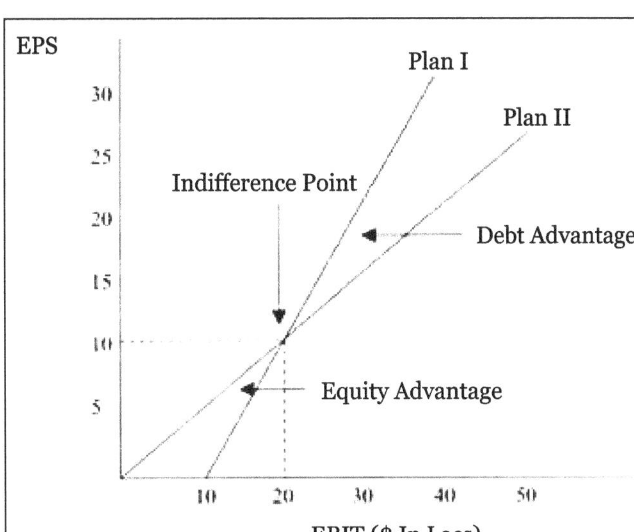

Graphics Presentation of Indifference Point.

The curve depicting Plan I in figure starts from the origin. For Plan-II EBIT will have some positive figure equal to the amount of interest to make EPS zero. So the curve depicting Plan-II in figure will start from the positive intercept of X axis. The two lines intersect at point E where the level of

EBIT and EPS both are same under both the financial plans. Point E is the indifference point. The value corresponding to X axis is EBIT and the value corresponding to 7 axis is EPS.

These can be found drawing two perpendiculars from the indifference point—one on X axis and the other on Taxis. Similarly we can obtain the indifference point between any two financial plans having various financing options. The area above the indifference point is the debt advantage zone and the area below the indifference point is equity advantage zone.

Above the indifference point the Plan-II is profitable, i.e. financial leverage is advantageous. Below the indifference point Plan I is advantageous, i.e. financial leverage is not profitable. This can be found by observing figure. Above the indifference point EPS will be higher for same level of EBIT for Plan II. Below the indifference point EPS will be higher for same level of EBIT for Plan I. The graphical approach of indifference point gives a better understanding of EBIT-EPS analysis.

Financial Breakeven Point

In general, the term Breakeven Point (BEP) refers to the point where the total cost line and sales line intersect. It indicates the level of production and sales where there is no profit and no loss because here the contribution just equals to the fixed costs. Similarly financial breakeven point is the level of EBIT at which after paying interest, tax and preference dividend, nothing remains for the equity shareholders.

In other words, financial breakeven point refers to that level of EBIT at which the firm can satisfy all fixed financial charges. EBIT less than this level will result in negative EPS. Therefore EPS is zero at this level of EBIT. Thus financial breakeven point refers to the level of EBIT at which financial profit is nil.

Financial Break Even Point (FBEP) is expressed as ratio with the following equation:

$$\text{FBEP} = \frac{(\text{EBIT} - I)(1-t) - P_d}{N} = 0$$

or

$$(\text{EBIT} - I)(1-t) - P_d = 0$$

or

$$(\text{EBIT} - I) = \frac{P_d}{(1-t)}$$

or.

$$\text{EBIT} = I + \frac{P_d}{(1-t)},$$

where, EBIT = Earnings before Interest and Tax,

I = Interest,

T = Rate of Tax,

P_d = Preference Dividend and

N = Number of Equity Shares.

It is to be noted here that beyond the financial breakeven point increase in EBIT will result in proportional increase in EPS.

Example: A company has formulated the following financing plans to finance Rs 15, 00,000 which is required for financing a new project.

	Plan 1 (Rs)	Plan II (Rs)	Plan III (Rs)
Equity share capital (Rs 10 each)	15,00,000	10,00,000	7,50,000
8% Debentures	-	5,00,000	2,50,000
10% preference share capital	-	-	5,00,000
	15,00,000	15,00,000	15,00,000

Compute the financial breakeven point for each alternative plan assuming tax rate at 50%.

Solution: We know that the financial breakdown point is the EBIT where EPS is 0.

$$\therefore \quad \text{FBEP}=\frac{(\text{EBIT-}I)(1-t)-P_d}{N}=0.$$

Financial breakdown point for plan I:

$$\frac{(\text{EBIT}-0)(1-0.5)-0}{1,50,000}=0$$

$$\Rightarrow \quad 0.5\,\text{EBIT}-0=0$$

$$\therefore \quad \text{EBIT}-0=0.$$

Financial breakeven point is 0.

Financial breakeven point for plan II:

$$\frac{(\text{EBIT}-40,000)(1-0.5)-0}{1,00,000}=0$$

$$\Rightarrow \quad 0.5\,\text{EBIT}-20,000=0$$

$$\therefore \quad \text{EBIT}=40,000.$$

Financial breakeven point is 40,000.

Financial breakeven point for plan III:

$$=\frac{(\text{EBIT}-20,000)(1-0.5)-50,000}{75,000}=0$$

$$\Rightarrow \quad 0.5\,\text{EBIT}-10,000-50,000=0$$

$$0.5\,\text{EBIT}=60,000$$

$$\therefore \quad \text{EBIT}=120,000.$$

Financial breakeven point is 120,000.

Leverage Analysis

In financial management leverage analysis means arranging fixed assets in such a way that fixed return is ensured. The types of leverage analysis are:

- Operating leverage: Firm generally purchases the assets, that its operation will produce revenue. When sale increases the fixed cost remains the same and operating revenue will increases. As fixed cost is constant, the % change in operating revenue is more than % change in sale. Hence there is a positive relation between operating leverage and breakeven point.

  Operating leverage= % change in operating profit/% change in sales.

- Financial leverage: It is also called trading on equity. Financial leverage means the use of preference share capital, equity share capital along with fixed interest bearing securities or debentures.

  Financial leverage= % change in earning per share/% change in earnings before interest and tax.

  Financial leverage assumes that the firm is capable of earning more on assets than that acquired by use of funds, on which fixed rate of dividend is paid.

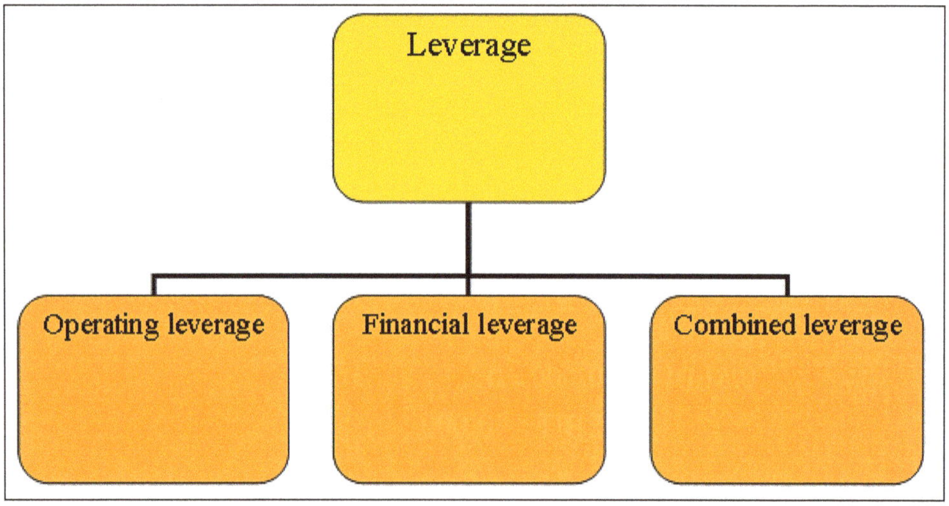

- Combined leverage: it measures the total leverage due to the both operating and financial leverage.

  Combined leverage= % change in earning per share/ % change in sales.

Thus, to conclude we can say that in operating leverage change in sale have effect on EBIT; in financial leverage change in EBIT have effect on EPS.

So the firm uses proper amount of both operating leverage and financial leverage as even a small change in sale changes EPS. EPS increase if sale increases and EPS decreases if sale decreases; there is a positive relation between the two.

Dividend

A dividend is the share of profits and retained earnings a company pays out to its shareholders. When a company generates a profit and accumulates retained earnings, those earnings can be either reinvested in the business or paid out to shareholders as a dividend. The annual dividend per share divided by the share price is the dividend yield.

Working Principle of Dividend

A dividend's value is determined on a per share basis and is to be paid equally to all shareholders of the same class (common, preferred, etc.). The payment must be approved by the by the board of directors.

When a dividend is declared, it will then be paid on a certain date, known as the payable date.

Steps for Working of Dividend

- The company generates profits and retained earnings.
- The management team decides some excess profits should be paid out to shareholders (instead of being reinvested).
- The board approves the planned dividend.
- The company announces the divided (the value per share, the date it will be paid, the record date, etc).
- The dividend is paid to shareholders.

Dividend Example

Below is an example from General Electric (GE)'s 2017 financial statements. As you can see in the screenshot, GE declared a dividend per common share or $0.84 in 2017, $0.93 in 2016, and $0.92 in 2015.

This figure can be compared to Earnings per Share (EPS) from continuing operations and Net Earnings for the same time periods.

Statement of Earnings (Loss)						
For the years ended December 31 (in millions: per share amounts in dollars)	General electric company and consolidated affiliates					
		2017		2016		2015
Per – share amount Earnings (loss) from continuing operations						
Diluted earnings (loss) per share	$	(0.68)	$	1.00	$	0.17
Basic earnings (loss) per share	$	(0.68)	$	1.01	$	0.17
Net earnings (loss)						
Diluted earnings (loss) per share	$	(0.72)	$	0.89	$	(0.61)
Basic earnings (loss) per share	$	(0.72)	$	0.90	$	(0.62)
Dividends declared per common share	$	0.84	$	0.93	$	0.92

Types of Dividends

There are various types of dividends a company can pay to its shareholders. Below are a list and a brief description of the most common types shareholders receive:

- Cash: This is the payment of actual cash from the company directly to the shareholders and is the most common type of payment. The payment is usually made electronically (wire transfer), but may also be paid by check or cash.
- Stock: Stock dividends are paid out to shareholders by issuing new shares in the company. These are paid out pro rata, based on the number of shares the investor owns.
- Assets: A company is not limited to paying distributions to its shareholders in the form of cash or shares. A company may also pay out other assets such as investment securities, physical assets, real estate, and others.
- Special: A special dividend is one that's paid outside of a company regular policy (i.e., quarterly, annual, etc.). It is usually the result of an excess cash build up.
- Common: This refers to the class of shareholders (i.e., common shareholders), not what's actually being received as payment.
- Preferred: This also refers to the class of shareholder receiving the payment.
- Other: Other, less common, types of financial assets can be paid out such as options, warrants, shares in a new spin-out company, etc.

Dividend vs. Buyback

Managers of corporations have several types of distributions they can make to the shareholders. The two most common types are dividends and share buybacks. A share buyback is when a company uses cash on the balance sheet to repurchase shares in the open market. This has two effects:

- It returns cash to shareholders.
- It reduces the number of shares outstanding.

The reason to perform share buybacks as an alternative means of returning capital to shareholders is that it can help boost a company's EPS. By reducing the number of shares outstanding, the denominator in EPS (net earnings/shares outstanding) is reduced and thus EPS increases. Manager of corporations are frequently evaluated on their ability to grow earnings per share, so they may be incentivized to use this strategy.

Impact of a Dividend on Valuation

When a company pays a divided it has no impact on the Enterprise Value of the business. However, it does lower the Equity Value of the business by the value of the dividend that's paid out.

-->			
$m	#1 start	#2Divident	#3End
Equity Value	$50.0	($3.0)	$47.0
Cash	$10.0	($3.0)	$7.0
Debt	$3.0		$3.0
Enterprise Value	$43.0		$43.0

Dividends in Financial Modeling

In financial modeling, it's important to have a solid understanding of how a dividend payment impacts a company's balance sheet, income statement, and cash flow statement. In CFI's financial modeling course, you'll learn how to link the statements together so that any dividends paid flow through all the appropriate accounts.

A well laid out financial model will typically have as assumptions section where any return of capital decisions is contained. For example, if a company is going to pay a cash dividend in 2021 there will be an assumption about what the dollar value will be, which will flow out of retained earnings and through the cash flow statement (investing activities), which will also reduce the cash balance.

Online company Inc. model	Historical Result				Forecast period				
	2014	2015	2016	2017	2018	2019	2020	2021	2022
Income Statement									
Balance Sheet									
Assets									
Cash	81,210	83,715	111,069	139,550	159,474	182,573	190,511	224,399	261,248
Account Receivable	5,904	6,567	7,117	7,539	8,179	8,997	9,896	10,758	11,650
Inventory	9,601	9,825	10,531	11,342	15,267	19,343	24,191	26,894	29,772
Current Assets	96,715	100,107	128,717	158,430	182,920	210,913	224,599	262,051	302,670
Property & Equipment	42,350	40,145	38,602	37,521	45,017	51,013	55,811	59,649	62,719
Good Will									
Total Assets	139,065	140,252	167,319	195,951	227,937	261,927	280,410	321,700	365,389

Liabilities									
Short Term Debt									
Account Payable	4,800	4,912	5,265	5,671	7,061	7,952	8,951	9,951	11,016
Current Liabilities	4,800	4,912	5,265	5,671	7,061	7,952	8,951	9,951	11,016
Long Term Debt	50,000	30,000	30,000	30,000	30,000	30,000	10,000	10,000	10,000
Total Liabilities	54,800	34,912	35,265	35,671	37,061	37,952	18,951	19,951	21,016
Shareholder's Equity									
Equity Capital	70,000	70,000	70,000	70,000	70,000	70,000	70,000	70,000	70,000
Retained Earnings	14,265	35,340	62,053	90,280	120,876	153,974	191,459	231,749	274,373
Shareholder's Equity	84,265	105,340	132,053	160,280	190,876	223,974	261,459	301,749	344,373
Total Liabilities Shareholder's Equity	139,065	140,252	167,319	195,951	227,937	261,927	280,410	321,700	365,389
Check	0.0000	0.0000	0.0000	0.0000	0.0000	0.0000	0.0000	0.0000	0.0000

Dividend Policy

A company's dividend policy dictates the amount of dividends paid out by the company to its shareholders and the frequency with which the dividends are paid out. When a company makes a profit, they need to make a decision on what to do with it. They can either retain the profits in the company (retained earnings on the balance sheet), or they can distribute the money to shareholders in the form of dividends.

Types of Dividend Policies

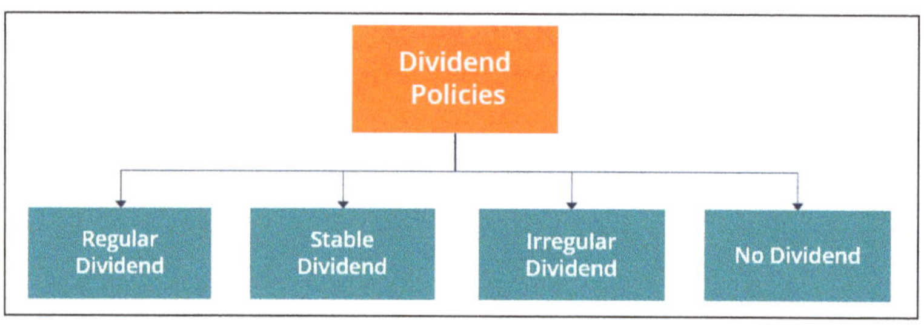

Regular Dividend Policy

Under this type of dividend policy, the company follows the procedure to pay out a dividend to its shareholders every year. If the company earns abnormal profit then it retains the extra profit whereas on the other side if it remains in loss any year then also it pays a dividend to its shareholders. This type of policy is adopted by the company who are having stable earnings and steady cash flow. In the eyes of investors, the company paying regular dividends are considered as low risk despite the fact the quantum of regular dividend might be comparatively low. Under this policy, the investors get dividends at a normal rate.

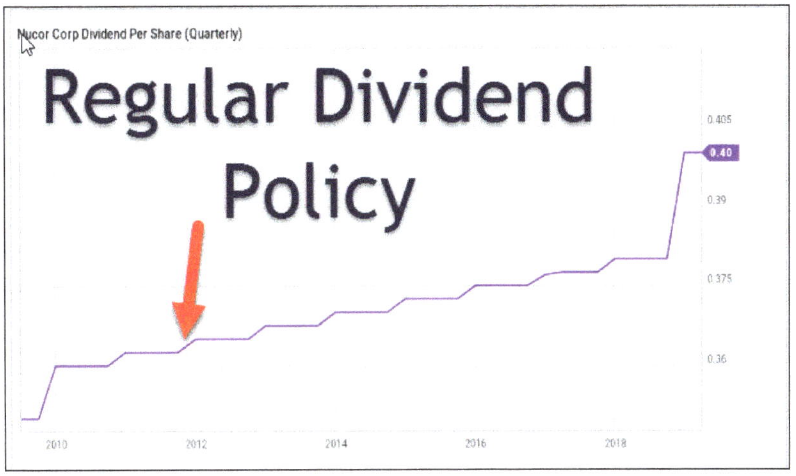

The class of investors putting their investments into these companies is generally risk-averse who mainly belongs to the retired or weaker section of the society and aims at regular income. This policy can be adopted by the company only if it is having a regular income. The main demerit regarding this policy is that investors cannot expect an increase in dividend even if the market is relatively booming high. This type of policy helps in creating confidence among the shareholders and also helps in stabilizing the market value of shares which results in an increase in goodwill of the company.

Stable Dividend Policy

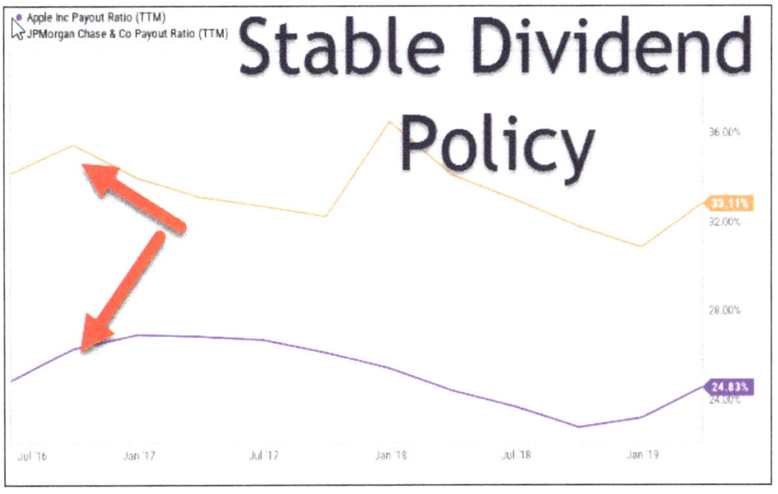

Under this type of dividend policy, the company follows the procedure to pay out a defined fixed percentage of profits as dividends every year. For example, suppose a company sets the payout rate at 10% then this percentage of profit will be paid out as dividends every year regardless of the quantum of profit. Whether a company makes a profit of $1 million or $200000, a fixed rate of dividend will be paid out to the shareholders. In the eyes of investors, the company adopting this policy is considered as risky reason being the amount of dividend fluctuates with the level of profit.

In it, the company makes three components for their dividends which are one part constant amount of dividend per share and the other part is a constant payout ratio and last is stable rupee dividend plus extra dividend. The constant dividend per share is paid through the reserve fund which is created for this purpose. The company actual volatility cannot be seen through the dividend payout. The stable dividend policy is defined by the target payout ratio. It also helps in stabilizing the market value of shares in the same line as regular dividend policy.

Irregular Dividend Policy

Under this type of dividend policy company states that it has no obligation in respect of paying a dividend to the shareholders. The quantum and rate of the dividend will be decided by the board of directors who will take the decision in respect of action to be taken with the earned profit. Their action in respect of paying dividend has nothing to do with the company's scenario of earning a profit or coming into the loss. It totally depends on the decision of the board of directors. The board might take the decision to distribute profit despite having low or no profit with the aim of gaining the confidence of investors so that they will invest more into the company and the company's liquidity will increase.

On the other hand, the company might retain all or major amounts of profit and distribute no or less amount of dividend with the aim of increasing the growth of the company by using the retained earnings. Moreover, this type of policy is adopted by the company who are having irregular cash flow and lacks liquidity. In the eyes of Investors Company paying irregular dividends is considered as risky and investing in this type of company is preferred by the class of investors who are risk lovers.

No Dividend Policy

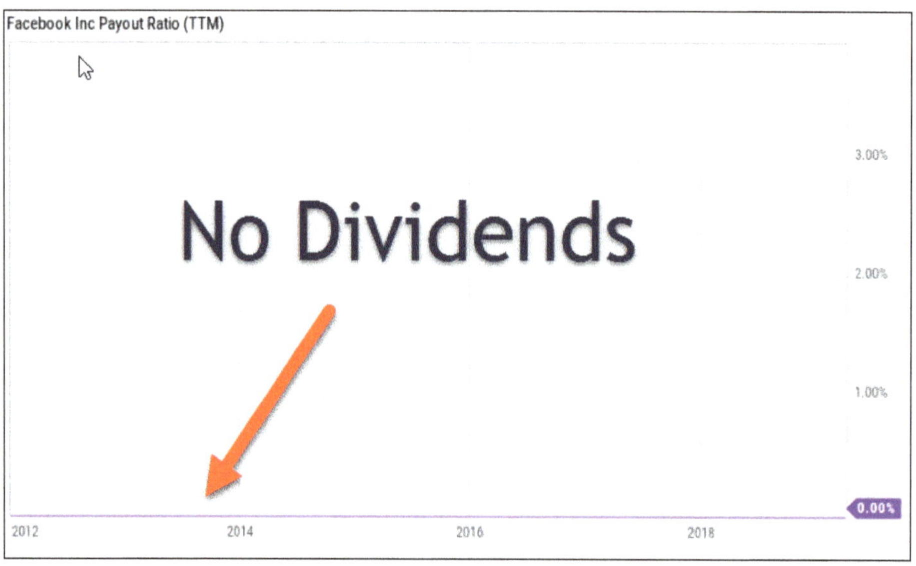

Under this type of dividend policy, the company follows the procedure of paying no dividend to the shareholders irrespective of its profit or loss scenario. The payout ratio will be 0%. The total earning will be retained by the company with the objective of reinvesting into the company model of business to expand it further with an increased rate and without hurdling into the issues like liquidity. The company gets funds through the earning for shareholders and it is the cheaper cost of financing resulting in an increase in profit.

These types of policy are adopted by the company who are generally startup or company who have already established the trust among the investors. For startups, it helps in expanding their business which will result in the overall growth of the business. The shareholders invest in the company's following no dividend policy with the aim that their overall value of an investment will increase with the growth of the company. For them, appreciation in share price is more important than the regular dividend. The class of investors investing in the company following this policy generally belongs to younger or middle ages that are not more bend towards regular income.

Pros and Cons

It reflects management thinking. Hence investors, based on their perception, can take the details given policy either as beneficial or in detriment.

However, the following are the advantages of the dividend policy:

- Intent of the company becomes visible: In the market, there is the company which is rigorously paying a dividend while there are companies whose main intention is to plough back the funds and reinvest the same in the business. Investors based on their fund requirements and earning strategy will invest by checking dividend policy.
- Trends of the dividend payout will be readily available: Investors will need to verify the past trend of the company to declare the dividend, in this policy, it will be readily available. Hence it will be kind of one-stop source of information about the dividends.

Also, the following are the cons, we have to consider while drafting the dividend policy:

- Deviation from the constant dividend pay-out: Any change in the dividend payout, in deviation to the policy or trend, will directly impact the market image of the company. This will give guidance to the analyst, and if anything goes in deviation to the same, it may crash the prices of the shares.
- Future borrowing of funds: This will give guidance to the market and fund providers. Fund providers will always make sure that their funds should be used for the business purpose and, not as a dividend get distributed to promoters.

Modification and Changes in the Dividend Policy

Any modification or changes in the dividend policies will require the approval of the shareholders. Also, if any, material changes are undertaken from statutory requirement per se, then there is also a requirement to intimate the concern state department.

Such modification will affect the mindset of the investors, analyst and credit rating agencies. Hence, it is of utmost importance to remain alert and cautious while making changes in the policy. Such policy changes require strategic thinking duly supported with future business aspects.

In the actual market scenario, corporates will always try to provide guidelines in the policy in a highly generalized manner which will give insight to the investor. No specific transaction related data will be disclosed, hence no additional disclosure will be needed to be added or modified in the future.

References

- Capital-structure-overview, finance, knowledge, resources: corporatefinanceinstitute.com, Retrieved 8 January, 2019
- Capital-structure-meaning-concept-importance-and-factors-accounting, capital-structure, financial-management: yourarticlelibrary.com, Retrieved 13 May, 2019
- Top-4-theories-of-capital-structure, capital-structure, financial-management: accountingnotes.net, Retrieved 25 February, 2019
- Trade-off-theory-capital-structure, business-finance: ebrary.net, Retrieved 16 January, 2019
- Ebit-eps-analysis-in-leverage-concept-advantages-and-other-details, financial-management: yourarticleli- br ary.com, Retrieved 29 March, 2019
- Leverage-analysis-and-types: managementation.com, Retrieved 30 April, 2019
- Dividend, finance, knowledge, resources: corporatefinanceinstitute.com, Retrieved 29 June, 2019
- Dividend-policy-types: wallstreetmojo.com, Retrieved 14 July, 2019

5

Capital Budgeting

The process which is used by businesses for determining which of the proposed fixed asset purchases to accept and which ones to decline is known as capital budgeting. Some of its objectives are selecting profitable projects and capital expenditure control. This chapter closely examines these key objectives of capital budgeting to provide an extensive understanding of the subject.

Capital budgeting, which is also called "investment appraisal," is the planning process used to determine which of an organization's long term investments such as new machinery, replacement machinery, new plants, new products, and research development projects are worth pursuing. It is to budget for major capital investments or expenditures.

Major Methods

Many formal methods are used in capital budgeting, including the techniques as followed:

- Net present value.
- Internal rate of return.
- Payback period.
- Profitability index.
- Equivalent annuity.
- Real options analysis.

Net Present Value

Net present value (NPV) is used to estimate each potential project's value by using a discounted cash flow (DCF) valuation. This valuation requires estimating the size and timing of all the incremental cash flows from the project. The NPV is greatly affected by the discount rate, so selecting the proper rate–sometimes called the hurdle rate–is critical to making the right decision.

This should reflect the riskiness of the investment, typically measured by the volatility of cash flows, and must take into account the financing mix. Managers may use models, such as the CAPM or the APT, to estimate a discount rate appropriate for each particular project, and use the weighted average cost of capital (WACC) to reflect the financing mix selected. A common practice in choosing a discount rate for a project is to apply a WACC that applies to the entire firm, but a higher discount rate may be more appropriate when a project's risk is higher than the risk of the firm as a whole.

Internal Rate of Return

The internal rate of return (IRR) is defined as the discount rate that gives a net present value (NPV) of zero. It is a commonly used measure of investment efficiency. The IRR method will result in the same decision as the NPV method for non-mutually exclusive projects in an unconstrained environment, in the usual cases where a negative cash flow occurs at the start of the project, followed by all positive cash flows. Nevertheless, for mutually exclusive projects, the decision rule of taking the project with the highest IRR, which is often used, may select a project with a lower NPV.

One shortcoming of the IRR method is that it is commonly misunderstood to convey the actual annual profitability of an investment. Accordingly, a measure called "Modified Internal Rate of Return (MIRR)" is often used.

Payback Period

Payback period in capital budgeting refers to the period of time required for the return on an investment to "repay" the sum of the original investment. Payback period intuitively measures how long something takes to "pay for itself". All else being equal, shorter payback periods are preferable to longer payback periods.

The payback period is considered a method of analysis with serious limitations and qualifications for its use, because it does not account for the time value of money, risk, financing, or other important considerations, such as the opportunity cost.

Profitability Index

Profitability index (PI), also known as profit investment ratio (PIR) and value investment ratio (VIR), is the ratio of payoff to investment of a proposed project. It is a useful tool for ranking projects, because it allows you to quantify the amount of value created per unit of investment.

Equivalent Annuity

The equivalent annuity method expresses the NPV as an annualized cash flow by dividing it by the present value of the annuity factor. It is often used when comparing investment projects of unequal lifespans. For example, if project A has an expected lifetime of seven years, and project B has an expected lifetime of 11 years, it would be improper to simply compare the net present values (NPVs) of the two projects, unless the projects could not be repeated.

Real Options Analysis

The discounted cash flow methods essentially value projects as if they were risky bonds, with the promised cash flows known. But managers will have many choices of how to increase future cash inflows or to decrease future cash outflows. In other words, managers get to manage the projects, not simply accept or reject them. Real options analysis try to value the choices–the option value–that the managers will have in the future and adds these values to the NPV.

These methods use the incremental cash flows from each potential investment or project. Techniques based on accounting earnings and accounting rules are sometimes used. Simplified and hybrid methods are used as well, such as payback period and discounted payback period.

The Goals of Capital Budgeting

The main goals of capital budgeting are not only to control resources and provide visibility, but also to rank projects and raise funds.

The purpose of budgeting is to provide a forecast of revenues and expenditures. That is, to construct a model of how a business might perform financially if certain strategies, events, and plans are carried out. It enables the actual financial operation of the business to be measured against the forecast, and it establishes the cost constraint for a project, program, or operation.

Budgeting helps to aid the planning of actual operations by forcing managers to consider how the conditions might change, and what steps should be taken in such an event. It encourages managers to consider problems before they arise. It also helps co-ordinate the activities of the organization by compelling managers to examine relationships between their own operation and those of other departments.

Other essential functions of a budget include:

- To control resources.
- To communicate plans to various responsibility center managers.
- To motivate managers to strive to achieve budget goals.
- To evaluate the performance of managers.
- To provide visibility into the company's performance.

Capital Budgeting, as a part of budgeting, more specifically focuses on long-term investment, major capital and capital expenditures. The main goals of capital budgeting involve:

Ranking Projects

The real value of capital budgeting is to rank projects. Most organizations have many projects that could potentially be financially rewarding. Once it has been determined that a particular project has exceeded its hurdle, then it should be ranked against peer projects (e.g. – highest Profitability index to lowest Profitability index). The highest ranking projects should be implemented until the budgeted capital has been expended.

Raising Funds

When a corporation determines its capital budget, it must acquire funds. Three methods are generally available to publicly-traded corporations: corporate bonds, preferred stock, and common stock. The ideal mix of those funding sources is determined by the financial managers of the firm and is related to the amount of financial risk that the corporation is willing to undertake.

Corporate bonds entail the lowest financial risk and, therefore, generally have the lowest interest rate. Preferred stock have no financial risk but dividends, including all in arrears, must be paid to the preferred stockholders before any cash disbursements can be made to common stockholders; they generally have interest rates higher than those of corporate bonds. Finally, common stocks entail no financial risk but are the most expensive way to finance capital projects. The Internal Rate of Return is very important.

Capital budgeting is an important task as large sums of money are involved, which influences the profitability of the firm. Plus, a long-term investment, once made, cannot be reversed without significant loss of invested capital. The implication of long-term investment decisions are more extensive than those of short-run decisions because of the time factor involved; capital budgeting decisions are subject to a higher degree of risk and uncertainty than are short-run decisions.

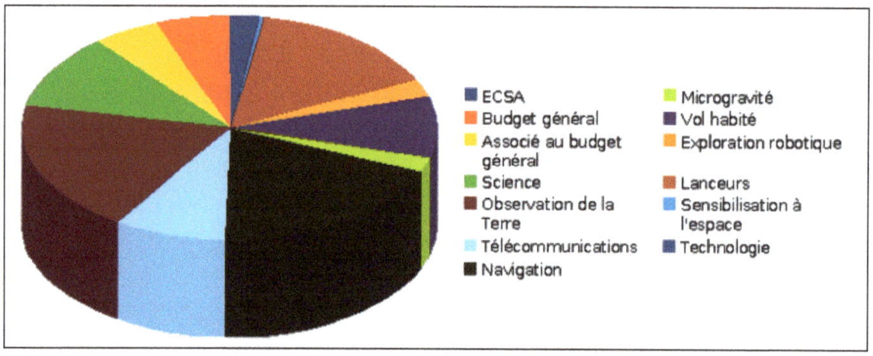

Goals of capital budgeting: The main goal of capital budgeting is to rank projects.

Accounting Flows and Cash Flows

Capital budgeting requires a thorough understanding of cash flow and accounting principles, particularly as they pertain to valuing processes and investments.

Accounting Flows

Accounting is the processes used to identify and transpose business transactions into permanent legal records of a business's operations and capital flows. The International Accounting Standards (IAS) and the Generally Accepted Accounting Principles (GAAP) are legislative descriptions of expectations and norms within the accounting field.

When it comes to the capital flows in accounting, it is easiest to visualize it based on each type of item:

Assets		Liabilities		Equity							
				Capital		Dividends		Revenues		Expenses	
↑ Debit **Increases** *Normal Balance*	↓ Credit **Decreases**	↓ Debit **Decreases**	↑ Credit **Increases** *Normal Balance*	↓ Debit **Decreases**	↑ Credit **Increases** *Normal Balance*	↑ Debit **Increases** *Normal Balance*	↓ Credit **Decreases**	↓ Debit **Decreases**	↑ Credit **Increases** *Normal Balance*	↑ Debit **Increases** *Normal Balance*	↓ Credit **Decreases**

Accounting Flows: This chart is a useful way to see the trajectory of accounting flows as they apply to different types of line items.

Understanding how to report each type of asset, and the impacts these asset changes have on income statements, balance sheets, and cash flow statements, is important in accurately depicting accounting flows.

Cash Flows

A cash flow is one element of accounting flows, and particularly important to understanding capital budgeting. A cash flow describes the transmission of payments and returns internally and/or externally as a byproduct of operations over time. Conducting cash flow analyses on current or potential projects and investments is a critical aspect of capital budgeting, and determines the profitability, cost of capital, and/or expected rate of return on a given project, organizational operation or investment.

Cash flow analyses can reveal the rate of return, or value of suggested project, through deriving the internal rate of return (IRR) and the net present value (NPV). They also indicate overall liquidity, or a business's capacity to capture existing opportunities through freeing of capital for future investments. Cash flows will also underline overall profitability including, but not limited to, net income.

Cash flows consolidate inputs from the following activities:

- Investing activities: Payments related to mergers or acquisitions, loans made to suppliers or received from customers, as well as the purchase or sale of assets are all considered investing activities and tracked as incoming or outgoing cash flows.
- Operating activities: Operating activities can be quite broad, incorporating anything related to the production, sale, or delivery of a given product or service. This includes raw materials, advertising, shipping, inventory, payments to suppliers and employee, interest payments, depreciation, deferred tax, and amortization.
- Financing activities: Financing activities primarily revolve around cash inflows from banks and shareholders, as well as outflows via dividends to investors. This includes, payment for repurchase of company shares, dividends, net borrowing and net repayment of debt.

Ranking Investment Proposals

The most valuable aim of capital budgeting is to rank investment proposals. To choose the most valuable investment option, several methods are commonly used.

Investment Proposal: Choosing the best investment proposal for business.

Several methods are commonly used to rank investment proposals, including NPV, IRR, PI, payback period, and ARR.

Net Present Value (NPV)

NPV can be described as the "difference amount" between the sums of discounted: cash inflows and cash outflows. In the case when all future cash flows are incoming, and the only outflow of cash is the purchase price, the NPV is simply the PV of future cash flows minus the purchase price (which is its own PV). The higher the NPV, the more attractive the investment proposal. NPV is a central tool in discounted cash flow (DCF) analysis and is a standard method for using the time value of money to appraise long-term projects. Used for capital budgeting and widely used throughout economics, finance, and accounting, it measures the excess or shortfall of cash flows, in present value terms, once financing charges are met.

$$\text{NPV}\left(i,N\right)=\sum_{t=1}^{N}\frac{R_t}{\left(1+i\right)^t},$$

In financial theory, if there is a choice between two mutually exclusive alternatives, the one yielding the higher NPV should be selected. The rules of decision making are:

NPV formula: Each cash inflow/outflow is discounted back to its present value (PV). Then they are summed. Therefore, NPV is the sum of all terms.

- When NPV > 0, the investment would add value to the firm so the project may be accepted.
- When NPV < 0, the investment would subtract value from the firm so the project should be rejected.
- When NPV = 0, the investment would neither gain nor lose value for the firm. We should be indifferent in the decision whether to accept or reject the project. This project adds no monetary value. Decision should be based on other criteria (e.g., strategic positioning or other factors not explicitly included in the calculation).

An NPV calculated using variable discount rates (if they are known for the duration of the investment) better reflects the situation than one calculated from a constant discount rate for the entire investment duration.

Internal Rate of Return (IRR)

The internal rate of return on an investment or project is the "annualized effective compounded return rate" or "rate of return" that makes the net present value (NPV as NET*1/(1+IRR)^year) of all cash flows (both positive and negative) from a particular investment equal to zero.

IRR calculations are commonly used to evaluate the desirability of investments or projects. The higher a project's IRR, the more desirable it is to undertake the project. Assuming all projects require the same amount of up-front investment, the project with the highest IRR would be considered the best and undertaken first.

Profitability Index (PI)

It is a useful tool for ranking projects, because it allows you to quantify the amount of value created per unit of investment. The ratio is calculated as follows:

Profitability index = PV of future cash flows / Initial investment.

As the value of the profitability index increases, so does the financial attractiveness of the proposed project. Rules for selection or rejection of a project:

- If PI > 1 then accept the project.
- If PI < 1 then reject the project.

Payback Period

Payback period intuitively measures how long something takes to "pay for itself. " All else being equal, shorter payback periods are preferable to longer payback periods. Payback period is widely used because of its ease of use despite the recognized limitations: The time value of money is not taken into account.

Accounting Rate of Return (ARR)

The ratio does not take into account the concept of time value of money. ARR calculates the return, generated from net income of the proposed capital investment. The ARR is a percentage return. Say, if ARR = 7%, then it means that the project is expected to earn seven cents out of each dollar invested. If the ARR is equal to or greater than the required rate of return, the project is acceptable. If it is less than the desired rate, it should be rejected. When comparing investments, the higher the ARR, the more attractive the investment. Basic formulae:

ARR = Average profit / Average investment,

where: Average investment = (Book value at beginning of year 1 + Book value at end of user life)/2

Reinvestment Assumptions

NPV and PI assume reinvestment at the discount rate, while IRR assumes reinvestment at the internal rate of return.

Reinvestment Rate

To some extent, the selection of the discount rate is dependent on the use to which it will be put. If the intent is simply to determine whether a project will add value to the company, using the firm's weighted average cost of capital may be appropriate. If trying to decide between alternative investments in order to maximize the value of the firm, the corporate reinvestment rate would probably be a better choice.

Reinvestment: Reinvestment to expand business.

$$\text{Year 3 Reinvesment factor} = \frac{\text{year 3 total distribution} \times \text{year 2 Reinvesment factor}}{\text{Year 3 share price}}$$

Reinvestment Factor: Describe how the reinvestment factors related to total return.

NPV Reinvestment Assumption

The rate used to discount future cash flows to the present value is a key variable of this process. A firm's weighted average cost of capital (after tax) is often used, but many people believe that it is appropriate to use higher discount rates to adjust for risk or other factors. A variable discount rate with higher rates applied to cash flows occurring further along the time span might be used to reflect the yield curve premium for long-term debt.

Another approach to choosing the discount rate factor is to decide the rate that the capital needed for the project could return if invested in an alternative venture. Related to this concept is to use the firm's reinvestment rate. Reinvestment rate can be defined as the rate of return for the firm's investments on average. When analyzing projects in a capital constrained environment, it may be appropriate to use the reinvestment rate, rather than the firm's weighted average cost of capital as the discount factor. It reflects opportunity cost of investment, rather than the possibly lower cost of capital.

PI Reinvestment Assumption

Profitability index assumes that the cash flow calculated does not include the investment made in the project, which means PI reinvestment at the discount rate as NPV method. A profitability index of 1 indicates break even. Any value lower than one would indicate that the project's PV is less than the initial investment. As the value of the profitability index increases, so does the financial attractiveness of the proposed project.

IRR Reinvestment Assumption

As an investment decision tool, the calculated IRR should not be used to rate mutually exclusive projects but only to decide whether a single project is worth the investment. In cases where one project has a higher initial investment than a second mutually exclusive project, the first project may have a lower IRR (expected return) but a higher NPV (increase in shareholders ' wealth) and, thus, should be accepted over the second project (assuming no capital constraints).

IRR assumes reinvestment of interim cash flows in projects with equal rates of return (the reinvestment can be the same project or a different project). Therefore, IRR overstates the annual equivalent rate of return for a project that has interim cash flows which are reinvested at a rate lower than the calculated IRR. This presents a problem, especially for high IRR projects, since there is frequently not another project available in the interim that can earn the same rate of return as the first project.

When the calculated IRR is higher than the true reinvestment rate for interim cash flows, the measure will overestimate–sometimes very significantly–the annual equivalent return from the project. This makes IRR a suitable (and popular) choice for analyzing venture capital and other private equity investments, as these strategies usually require several cash investments throughout the project, but only see one cash outflow at the end of the project (e.g., via IPO or M&A).

When a project has multiple IRRs, it may be more convenient to compute the IRR of the project with the benefits reinvested. Accordingly, MIRR is used, which has an assumed reinvestment rate, usually equal to the project's cost of capital.

$$\mathrm{MIRR} = \sqrt[n]{\frac{FV\,(positive\,cash\,flows, \text{reinvesment rate})}{-PV\,(\text{negetive cash flows, finance rate})}} - 1$$

Calculation of the MIRR.

Long-term vs. Short-term Financing

Long-term financing is generally for assets and projects and short term financing is typically for continuing operations.

Achieving the goals of corporate finance requires appropriate financing of any corporate investment. The sources of financing are, generically, capital that is self-generated by the firm and capital from external funders, obtained by issuing new debt and equity.

Management must attempt to match the long-term or short-term financing mix to the assets being financed as closely as possible, in terms of both timing and cash flows.

Financing: To manage business often requires long-term and short-term financing.

Long-term Financing

Businesses need long-term financing for acquiring new equipment, R&D, cash flow enhancement and company expansion. Major methods for long-term financing are as follows:

Equity Financing

This includes preferred stocks and common stocks and is less risky with respect to cash flow commitments. However, it does result in a dilution of share ownership, control and earnings. The cost of equity is also typically higher than the cost of debt – which is, additionally, a deductible expense – and so equity financing may result in an increased hurdle rate which may offset any reduction in cash flow risk.

Corporate Bond

A corporate bond is a bond issued by a corporation to raise money effectively so as to expand its business. The term is usually applied to longer-term debt instruments, generally with a maturity date falling at least a year after their issue date.

Some corporate bonds have an embedded call option that allows the issuer to redeem the debt before its maturity date. Other bonds, known as convertible bonds, allow investors to convert the bond into equity.

Capital Notes

Capital notes are a form of convertible security exercisable into shares. They are equity vehicles. Capital notes are similar to warrants, except that they often do not have an expiration date or an exercise price (hence, the entire consideration the company expects to receive, for its future issue of shares, is paid when the capital note is issued). Many times, capital notes are issued in connection with a debt-for-equity swap restructuring: instead of issuing the shares (that replace debt) in the present, the company gives creditors convertible securities – capital notes – so the dilution will occur later.

Short-term Financing

Short-term financing can be used over a period of up to a year to help corporations increase inventory orders, payrolls and daily supplies. Short-term financing includes the following financial instruments:

Commercial Paper

This is an unsecured promissory note with a fixed maturity of 1 to 364 days in the global money market. It is issued by large corporations to get financing to meet short-term debt obligations. It is only backed by an issuing bank or corporation's promise to pay the face amount on the maturity date specified on the note. Since it is not backed by collateral, only firms with excellent credit ratings from a recognized rating agency will be able to sell their commercial paper at a reasonable price.

Asset-backed commercial paper (ABCP) is a form of commercial paper that is collateralized by other financial assets. ABCP is typically a short-term instrument that matures between 1 and 180 days from issuance and is typically issued by a bank or other financial institution.

Promissory Note

This is a negotiable instrument, wherein one party (the maker or issuer) makes an unconditional promise in writing to pay a determinate sum of money to the other (the payee), either at a fixed or determinable future time or on demand of the payee, under specific terms.

Asset-based Loan

This type of loan, often short term, is secured by a company's assets. Real estate, accounts receivable (A/R), inventory and equipment are typical assets used to back the loan. The loan may be backed by a single category of assets or a combination of assets (for instance, a combination of A/R and equipment).

Repurchase Agreements

These are short-term loans (normally for less than two weeks and frequently for just one day) arranged by selling securities to an investor with an agreement to repurchase them at a fixed price on a fixed date.

Letter of Credit

This is a document that a financial institution or similar party issues to a seller of goods or services which provides that the issuer will pay the seller for goods or services the seller delivers to a third-party buyer. The issuer then seeks reimbursement from the buyer or from the buyer's bank. The document serves essentially as a guarantee to the seller that it will be paid by the issuer of the letter of credit, regardless of whether the buyer ultimately fails to pay.

Objectives of Capital Budgeting

Capital expenditures are huge and have a long-term effect. Therefore, while performing a capital budgeting analysis an organization must keep the following objectives in mind:

Selecting Profitable Projects

An organization comes across various profitable projects frequently. But due to capital restrictions, an organization needs to select the right mix of profitable projects that will increase its shareholders' wealth.

Capital Expenditure Control

Selecting the most profitable investment is the main objective of capital budgeting. However, controlling capital costs is also an important objective. Forecasting capital expenditure requirements and budgeting for it, and ensuring no investment opportunities are lost is the crux of budgeting.

Finding the Right Sources for Funds

Determining the quantum of funds and the sources for procuring them is another important objective of capital budgeting. Finding the balance between the cost of borrowing and returns on investment is an important goal of Capital Budgeting.

Capital Budgeting Process

The process of capital budgeting is as follows:

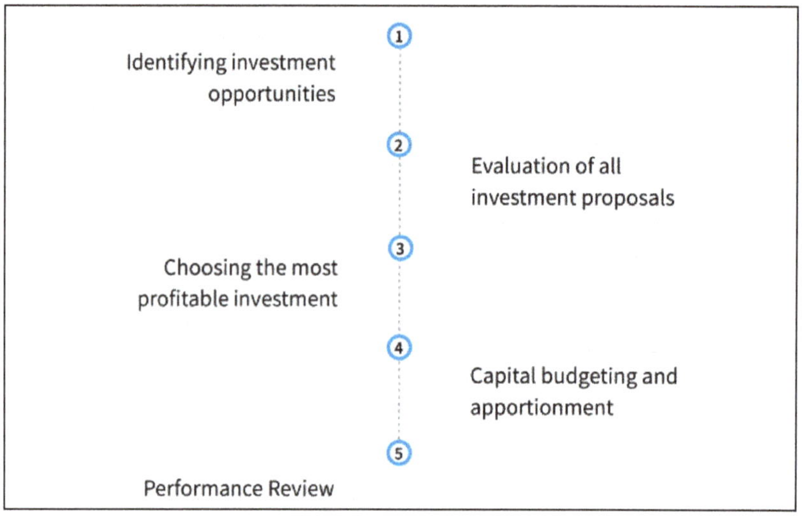

Capital Budgeting Process.

Identifying Investment Opportunities

An organization needs to first identify an investment opportunity. An investment opportunity can be anything from a new business line to product expansion to purchasing a new asset. For example, a company finds two new products that they can add to their product line.

Evaluating Investment Proposals

Once an investment opportunity has been recognized an organization needs to evaluate its options for investment. That is to say, once it is decided that new product/products should be added to the product line, the next step would be deciding on how to acquire these products. There might be multiple ways of acquiring them. Some of these products could be:

- Manufactured In-house,
- Manufactured by Outsourcing manufacturing the process, or
- Purchased from the market.

Choosing a Profitable Investment

Once the investment opportunities are identified and all proposals are evaluated an organization needs to decide the most profitable investment and select it. While selecting a particular project an organization may have to use the technique of capital rationing to rank the projects as per returns and select the best option available.

In our example, the company here has to decide what is more profitable for them. Manufacturing or purchasing one or both of the products or scrapping the idea of acquiring both.

Capital Budgeting and Apportionment

After the project is selected an organization needs to fund this project. To fund the project it needs to identify the sources of funds and allocate it accordingly.

The sources of these funds could be reserves, investments, loans or any other available channel.

Performance Review

The last step in the process of capital budgeting is reviewing the investment. Initially, the organization had selected a particular investment for a predicted return. So now, they will compare the investments expected performance to the actual performance.

In our example, when the screening for the most profitable investment happened, an expected return would have been worked out. Once the investment is made, the products are released in the market, the profits earned from its sales should be compared to the set expected returns.

Investment Criteria

Investment criteria refers to the problem of determining the best utilisation of investment resources to minimize capital intensity, to maximize social marginal productivity of capital and employment absorption.

Objectives of Factor Allocation of Investment

The primary objective of a developing economy is to secure a greater and faster increase in its income from its available resources. Therefore, the objectives of investment criteria are summarized below:

- Equal distribution of income and wealth.
- Balanced and rapid growth of the economy.
- To raise the gross and national product and per capita income.
- Proper allocation of existing resources.
- Efforts to correct the balance of payment.
- All-round development of the country.
- To keep watch the interest of the future generation.

Practical Application of Investment Criteria

Out of the various investment criteria discussed, it is difficult to suggest any one criterion of the allocation of investment resources in underdeveloped countries. Since the problems facing these countries are manifold any one criterion can only have limited application. Hence the choice of a suitable criterion will very much depend upon the circumstances prevailing in a country and the problems with which it is faced. In addition to that the practical application of the investment criteria may be limited due to the following factors:

- It is difficult to define correctly the objectives of an investment policy. There may be various conflicting objectives and it may be difficult to choose the most desirable ones.
- The principles of investment recommended by different writers are defective as theories. It is doubtful whether a sound theory can be laid down in respect of the complicated problems of investment.
- The investment criteria generally fail because of the various non-measurable aspects of investment projects.

Types of Investment Criteria

Social Marginal Productivity Criteria

This theory was put forward by Hollis B. Chenery. Social Marginal Productivity of Investment may be defined as the return to the private investor plus the net contribution of the investment to the national product. According to this criterion, the projects must be ranked according to their social value, determine the marginal project from the total funds and exclude all lower- ranking projects. In order to measure social marginal product (SMP) Chenery used the following method:

Let the welfare function be $U = f(Y, B, D,)$,

where:

Y = effect on income,

B, effect on balance of payments,

D = effect on distribution of income, and

U = index of social welfare.

Then increment in U corresponding to a given increment in investment can be written as:

$$\Delta U = \frac{\delta U}{\delta Y}\Delta Y + \frac{\delta U}{\delta B}\Delta B + \Delta D + ,$$

This implies, the increase in SMP is the sum of the effects of a change in income, balance of payments portion, distribution of income etc. For simple explanation, all other variables are ignored excepting Y and B to express SMP.

Accordingly

$$SMP = \Delta U = \Delta Y + r\Delta B,$$

Mathematically, "r" represents an amount of increase in national income which would be equivalent to an improvement of one unit in the balance of payments under specified conditions. Therefore, r measures the average over-valuation of the domestic currency, at the existing rates of exchange.

If r=0, balance of payments is in equilibrium, if r is positive (>0), the domestic currency is overvalued and if r is negative (<0) the domestic currency is undervalued. In underdeveloped countries r may be appreciably greater than zero because of the relative inelasticity of imports and exports. This follows:

$$SMP = \frac{X+E-M_i}{K} - \frac{L+M_d+O}{K} + \frac{1}{K}(\alpha B_1 + B_2),$$

or,

$$SMP = \frac{V}{K} - \frac{C}{K} + \frac{B_r}{K},$$

where: All Variables (except B_1 and K) are Annual Flows.

SMP = Average annual increment in national income from marginal unit of investment in a given productive use;

- K = Increment to Capital (Investment),
- X = Increased market value of output,
- E = Added value of output due to external economies,
- M_1 = Cost of imported materials,
- V = Social value added domestically, i.e., V = X+E—M_i,
- L = Labour cost,
- M_i = Cost of domestic materials,
- O = Cost of overheads,
- C = Total cost of domestic factors = L + M_d + O,
- B_r = Total balance of payments effect = $\alpha B_1 + B_2$,
- α = current amortization and interest rate on current borrowings,
- B_1 = Effect of investment on balance of payments,
- B_2 = Effect of operation on balance of payments.

Thus, the social marginal product is divided into three elements, viz.:

- Value added in the domestic economy for unit of investment;
- Total operating costs per unit of investment; and
- Balance of payments premium per unit of investment.

SMP is thus the product of the percentage margin of social value over cost (V-C/V) and the rate of capital turnover plus the balance of payments premium. This form of equation shows that a decrease in the rate of capital turnover may be offset by a proportionate increase in the value margin and vice-versa.

Limitations

- It presupposes the attainment of an optimal income distribution by purely fiscal means.
- The concept is vague. It is less definite than the private profit criterion although it is more generally applicable.
- The market prices do not exactly reflect social values and as such, quantitative assessment of the costs and benefits arising out of investment is extremely difficult.
- It is difficult to measure the costs of a larger number of items which contribute to the total cost of a project.
- It is pointed out that the effect of an investment on balance of payments arises not only from the cost incurred in connection with installation and operation of the plant but also on the availability of foreign loans, their expected flow over time and conditions of repayment;
- This criterion does not consider structural interdependence and the nature and value of external economies.
- SMP criterion helps in the maximization of output that can be attributed to the current investment effort but it does not take into consideration as to what happens to the final product during any period, which in turn, influences the investment rate in future.
- Harvey Leibenstein criticizes that it does not emphasize the need for generating the forces of economic development in an underdeveloped country. According to him, the object should be to maximize the amount of capital per worker and improve the quality of labour force.

Capital Turnover Criterion or Capital Intensity Criterion

J.J. Polak and N.S. Buchanan have propounded this criterion. This criterion is based on capital-output ratio, i.e., K/Y of a project. In those countries where capital is scarce, funds should be invested in those projects which have the lowest capital intensity.

This criterion is also used in its reverse form and then it is called capital—turnover criterion. According to this criterion, those projects should be selected which have a high rate of capital turnover or low capital output ratio.

Since capital is scarce in underdeveloped countries, those projects should be chosen which yield maximum output per unit of capital invested, i.e., where the capital—turnover is the highest. Quick yielding projects with low capital intensity are also desirable because they make it possible for the scarce capital resources to be released soon for investment in other projects.

Such projects also generate more employment which may be very desirable in the context of underdeveloped countries.

Criticism

This present criterion has been criticised on the following grounds:

- The difficulty arises in estimating capital -output ratio in poor countries and comparing it with that of advanced countries due to lack of data. Hence, any criterion based on capital output ratio is likely to create practical difficulties.
- This criterion does not take into account the element of time. A particular project may be less capital intensive in the short run but may turn out to be more capital intensive in the long run.
- The supplementary benefits conferred by a project have not been taken into account while laying down this criterion. It is possible that a project may be more capital intensive but it confers important supplementary benefits on the economy which may outweigh its high capital cost. Thus the projects with low capital-output ratio have also got their importance for a developing economy.
- The employment argument in favour of less capital intensive projects does not hold good. A more capital-intensive project can also contribute substantially in providing more employment in the long-run.
- Labour intensive projects may generate more employment but they tend to reduce productivity. Hence, capital intensive projects are also quite important for underdeveloped countries if the level of output is to be raised substantially.
- The maximization of employment argument implied in this concept may hold good in short run. A capital intensive project may absorb little labour to start with, but may maximize the amount of labour per unit of investment in the long run.
- These techniques often produce sub-standard projects such products are often subsidised by Govt., and entail high social costs.
- The supplementary benefits of a project are not taken into consideration. It is possible that a project may be more capital intensive but it confers important supplementary benefits on the economy which may outweigh its high capital cost. Thus the projects with low capital output ratio have greater importance for developing economy.

Reinvestment Criteria or Criteria of Investment for Accelerated Growth

Walter Galenson and Harvey Leibenstein introduced the concept of marginal per capita reinvestment quotient criterion for investment in the underdeveloped countries. The rate of investment per unit of capital invested is given by:

$$r = p - ew/c$$

where p=output per machine; e=number of workers for machine; w = real wage rate; c = cost per machine and r = rate of reinvestment per unit of capital.

This model explains the employment provided by any combination of men and machines through the following equation:

$$E_{1+1} = E_1 \left(1 + \frac{p - e\omega}{c}\right)^t,$$

where E = Total employment.

It is assumed that I = P—W,

i.e., the total amount invested in any period is the difference between the total gross value added (P=Np) and the real compensation paid to labour (Ew) Then:

I = P—Ew,

I = NP—Ew,

I = N_p — eNw = N(p— ew),

Net investment I = cost per machine (c) multiplied AN, the increase in number of machines,

Is given by (ΔN/N) and is equal to the rate of reinvestment for unit of capital i.e.

r = ΔN/N = P — ew/c,

This criterion is thus designed to take into account the influence of choice of projects on the rate of capital accumulation. If we assume that all profits are reinvested while all wages are consumed, this reinvestment quotient is nothing but the rate of profit. This reinvestment quotient is likely to be higher in capital intensive than in labour intensive projects.

Criticism

This criterion focuses its attention on the maximization of the current rate of investment so that the economy could grow at a rapid rate in the years to come but it fails to take into account the reality of the situation in the LDC's. Its main shortcomings are as follows:

- This criterion would have adverse effect on income distribution and employment. In many countries reduction of income disparities and unemployment are the main objectives of planning so this criterion cannot be adopted in these countries.
- It is against the principle of marginal productivity of capital. As the amount of capital is increased in successive doses and offers a point where its productivity starts declining and hence there is fall in output per capita.

- It does not consider the effect of balance of payments on investment. In an under developed economy there is an acute scarcity of capital goods which have to be imported and they worsen the already tight balance of payments position.
- It neglects the importance of consumption; rather it advocates its curtailment. But current consumption may be more important than future consumption and the reinvestible surplus may have to be cut down in the interest of the community. The ignorance of consumer goods sector in favour of capital goods sector brings serious consequences both for economy and the state.
- Adoption of highly capital intensive techniques may create certain practical difficulties in underdeveloped countries. These countries are generally short of capital and due to this it is not possible for them to concentrate on capital intensive project. Shortage of skilled manpower and entrepreneurial ability may create another difficulty.
- Capital deepening of investment does not ensure the best utilization of the available capital resources. It may result in such an inefficient allocation of capital resources that the increase in income may be very small.
- Growth rate cannot be maximized by choosing the investment which has higher re-investible profit per unit of capital. Choice of investment with a higher reinvestment quotient cannot ensure a higher rate of economic growth. The surplus may be large per unit of capital but if the propensity to consume of the people engaged in the production goes up, investible surplus is adversely affected.
- This criterion violates the social welfare objectives of a developing economy. The adoption of this criterion will lead to the concentration of wealth in the hands of the profit earning class. It also results in the displacement of labour which is against the basic norms of a developing society.
- The use of reinvestment criterion perpetuates the problem of unequal distribution of income in such economies. There is greater degree of unequal distribution of income between the wage earners and capitalists and between those who obtain immediate employment and those who are left unabsorbed.
- O. Eckestein is of the view that instead of depending on the reinvestment criterion for planned investment, it may be better to use fiscal measures to attain an income distribution which will yield sufficient savings for purpose of investment.
- The contention that highly capital intensive processes have a large investment potential does not appear to be correct. A highly capital intensive industry like the iron and steel will not yield output until several years have lapsed.

Time Series Criterion

Time factor is an important factor in the choice of techniques. If the capital output ratio and the rate of savings, the time path of two techniques can be drawn. It can be found out which of the techniques yields the highest returns over time horizon.

For that, a time horizon is fixed up and returns for both the projects for different years are calculated. On the basis of this we can find out a period of recovery for any pair of techniques. In choosing the technique we compare this period of recovery with the period we are ready to take into account.

Table: Suppose that there are two projects H and L and time horizon is ten years at the end of which total returns in each case are 100 million.

Period in year	Project 1 capital intensive (H) return in lakhs	Project II capital intensive (L) return in lakhs
1	2.5	6.5
2	4.0	7.0
3	6.0	8.5
4	9.5	9.0
5	10.5	10.0
6	11.5	11.0
7	12.5	12.5
8	13.0	12.0
9	14.0	12.5
10	15.5	13.0
	100	100

The returns of the H project are less in comparison to project L over the first six years while in the remaining four years the returns of H rise more than the project L. Since the total returns are the same for both the projects, the overall position is one of indifference.

The point to be noted is that whether the initial loss in output by adopting a capital intensive projects recovered within the period of ten years or not. The time taken by the capital intensive technique to overcome its initial deficiency in output over the labour intensive technique is called the period of recovery. This is explained with the help of diagram given below:

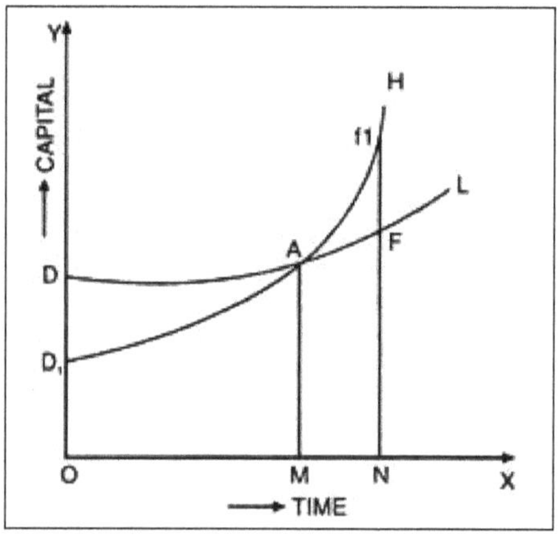

In diagram I, H and L curves show the flow of real output during a given time horizon with two techniques. The period ON is the period of recovery which makes the area DAD_1 = area FAf_1.

Thus for any pair of techniques a period of recovery can be found. In the selection of techniques the period of recovery should be compared with the period we already taken into account. If it is found that period of recovery is longer i.e. if within the time horizon the loss in output by adopting technique H is not recovered by excess of output we should choose technique L and vice-versa. If there is some conflict between present and future, the choice will depend on the time discounted use.

Limitations

The limitations of this criterion:

- It is arbitrary to fix up time horizon of ten years. There is no specific law on the basis of which period of recovery for a particular project can be fixed up.
- It is not possible to derive the time series for all times to come. Therefore, the planning period has to be definitely fixed but this creates some serious problems. When the time limit is about to end, labour intensive technique might be selected in order to inflate the quality of output and thus capital formation is neglected.
- The factors like technological change, wage rate, propensity to consume etc. on which the study of time series depends may all be changing and make the forecasting of future investment.

Balance of Payments Criterion

The balance of payments effect of investment projects is important in case of underdeveloped countries. According to this criterion the allocation of investment should be done to minimize the adverse effect on balance of payments. Balance of payments difficulties of underdeveloped countries are due to the fact that they are heavily dependent on foreign countries for their capital equipment. They also require foreign exchange for import of materials for keeping this equipment into operation.

Buchanan had called this type of imports as the direct drain on foreign exchange. The rise in income due to investment and industrialisation leads to imports of consumer's goods. These are called circulation drain on foreign exchange. On the basis of the effect on the balance of payment. Polak divides investment into three categories:

- Investment, yielding goods which add to the exports of a country or replacing goods formerly imported. The next effect of such an investment will be to create export surplus.
- Investment, replacing goods previously sold in the country or exported from the country; the effect of this sort of investment on balance of payments will be neutral.
- Investment, which would result in addition of goods to those sold in the country and in excess at demand. Such an investment will have a negative effect on the balance of payments.

The first two types of investment should be preferred because they will have a favourable effect on balance of payments. The third type may be avoided. Thus according to this criterion investment projects with least bad effects on the balance of payments must be chosen.

Limitations

The concept of payment criterion is subject to following drawbacks:

- Investment may raise real incomes without increasing money incomes which can be spent on imports here and fear of increased imports there only when money incomes rise.
- If money incomes rise along with real incomes, import may not rise.
- The investment may also lead to less imports rather than investments of first type.

Net Present Value (NPV)

Net Present Value (NPV) is the value of all future cash flows (positive and negative) over the entire life of an investment discounted to the present. NPV analysis is a form of intrinsic valuation and is used extensively across finance and accounting for determining the value of a business, investment security, capital project, new venture, cost reduction program, and anything that involves cash flow.

The formula for Net Present Value is:

$$NPV_{XYZ} = \frac{Z_1}{1+r} + \frac{Z_2}{(1+r)^2} - X_0,$$

where:

- Z_1 = Cash flow in time 1.
- Z_2 = Cash flow in time 2.
- r = Discount rate.
- X_0 = Cash outflow in time 0 (i.e. the purchase price / initial investment).

Need of Net Present Value (NPV) Analysis

NPV analysis is used to help determine how much an investment, project, or any series of cash flows is worth. It is an all-encompassing metric, as it takes into account all revenues, expenses, and capital costs associated with an investment in its Free Cash Flow (FCF).

In addition to factoring all revenues and costs, it also takes into account the timing of each cash flow that can result in a large impact on the present value of an investment. For example, it's better to see cash inflows sooner and cash outflows later, compared to the opposite.

Reasons for Discontinuity of Cash Flows

The cash flows in net present value analysis are discounted for two main reasons, (1) to adjust for the risk of an investment opportunity, and (2) to account for the time value of money (TVM).

The first point (to adjust for risk) is necessary because not all businesses, projects, or investment opportunities have the same level of risk. Put another way, the probability of receiving cash flow from a US Treasury bill is much higher than the probability of receiving cash flow from a young technology startup.

To account for the risk, the discount rate is higher for riskier investments and lower for a safer one. The US treasury example is considered to be the risk-free rate, and all other investments are measured by how much more risk they bear relative to that.

The second point (to account for the time value of money) is required because due to inflation, interest rates, and opportunity costs, money is more valuable the sooner it's received. For example, receiving $1 million today is much better than $1 million received five years from now. If the money is received today, it can be invested and earn interest, so it will be worth more than $1 million in five years' time.

Example of Net Present Value (NPV)

Let's look at an example of how to calculate the net present value of a series of cash flows. As you can see in the screenshot below, the assumption is that an investment will return $10,000 per year over a period of 10 years, and the discount rate required is 10%.

Discount rate	10.0%									
Year	1	2	3	4	5	6	7	8	9	10
Discount factor	0.91	0.83	0.75	0.68	0.62	0.56	0.51	0.47	0.42	0.39
Undiscounted cash flow	10,000	10,000	10,000	10,000	10,000	10,000	10,000	10,000	10,000	10,000
Present value	9,091	8,264	7,513	6,830	6,209	5,645	5,132	4,665	4,241	3,855
Net present value	61,446									

The final result is that the value of this investment is worth $61,446 today. It means a rational investor would be willing to pay up to $61,466 today to receive $10,000 every year over 10 years. By paying this price, the investor would receive an internal rate of return (IRR) of 10%. By paying anything less than $61,000, the investor would earn an internal rate of return that's greater than 10%.

NPV Functions in Excel

Excel offers two functions for calculating net present value: NPV and XNPV. The two functions use the same math formula shown above, but save an analyst the time for calculating it in long form.

The regular NPV function =NPV () assumes that all cash flows in a series occur at regular intervals (i.e. years, quarters, month) and doesn't allow for any variability in those time period.

The XNPV function =XNPV () allows for specific dates to be applied to each cash flow so they can be at irregular intervals. The function can be very useful as cash flows are often unevenly spaced out, and this enhanced level of precision is required.

Internal Rate of Return (IRR) and NPV

The internal rate of return (IRR) is the discount rate at which the net present value of an investment is equal to zero. Put another way, it is the compound annual return an investor expects to earn (or actually earned) over the life of an investment.

For example, if a security offers a series of cash flows with an NPV of $50,000 and an investor pays exactly $50,000 for it, then the investor's NPV is $0. It means they will earn whatever the discount rate is on the security. Ideally, an investor would pay less than $50,000 and therefore earn an IRR that's greater than the discount rate.

Negative vs. Positive Net Present Value

If the net present value of a project or investment, is negative it means the expected rate of return that will be earned on it is less than the discount rate (required rate of return or hurdle rate). This doesn't necessarily mean the project will "lose money." It may very well generate accounting profit (net income), but, since the rate of return generated is less than the discount rate, it is considered to destroy value. If the NPV is positive, it creates value.

Applications in Financial Modeling

NPV of a Business

To value a business an analyst will build a detailed discounted cash flow DCF model in Excel. This financial model will include all revenues, expenses, capital costs, and details of the business. Once the key assumptions are in place, the analyst can build a five-year forecast of the three financial statements (income statement, balance sheet, and cash flow) and calculate the free cash flow of the firm (FCFF), also known as the unlevered free cash flow. Finally, a terminal value is used to value the company beyond the forecast period, and all cash flows are discounted back to the present at the firm's weighted average cost of capital.

NPV of a Project

To value a project is typically more straightforward than an entire business. A similar approach is taken, where all the details of the project are modeled into Excel, however, the forecast period will be for the life of the project and there will be no terminal value. Once the free cash flow is calculated, it can be discounted back to the present at either the firm's WACC or the appropriate hurdle rate.

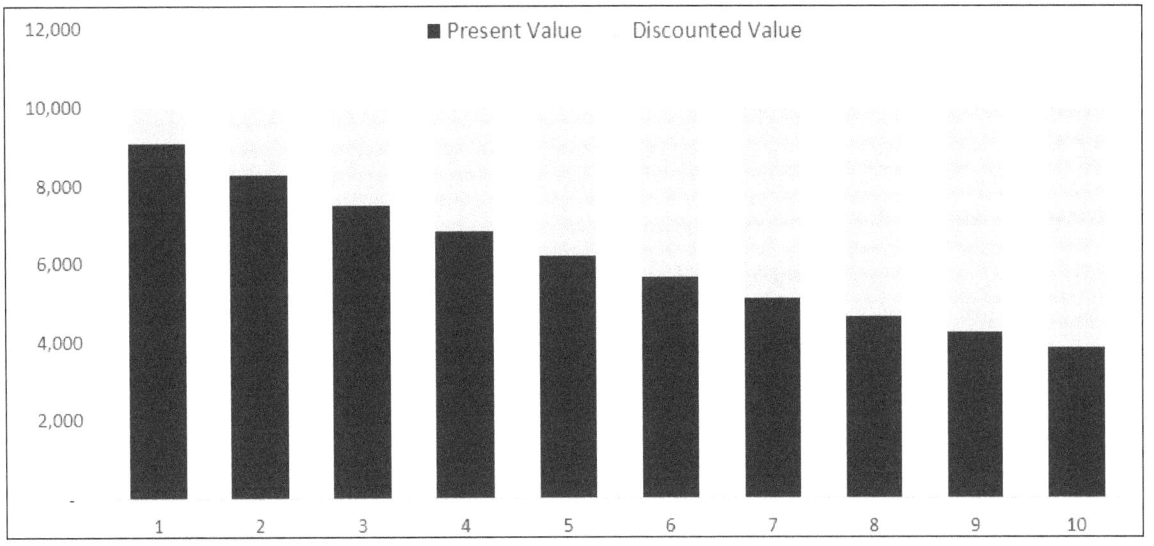

Drawbacks of Net Present Value

While net present value (NPV) is the most commonly used method for evaluating investment opportunities, it does have some drawbacks that should be carefully considered.

Key challenges to NPV analysis include:

- A long list of assumptions has to be made.
- Sensitive to small changes in assumptions and drivers.
- Easily manipulated to produce the desired output.
- May not capture second- and third-order benefits/impacts (i.e. on other parts of a business).
- Assumes a constant discount rate over time.
- Accurate risk-adjustment is challenging to perform (hard to get data on correlations, probabilities.

Profitability Index

Profitability index method measures the present value of benefits for every dollar investment. In other words, it involves the ratio that is created by comparing the ratio of the present value of future cash flows from a project to the initial investment in the project. The Profitability Index Method is often times compared similarly to the Net Present Value Method for their close proximity. One should use caution when utilizing both the NPV and profitability index methods in tandem.

Often times, it has been found that both methods can rank projects in a different way. One project could possibly be ranked number 1 for one of the methods while it ranks dead last in the other.

Profitability Index Method Formula

Profitability Index = (PV of future cash flows) ÷ Initial investment. Or = (NPV + Initial investment) ÷ Initial Investment: As one would expect, the NPV stands for the Net Present Value of the initial investment.

Profitability Index Calculation

Example: a company invested $20,000 for a project and expected NPV of that project is $5,000. Profitability Index = (20,000 + 5,000) / 20,000 = 1.25. That means a company should perform the investment project because profitability index is greater than 1.

Example of Profitability Index

Texabonds Inc has decided to consider a project where they predict the annual cash flows to be $5,000, $3,000 and $4,000, respectively for the next three years. At the beginning of the project, the initial investment put into the project is $10,000. Use the Profitability Index Method and a discount rate of 12% to determine if this is a good project to undertake. In order to solve this problem, it is probably a good idea to make a table so that the numbers can be organized by year.

Using a PI table, the following PVIF's are found respectively for the 3 years: .893, .797, .712. Once the PVIF's are determined, simply multiply the cash flows and the PVIF's together in order to get the PV of cash flows for each respective year ($4,465, $2,391, $2,848). Adding up all the PV's will get the total present value of the project which is $9,704. Divide that final number by the original investment $10,000 and the PI has been determined: .9704. As one can see, the Profitability Index- is less than 1 so the project should be scrapped. The NPV can also be determined by subtracting the initial investment ($10,000) from the total PV of the project ($9,704) and you are left with -$296. In this case, because the number is negative, NPV also says that the project should be rejected.

Application

Profitability index is primarily used as a tool to rank projects. The higher the value of profitability index, the more attractiveness of a proposed project is. For a single project, profitability index value of 1 or greater is acceptable. If a project has profitability index (>1), then a company should perform the project. However if a project has profitability index (<1), a company should reject the project.

There is relationship between profitability index and net present value method. If profitability index >1, the NPV is positive. If profitability index <1, NPV is negative. The profitability index is a relative measure of an investment's value while NPV is an absolute measure. The profitability index method can be a useful substitute for NPV method when presenting a project's benefits per dollar of investment. It makes the most sense to look at the concept from a project-by-project basis. The profitability index gives a company the opportunity to determine whether a project should be pursued or not. If the profitability index is above one, then a company can execute and pursue the project. If the profitability index is below one, then the project should be scrapped for the detrimental cash flow problems.

Internal Rate of Return

The Internal Rate of Return (IRR) is the discount rate that makes the net present value (NPV) of a project zero. In other words, it is the expected compound annual rate of return that will be earned on a project or investment. In the example below, an initial investment of $50 has a 22% IRR. That is economically equal to earning a 22% compound annual growth rate.

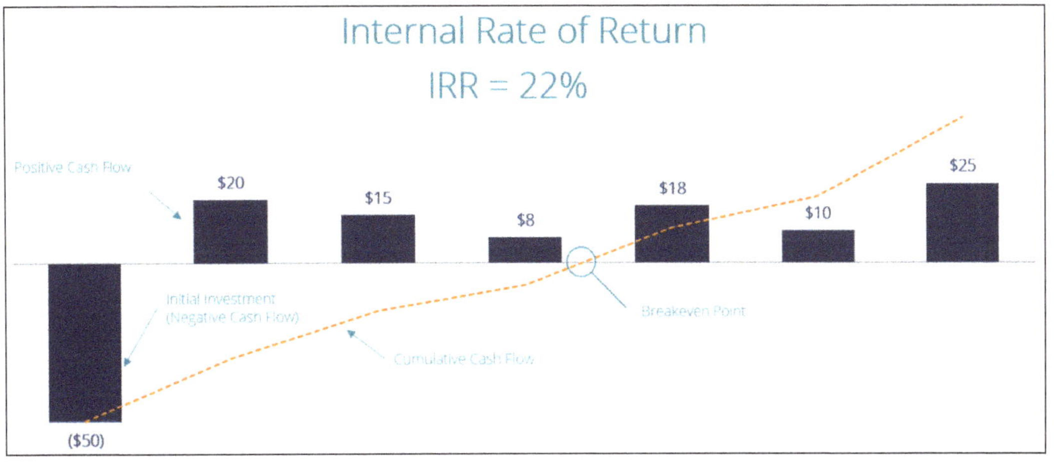

When calculating IRR, expected cash flows for a project or investment are given and the NPV equals zero. Put another way, the initial cash investment for the beginning period will be equal to the present value of the *future* cash flows of that investment. (Cost paid = present value of future cash flows, and hence, the *net* present value = 0).

Once the internal rate of return is determined, it is typically compared to a company's hurdle rate or cost of capital. If the IRR is greater than or equal to the cost of capital, the company would accept the project as a good investment. (That is, of course, assuming this is the sole basis for the decision. In reality there are many other quantitative and qualitative factors that are considered in an investment decision.) If the IRR is lower than the hurdle rate, then it would be rejected.

IRR Formula

The IRR formula is as follows:

$$0 = CF_0 + \frac{CF_1}{(1+IRR)} + \frac{CF_2}{(1+IRR)^2} + \frac{CF_3}{(1+IRR)^3} + \ldots + \frac{CF_n}{(1+IRR)^n}$$

or

$$0 = NPV = \sum_{n=0}^{N} \frac{CF_n}{(1+IRR)^n}$$

where:

$$CF_0 = \text{Initail Invesment / outlay}$$
$$CF_1, CF_2, CF_3 ... CF_n = \text{cash flow}$$
$$n = \text{Each period}$$
$$N = \text{Holding period}$$
$$NPV = \text{Net present value}$$
$$IRR = \text{Internal rate of return}$$

Calculating the internal rate of return can be done in three ways:

- Using the IRR or XIRR function in Excel or other spreadsheet programs.
- Using a financial calculator.
- Using an iterative process where the analyst tries different discount rates until the NPV equals to zero.

Example of Calculating IRR

A company is deciding whether to purchase new equipment that costs \$500,000. Management estimates the life of the new asset to be four years and expects it to generate an additional \$160,000 of annual profits. In the fifth year, the company plans to sell the equipment for its salvage value of \$50,000.

Meanwhile, another similar investment option can generate a 10% return. This is higher than the company's current hurdle rate of 8%. The goal is to make sure the company is making better use of its cash.

To make a decision, the IRR for investing in the new equipment is calculated below.

Excel was used to calculate the IRR of 13%, using the function, *=IRR()*. From a financial standpoint, the company should make the purchase, because the IRR is both greater than the hurdle rate and the IRR for the alternative investment.

Year	Cash flow	PV of cash flow
0	-\$500,000	-\$500,000
1	\$160,000	\$141,247
2	\$160,000	\$124,692
3	\$160,000	\$110,077
4	\$160,000	\$97,176
5	\$50,000	\$26,808

NPV	0
IRR	13%

Use of Internal Rate Return

Companies take on various projects to increase their revenues or cut down costs. A great new business idea may require, for example, investing in the development of a new product.

In capital budgeting, senior leaders like to know the reasonably projected returns on such investments. The internal rate of return is one method that allows them to compare and rank projects based on their projected yield. The investment with the highest internal rate of return is usually preferred.

Internal Rate of Return is widely used in analyzing investments for private equity and venture capital, which involves multiple cash investments over the life of a business and a cash flow at the end through an IPO or sale of the business.

Thorough investment analysis requires an analyst to examine both the net present value (NPV) and the internal rate of return, along with other indicators, such as the payback period, in order to select the right investment. Since it's possible for a very small investment to have a very high rate of return, investors and managers sometimes choose a lower percentage return but higher absolute dollar value opportunity. Also, it's important to have a good understanding of your own risk tolerance, or a company's investment needs, risk aversion, and other available options.

Disadvantages of IRR

Unlike net present value, the internal rate of return doesn't give you the return on initial investment in terms of real dollars. For example, knowing an IRR of 30% alone doesn't tell you if it's 30% of $10,000 or 30% of $1,000,000.

Using IRR exclusively can lead you to make poor investment decisions, especially if comparing two projects with different durations.

Let's say a company's hurdle rate is 12%, and one-year project A has an IRR of 25%, whereas five-year project B has an IRR of 15%. If the decision is solely based on IRR, this would lead to unwisely choosing project A over B.

Another very important point about the internal rate of return is that it assumes all positive cash flows of a project will be reinvested at the same rate as the project, instead of the company's cost of capital. Therefore, internal rate of return may not accurately reflect the profitability and cost of a project. A smart financial analyst will alternatively use the modified internal rate of return (MIRR) to arrive at a more accurate measure.

Payback and Discounted Payback Period

The payback period of an investment is the length of the time period required for cumulative total net cash flows to total initial cash outlays. In other words, at payback period the investor has recovered the money invested in the project.

Steps to Calculate Payback Period:

- The first step in calculating the payback period is determining the initial capital investment, and
- The next step is calculating/estimating the annual expected after-tax net cash flows over the useful life of the investment.

Payback Period Calculation with Uniform Cash Flows

When cash flows are uniform over the useful life of the asset then the calculation of payback period is made through following formula.

Payback period Formula = Total initial capital investment / Expected annual after-tax cash inflow

Let us see an example of how to calculate payback period when cash flows are uniform over using full life of the asset.

Payback Period Example

A project costs $2Mn and yields a profit of $30,000 after depreciation of 10% (straight line) but before tax of 30%. Let's us calculate the payback period of the project.

Profit before tax $ 30,000

Less: Tax@30%(30000*30%) $ 9,000

Profit after tax $ 21,000

Add: Depreciation(2Mn*10%) $ 2,00,000

Total cash inflow $ 2,21000

While calculating cash inflow, generally depreciation is added back as it does not result into cash out flow. Payback Period Formula = Total initial capital investment/Expected annual after-tax cash inflow = $ 20,00,000/$2,21000 = 9 Years(Approx).

Payback Period Calculation with Nonuniform Cash Flows

When cash flows are NOT uniform over the use full life of the asset then the cumulative cash flow from operations must be calculated for each year. In this case, the payback period shall be the corresponding period when cumulative cash flows is equal to the initial cash outlay.

In case, the sum does not match, then the period in which it lies should be identified. After that, we need to compute the fraction of the year that is needed to complete the payback.

Payback Period Example

Suppose ABC ltd is analysing a project which requires investment of $2, 00,000 and it is expected to generate cash flows as follows:

Year	Annual cash inflows
1	80,000

2	60,000
3	60,000
4	20,000

Table: In this cash payback period can be computed as follows by calculating cumulative cash flows.

Year	Annual cash inflows	Cumulative Annual cash inflows	Payback period
1	80,000	80,000	
2	60,000	1,40,000(80,000+60,000)	
3	60,000	2,00,000(1,40,000+60,000)	In this Year 3 we got initial investment of $ 2,00,000 so this is the payback year
4	20,000	2,20,000(2,00,000+20,000)	

Table: Suppose, in the above case, if the cash outlay is $2, 05,000 then pay back period is.

Year	Annual cash inflows	Cumulative Annual cash inflows	Payback period
1	80,000	80,000	
2	60,000	1,40,000(80,000+60,000)	
3	60,000	2,00,000(1,40,000+60,000)	
4	20,000	2,20,000(2,00,000+20,000)	Payback period is between 3 and 4 years

Since up to three years a sum of $2, 00,000 is recovered, the balance amount of $ 5,000($2, 05,000-$2, 00,000) is recovered in fraction of year which is as follows.

Forgetting $20,000 additional cash flows the project is taking complete 12 months. So for getting additional of $ 5,000($2, 05,000-$2, 00,000) it will take (5,000/20,000) 1/4th Year. i.e 3 months.

So, the project payback period is 3 years 3 months.

Advantages of Payback Period Method

- It is easy to calculate.
- It is easy to understand as it gives a quick estimate of the time needed for the company to get back the money it has invested in the project.
- The length of the project payback period helps in estimating the project risk. The longer the payback period, the riskier the project is. This is because the long-term predictions are less reliable.
- In the case of industries where there is a high obsolescence risk like software industry or mobile phone industry short payback periods often become determining a factor for investments.

Disadvantages of Payback Period Method

Following are the disadvantages of the payback period.

- It ignores the time value of money.

- It fails to consider the investment total profitability i.e it considers cash flows from the initiation of the project till the payback period and fails to consider the cash flows after the payback period.
- It may cause company to place importance on projects which are short payback period thereby ignoring the need to invest in long-term projects (i.e A company cannot just determine a project feasibility only based on the number of years in which it is going to give your return back, there are number of other factors which it does not consider).
- It does not take into account the social or environmental benefits in the calculation.

Payback Reciprocal

Payback reciprocal is the reverse of the payback period.This reciprocal of payback period is calculated by using following formula:

Payback reciprocal = Annual average cash flow/Initial investment.

For example, a project cost is $ 20,000 and annual cash flows are uniform at $4,000 per anum and life of asset acquire is 5 years then payback period reciprocal will be as follows:

$ 4,000/20,000 = 20%.

This 20% represents the rate of return the project or investment gives every year.

Discounted Payback Period

Discounted payback period is next level of payback period where the cashflows are discounted before calculating the period of payback.

Some companies prefer to calculate the payback period as it considers the time value of money.

The discounting can be done using the WACC (Weighted average cost of capital) or IRR (Internal rate of return) or bank rate company got the lending or government risk-free bond rate.

The most appropriate rate to discount cash flows is WACC (Weighted average cost of capital) or IRR (Internal rate of return). Let's take an example for calculating the discounted payback period.

Example of Discounted Payback Period

A project is having a cash outflow of $ 30,000 with annual cash inflows of $ 6,000, so let us calculate the discounted payback period, in this case, assuming companies WACC is 15% and life of the project is 10 years.

Year	Cash flow	Present value factor @ 15%	Present value of cash flows	Cumulative present value of cash flows
1	$ 6,000	0.870	$ 5,220	$ 5,220
2	$ 6,000	0.756	$ 4,536	$ 9,756
3	$ 6,000	0.658	$ 3,948	$ 13,704

4	$ 6,000	0.572	$ 3,432	$ 17,136
5	$ 6,000	0.497	$ 2,982	$ 20,118
6	$ 6,000	0.432	$ 2,592	$ 22,710
7	$ 6,000	0.376	$ 2,256	$ 24,966
8	$ 6,000	0.327	$ 1,962	$ 26,928
9	$ 6,000	0.284	$ 1,704	$ 28,632
10	$ 6,000	0.247	$ 1,482	$ 30,114

In this case, the cumulative cash flows are $ 30,114 in 10th year as, so payback period is approx. 10 years

But, if you calculate the same in simple payback, the payback period is 5 years($30,000/$6,000)

Please note that if the discount rate increases, the distortion between the simple rate of return and discounted payback period increases. Let me explain this further. Let us take 10% discount rate in the above example and calculate the discounted payback period.

Year	Cash flow	Present value factor @ 10%	Present value of cash flows	Cumulative present value of cash flows
1	$6,000	0.909	$5,454	$5,454
2	$6,000	0.826	$4,956	$10,410
3	$6,000	0.751	$4,506	$14,916
4	$6,000	0.683	$4,098	$19,014
5	$6,000	0.621	$3,726	$22,740
6	$6,000	0.564	$3,384	$26,124
7	$6,000	0.513	$3,078	$29,202
8	$6,000	0.466	$2,796	$31,998
9	$6,000	0.424	$2,544	$34,542
10	$6,000	0.385	$2,310	$36,852

In this case, the discounting rate is 10% and discounted payback period is around 8 years, whereas the discounted payback period is 10 years if the discount rate is 15%. But simple payback period is 5 years in both the cases. So, this means as the discount rate increases, the difference in payback periods of discounted pay period and simple payback period increases.

Discount Rate	Simple Payback(a)	Discounted Payback(b)	Difference in payback period (b)- (a)
10%	5 Years	8 Years	3 Years
15%	5 Years	10 Years	5 years

A company wants to replace its old semi automatic machine with a new fully automatic machine. In the market there are two models available in the market (Model A & Model B) at a cost of $ 5,00,000 each. Salvage value of old machine is $ 1,00,000.The utilities of existing machinery can be used is company purchases model A and additional utilities to be bought is only $1,00,000. However in case the company buys the model B then all the existing utilities will have to be replaced and new utilities cost$ 2,00,000 and salvage value of old utilities is $20,000 , The cash flows expected are as follows and discount rate is 15%.

Year		
	A	B
1	$ 1,00,000	$ 2,00,000
2	$ 1,50,000	$ 2,10,000
3	$ 1,80,000	$ 1,80,000
4	$ 2,00,000	$ 1,70,000
5	$ 1,70,000	$ 40,000
Salvage value expected	$ 50,000	$ 60,000

Table: Expenditure at Year of investment (Year Zero).

Particulars	A	B
Cost of machine	$ 5,00,000	$ 5,00,000
Cost of utilities	$ 1,00,000	$ 2,00,000
Salvage of old machine	($ 1,00,000)	($ 1,00,000)
Salvage of old machine	–	($ 20,000)
Total Exp	$ 5,00,000	$ 5,80,000

Year	Present value factor @ 15%	Machine A			Machine B		
		Cash in flows	Present value of cash flows	Cumulative present value of cash flows	Cash in flows	Present value of cash flows	Cumulative present value of cash flows
0 (As calculated above)	1.00	$500,000	$500,000	$500,000	$580,000	$580,000	$580,000
1	0.87	$100,000	$87,000	$87,000	$200,000	$174,000	$174,000
2	0.76	$150,000	$114,000	$201,000	$210,000	$159,600	$333,600
3	0.66	$180,000	$118,800	$319,800	$180,000	$118,800	$452,400
4	0.57	$200,000	$114,000	$433,800	$170,000	$96,900	$549,300
5(Including salvage value of $ 50,000 for Mach A and $ 60,000 for Mach B)	0.50	$ 170000+ $50,000	$110,000	$543,800	$100,000	$50,000	$599,300

In this case, the discounted payback for Machine A is as follows:

Machine A is getting $ 4,33,800 at the end of year 4 and only $66,200($50000-$433800) has to get in year 5. So, pay back here is:

4 years+ (66,200/1,10,000) = 4.6 Years

Machine B is getting $ 5,49,300 at the end of year 4 and only $30,700 ($5,80,000- $5,49,300) has to get in year 5. So, pay back here is:

4 years+ (30,700/50,000) = 4.6 Years

The discounted payback in both cases is same.

Calculation of Cash Flows for Payback Period or Discounted Payback Period

Generally, companies use one or more techniques for capital investment decisions. Some of them use different methods for different projects while others use multiple methods for each project.

For any technique, the calculation of projected cash flow is very important.

Since the timing of cash flows does not match with a period of profit, normally firms are more interested in cash flows. A firm may earn $ 100 Million profit but actual cash receipt may be lesser. This is because all sales and purchases and sales are not on a cash basis. Further depreciation is a noncash item and profit is calculated after considering depreciation.

Calculating Payback Cash Flows

Various factors to keep in mind while arriving cash flows:

- Depreciation: Since depreciation is a noncash item it does not affect the cash flow. However, the tax benefit from depreciation from depreciation affects cash flow.
- Opportunity cost: Opportunity cost is the income that would have been earned or cost that would have been incurred had the activity is done. For example, A company acquired a land at $ 10 Million 5 years ago and the cost of land, if sold now, is $ 25 Million. Assume that if the company uses this land now for the project, then its sale value if $ 25 Million forms part of initial cash outflow, The cost of acquisition of land 5 years ago at $ 10 million is irrelevant for decision making.
- Sunk cost: Sunk cost is the cost that is already spent and hence irrelevant for decision making. For example: If a company has paid $ 50,000 for consultancy charges for preparation of feasibility report whether to take a project or not. In this case, the charges of $ 50,000 paid are irrelevant as sum has already paid and shall not affect the decision whether the project should be undertaken or not.
- Working capital: Every project requires working capital to run the project. Therefore while calculating cash flows, the initial working capital requirement should be treated as cash outflows and at the end of the project, its release should be treated as a cash inflow. In case additional working capital is required during the life of a project, then the additional working capital required is treated as cash outflow at that period of time.
- Allocated overheads: Some overheads are allocated based on machine hours, labor hours etc, They may be allocated to the new project as well. Since those expenses are already incurred and are just allocated they should not be considered while calculating cash flows. However, sometimes the overhead costs increase due to acceptance of some project.Then, in that case, the incremental overhead costs should be considered as cash outflows while calculating cash flows.
- Additional Capex: Generally entire CapEx is not incurred only during initial year, it may be incurred in subsequent years as well. In such as cases such cash outflows to be taken as outflows during those respective years.

- Exclusion of Finance costs: When cash flows relating to long term funds are being calculated, the financing costs of long-term funds should be excluded. Because the WACC used for discounting cash flows already takes into account the interest and dividend payments.
- Post-tax cash flows: The cash flows should be taken the net of tax. It is always better to avoid using pre-tax cash flows and pre-tax discounting rate.

Cost of Capital

Cost of capital is the opportunity cost of funds available to a company for investment in different projects. The most common measure of cost of capital is the weighted average cost of capital, which is a composite measure of marginal return required on all components of the company's capital, namely debt, preferred stock and common stock.

Most companies are for-profit entities which must generate wealth for its shareholders and debt-holders. The projects they invest in must earn enough to pay off the interest on bonds and other debt and pay cash dividends to shareholders and generate enough growth to cause an increase in their stock price. It is important for companies to calculate the cost of different components of capital, identify their target mix of debt and equity and work out their weighted average cost of capital. In deciding whether to invest in a project or not, through the capital budgeting process, they must compare the return available on the project with the cost of capital and accept the project only where the return is higher than the cost of capital. If they invest in projects with return lower than the cost of capital, they are effectively destroying their shareholders wealth.

Weighted average cost of capital is calculated by multiplying the after-tax cost of debt with the percentage of debt in total capital, multiplying the cost of preferred stock with the percentage of preferred stock in total capital, multiplying the cost of common stock with the percentage of common stock in total capital and summing all the products together.

The following equation mathematically expresses the definition of WACC:

$$\text{Cost of Capital} = w_d \times r_d \times (1-t) + w_p \times r_p + w_e \times r_e,$$

where w_d, w_p and w_e refer to the relative percentage of debt, preferred stock and common stock in the total target capital. r_d, r_p and r_e are cost of debt, cost of preferred stock and cost of common stock respectively. r_d is multiplied by (1 – t), where t refers to the tax rate, because interest expense is allowed as deduction while calculating taxes and this tax-deductibility creates a saving which must be accounted for.

WACC Calculator			
Capital	Common	Preferred	Debt
Weight ($ or %):	68.5	0	31.5
Cost %:	10.88	0	4.50
Tax Rate %:			30
WACC %	8.45		

Component Cost of Capital

If a company's debt is publicly traded and market prices are available, cost of debt can be determined as equal to its yield to maturity. If no reasonable estimate of market price is available but a bond rating is available, a company's cost of debt can be estimated as equal to the average cost of debt of companies in the same industry which have the same bond rating. If no market price or bond rating is available for the company's debt, a rating might be estimated based on financial ratios.

Cost of preferred stock can be calculated using the following formula,

Cost of Preferred Stock:

$$= \frac{\text{Preferred Divideds per Share}}{\text{Current Preferred Stock Price}},$$

Cost of common stock can be estimated using either the capital asset pricing model. Under the capital asset pricing mode, cost of common equity is calculated as follows,

Cost of Common Stock:

$$= r_f + \text{beta} \times \text{MRP},$$

Where r_f stands for risk-free rate, typically estimated as equivalent to 10-year government bond rate. Beta is the beta coefficient of the company, a measure which assesses the sensitivity of the company's common stock to movement in market interest rates.

MRP stands for market risk premium (also called equity risk premium) which equals the expected return on the broad market index such as S&P500 i.e E_m minus the risk-free rate i.e. r_f.

$$\text{Market Risk Premium}(\text{MRP}):$$
$$= E_m - r_f,$$

If no reliable estimate of MRP is available, the historical risk premium approach maybe used, which bases market risk premium on the historical average of market risk premium.

Under the dividend discount model, cost of common stock can be estimated as follows:

$$\text{Cost of Common Stock} = \frac{D_1}{P_0} + g,$$

Where D_1 is the dividend per share expected in 1 year and P_0 is the current market price of the stock and g is the sustainable growth rate.

Classification of Cost of Capital

- Explicit cost of capital: It is the cost of capital in which firm's cash outflow is oriented towards utilisation of capital which is evident, such as payment of dividend to the shareholders, interest to the debenture holders, etc.

- Implicit cost of capital: It does not involve any cash outflow, but it denotes the opportunity foregone while opting for another alternative opportunity.

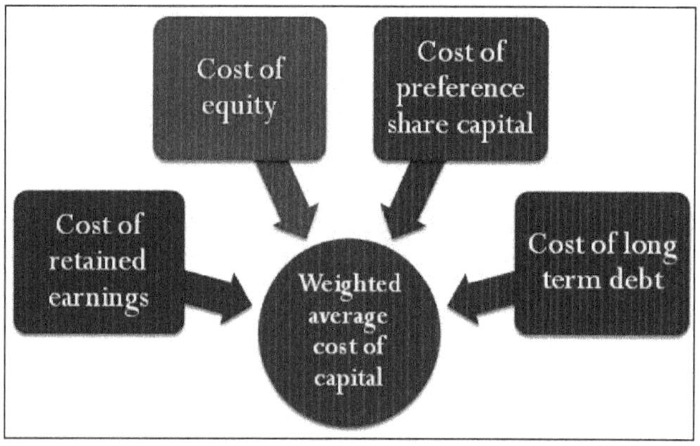

To cover the cost of raising funds from the market, cost of capital must be obtained. It helps in assessing firm's new projects because it is the minimum return expected by the shareholders, lenders and debtholders for supplying capital to the business, as a consideration for their share in the total capital. Hence, it establishes a benchmark, which must be met out by the project.

However, if a firm is incapable of reaping the expected rate of return, the value of shares in the market will tend to decline, which will lead to the reduction in the wealth of the shareholders as a whole.

Importance of Cost of Capital

- It helps in evaluating the investment options, by converting the future cash flows of the investment avenues into present value by discounting it.
- It is helpful in capital budgeting decisions regarding the sources of finance used by the company.
- It is vital in designing the optimal capital structure of the firm, wherein the firm's value is maximum, and the cost of capital is minimum.
- It can also be used to appraise the performance of specific projects by comparing the performance against the cost of capital.
- It is useful in framing optimum credit policy, i.e. at the time of deciding credit period to be allowed to the customers or debtors, it should be compared with the cost of allowing credit period.

Weighted Average Cost of Capital

WACC stands for weighted average cost of capital which is the minimum after-tax required rate of return which a company must earn for all its investors. It is calculated as the weighted average of cost of equity, cost of debt and cost of preferred stock.

WACC is an important input in capital budgeting and business valuation. It is the discount rate used to find out the present value of cash flows in the net present value technique. It is the hurdle rate to which the internal rate of returns of different projects are compared to decide whether the projects are feasible. It is also used in the free cash flow valuation model to discount the free cash flow to firm to find a company's intrinsic value.

Formula Weighted Average Cost of Capital

For a company which has two sources of finance, namely equity and debt, WACC is calculated using the following formula:

$$WACC = k_e \times \frac{E}{E+D} + k_d \times (1-t) \times \frac{D}{E+D},$$

where,

k_e is the cost of equity,

E is the market value of equity,

k_d is the pre-tax cost of debt,

t is the tax rate,

D is the market value of debt, and

E/(E + D) and D/(E + D) are the respective weights of equity and debt in the company's capital structure.

Cost of Equity

Cost of equity is the required rate of return on common stock of the company. It is the minimum rate of return which a company must earn to keep its common stock price from falling. Cost of equity is estimated using different models, such as dividend discount model (DDM) and capital asset pricing model (CAPM).

After-tax Cost of Debt

After-tax cost of debt represents the after-tax rate of return which the debt-holders need to earn till the maturity of the debt. Cost of debt of a company is calculated by finding the yield to maturity of the company's bonds and other loans. If no yield to maturity is available, the cost can be estimated using the instrument's current yield, etc.

After-tax cost of debt is included in the calculation of WACC because debt offers a tax shield i.e. interest expense on debt reduces taxes. This reduction in taxes is reflected in reduction in cost of debt capital.

Equity and Debt Weights

E/A is the weight of equity in the company's total capital. It is calculated by dividing the market value of the company's equity by sum of the market values of equity and debt.

D/A is the weight of debt component in the company's capital structure. It is calculated by dividing the market value of the company's debt by sum of the market values of equity and debt.

Ideally, WACC should be estimated using target capital structure, which is the capital structure the company's management intends to maintain in the long-run.

Example: ABC, Inc. went public by issuing 1 million shares of common stock @ $25 per share. The shares are currently trading at $30 per share. Current risk free rate is 4%, market risk premium is 8% and the company has a beta coefficient of 1.2.

During last year, it issued 50,000 bonds of $1,000 par paying 10% coupon annually maturing in 20 years. The bonds are currently trading at $950. If the tax rate is 30%, calculate the weighted average cost of capital.

Solution: First we need to calculate the proportion of equity and debt in ABC, Inc. capital structure.

Calculating Capital Structure Weights

Current Market Value of Equity:

= 1,000,000 × $30

= $30,000,000

Current Market Value of Debt:

= 50,000 × $950

= $47,500,000

Total Market Value of Debt and Equity:

= $77,500,000

Weight of Equity:

= $30,000,000 ÷ $77,500,000

= 38.71%

Weight of Debt:

= $47,500,000 ÷ $77,500,000

= 61.29%, or

Weight of Debt:

= 100% minus cost of equity

= 100% − 38.71%

= 61.29%

Now, we need estimates for cost of equity and after-tax cost of debt.

Estimating Cost of Equity

We can estimate cost of equity using either the dividend discount model (DDM) or capital asset pricing model (CAPM).

Cost of equity (DDM):

= Expected Dividend in 1 year ÷ Current Stock Price + Growth Rate.

Cost of equity (CAPM):

= Risk Free Rate + Beta Coefficient × Market Risk Premium.

In the current example, the data available allow us to use only CAPM to calculate cost of equity.

Cost of Equity:

= Risk Free Rate + Beta × Market Risk Premium

= 4% + 1.2 × 8%

= 13.6%.

Estimating Cost of Debt

Cost of debt is equal to the yield to maturity of the bonds. With the given data, we can find that yield to maturity is 10.61%. It is calculated using hit and trial method. We can also estimate it using MS Excel RATE function.

For inclusion in WACC, we need after-tax cost of debt, which is 7.427% [= 10.61% × (1 – 30%)].

Calculating WACC

Having all the necessary inputs, we can plug the values in the WACC formula to get an estimate of 9.82%.

WACC

= 38.71% × 13.6% + 61.29% × 7.427%

= 9.8166%

It is called weighted average cost of capital because as you see the cost of different components is weighted according to their proportion in the capital structure and then summed up.

WACC represents the average risk faced by the organization. It would require an upward adjustment if it has to be used to calculate NPV of projects which are riskier than the company's average projects and a downward adjustment in case of less risky projects. Further, WACC is after all estimation. Further, different models for calculation of cost of equity may yield different values.

Common Stock

Common stock is a type of security that represents ownership of equity in a company. There are other terms – such as common share, ordinary share, or voting share – that are equivalent to common stock.

Holders of common stock own the rights to claim a share in the company's profits and exercise control over it by participating in the elections of the board of directors, as well as in the voting regarding important corporate policies.

Common stock owners can profit from the capital appreciation of the securities. On average, the shares offer a higher return relative to preferred stock or bonds. However, the higher returns come with the higher risks associated with such securities.

Shareholder Rights

The main sources of shareholder rights are legislation in the company's incorporation, corporate charter, and governance documents. Therefore, the rights of shareholders can vary from one jurisdiction to another and from one corporation to another.

Nevertheless, there are a few shareholder rights that are almost uniform for every corporation. First, the right of shareholders to claim a portion of company's profits. The shareholders usually receive a portion of profits through dividends. In addition, in case of a company's liquidation, holders of common stock own rights to the company's assets. However, since common shareholders are at the bottom of the priority ladder, it is very unlikely that they would receive compensation in the event of liquidation.

Moreover, common shareholders can participate in important corporate decisions through voting. They can participate in the election of the board of directors and vote on different corporate matters such as corporate objectives, policies, and stock splits.

Classifications of Common Stock

There is no unified classification of common stock. However, some companies may issue two classes of common stock. In most cases, a company will issue one class of voting shares and another class of non-voting (or with lesser voting power) shares. The main rationale for using dual classification is to preserve control over the company.

Despite the difference in voting rights, different classes of common stock usually enjoy the same rights to the company's profits.

Preferred Stock

Preferred stock is a type of capital stock issued by some corporations. Preferred stock is also known as preference stock.

The word "preferred" refers to the dividends paid by the corporation. Each year, the holders of the preferred stock are to receive their dividends before the common stockholders are to receive any dividend. In exchange for this preferential treatment for dividends, the preferred stockholders (or shareholders) generally will never receive more than the stated dividend. For example, the holder of 100 shares of a corporation's 8% $100 par preferred stock will receive annual dividends of $800 (8% X $100 = $8 per share X 100 shares) before the common stockholders are allowed to receive any cash dividends for the year. Unless the preferred stock has a participating feature, this preferred stockholder will never receive more than $8 per share no matter how successful the corporation becomes.

Types of Preferred Stock

Convertible Preferred Stock

Convertible preferred stock is preferred stock that holders can exchange for common stock at a set price after a certain date.

Example: Let's assume you purchase 100 shares of XYZ Company convertible preferred stock on June 1, 2006. According to the registration statement, each share of preferred stock is convertible after January 1, 2007, (the conversion date) to three shares of XYZ Company common stock. (The number of common shares given for each preferred share is called the conversion ratio. In this example, the ratio is 3.0.).

If after the conversion date arrives XYZ Company preferred shares are trading at $50 per share, and the common shares are trading at $10 per share, then converting the shares would effectively turn $50 worth of stock into only $30 worth (the investor has the choice between holding one share valued at $50 or holding three shares valued at $10 each). The difference between the two amounts, $20, is called the conversion premium (although it is typically expressed as a percentage of the preferred share price; in this case it would be $20/$50, or 40%).

By dividing the price of the preferred shares ($50) by the conversion ratio (3), we can determine what the common stock must trade at for you to break even on the conversion. In this case, XYZ Company common must be trading at a minimum of $16.67 per share for you to seriously consider converting.

Convertible preferred shares trade like other stocks, but the conversion premium influences their trading prices. The lower the conversion premium, (that is, the closer the preferred shares are to being "in the money,") the more the price of the preferred shares will follow the price movements of the common stock. The higher the conversion premium, the less the convertible preferred shares follow the common stock.

Usually, holders of convertible preferred can convert at any time after the conversion date, but sometimes the issuer can force conversion. Either way, converting preferred stock into common stock dilutes the common shareholders, which is why companies sometimes offer to buy back converted shares.

Also, as with traditional preferred, holders of convertible preferred stock generally do not have the voting privileges enjoyed by holders of common stock.

Importance of Convertible Preferred Stock

Like common stock, preferred shares represent an ownership stake in a company; in other words, a claim on its assets and earnings.

Return

The primary difference between preferred stock and common stock relates to the order in which shareholders are paid in the event of bankruptcy or other corporate restructuring. If the issuing company seeks bankruptcy protection, then the owners of preferred shares take priority over common shareholders when it comes time to pay dividends and liquidate the company's assets.

Further, although dividends paid on common stock are not guaranteed and can fluctuate from quarter to quarter, preferred shareholders are usually guaranteed a fixed dividend paid on a regular basis. This means that interest rates affect the pricing of preferred stock. High rates could make a preferred dividend seem unattractive and low rates could make it seem attractive.

Risk

Issuing convertible preferred is a way for companies to raise capital on better terms than they could with traditional equity financing, especially if they have low stock prices already (new equity would dilute shareholders considerably) or if they have poor credit and cannot borrow at reasonable rates. With convertible preferred, a company can secure a lower interest rate than with pure debt financing and use the promise of a dividend to sell shares at a higher price. However, since companies with poor credit sometimes use preferred shares to gain revenue, the risk of default may be slightly higher.

Ratings

Like corporate bonds, most convertible preferred stocks are rated by one of the major ratings agencies, the largest and most widely known being Standard & Poor's and Moody's. If the stock is rated only by one of the smaller rating agencies, such as Duff & Phelps or Fitch, then investors should be aware that the organization may not have been able to obtain a positive rating from either S&P or Moody's.

Regulators generally classify convertible preferred as equity rather than debt. This classification is helpful to issuers because the interest payments come with tax breaks and the securities don't increase issuers debt-to-equity ratios. However, analysts sometimes consider preferred and convertible preferred as debt when performing ratio analyses.

Convertible preferred stock is just one of many types of hybrid issues on the market these days, and in general, the securities are a way to increase yields and lower risk. Ultimately, investors must consider whether the higher yield of convertible preferred compensates them for the higher risk of an equity security.

Cumulative Preferred Stock

Cumulative preferred stock is an equity instrument that pays a fixed dividend on a predetermined schedule, and prior to any distributions to the holders of a company's common stock. The amount of the dividend is usually based on the par value of the stock. Thus, a 5% dividend on preferred shares that have a $100 par value equates to a $5 dividend.

This dividend payment is cumulative, so any delayed prior payments must also be paid before dividend distributions can be made to the holders of a company's common stock. This situation typically arises when a company has cash flow difficulties, and so its board of directors elects to temporarily suspend dividend payments until such time as cash flows improve.

As long as a company has not paid scheduled dividends, the amount of the unpaid dividends is said to be in arrears, and is disclosed in the notes accompanying its financial statements.

In the event of liquidation, the holders of preferred stock must be paid off before common stockholders, but after secured debt holders have been paid. Preferred stockholders can have a broad range of voting rights, ranging from none to having control over the eventual disposition of the entity.

Convertible Exchangeable Preferred Stock

The term convertible exchangeable preferred stock refers to a security that allows the issuer to exchange it for convertible bonds. Empirical evidence suggests issuing convertible exchangeable preferred stock is oftentimes accompanied by a negative earnings outlook.

Convertible exchangeable preferred stock allows the issuing company to exchange a non-taxable expense (the preferred dividend) for a taxable expense (the interest expense on bonds). These securities combine two features, one that benefits the issuer and one that benefits the holder:

- Exchangeability: at the issuer's discretion, the preferred stock may be exchanged for convertible bonds at a predetermined rate.
- Convertibility: at the holder's discretion, the bonds can be converted at a predetermined rate for common stock.

While these securities should be more popular with investors and issuers than preferred stock carrying only one of the above features, their popularity in the market lags behind both exchangeable preferred and convertible preferred.

Perpetual Preferred Stock

A perpetual preferred stock is a type of preferred stock that pays a fixed dividend to the investor for as long as the company is in business. It doesn't have a maturity, or specific buyback, date but does have redemption features. Unless redeemed, issued perpetual preferred stock will pay dividends indefinitely, provided the issuer is still extant. They trade on stock exchanges similar to common stock.

There are two types of preferred stocks - perpetual and non-perpetual. Perpetual preferred stock does not have an expiration date and pays the investor a fixed dividend for as long as the issuing company is in existence. The company does, however, hold the right to buy back the stock at any time under specific terms defined in the prospectus. This buyback period is basically a call feature that is common place in the bond market.

Companies buyback perpetual preferred shares for several reasons, most notably changes in interest rates and tax laws. Investors must bear this in mind because losing their shares to a redemption means they will suddenly lose an income stream. For example, if the interest rates fall below the yield paid to stockholders then the company would, most likely, buy back the outstanding perpetual preferred stock. This means that the investors will not be able to reinvest their money and receive the same dividend rate that had been instrumental in them receiving a steady income stream. Though not exactly identical, a perpetual preferred stock has characteristics that are similar to a bond with an extremely long maturity date.

Since, in theory, perpetual preferred stock can exist indefinitely, so too must the dividend payments. Hence, to price these one would calculate the present value (PV) of a perpetuity, which is the fixed dividend amount divided by the dividend yield:

Perpetual Preferred Stock Price = Fixed Dividend ÷ Dividend Yield

A non-perpetual preferred stock has a particular buyback price and buyback date, usually 30 or more years from the date of issue. It also has a defined maturity date and therefore has more certainty regarding cash flows.

Advantages of Preferred Stock - Company's Point of View

- The dividend payable on this stock is fixed which is usually lower as compared to payable on equity shares. As a results they facilitates the company to enhancing the profits convenient for the dividend available to equity shareholders.
- Preferred shareholders have no voting right on matters that not effecting their right from now promoters or management can keep command over the circumstances of the corporate.
- The corporate or the organisation should continue limberness in its capital structure through issuing of redeemable preference stock or shares as they will be redeemed under the conditions of issue.
- Issue of preferred stock does not prove or state a burden on finance of the company because the reason behind this is, the dividends are paid only if the sufficient amount of financial surplus available or on dividends are to be paid.
- Non-availability of payment of dividend on preference stock does not generate a charge on the company's assets.
- The issue of this stock spread the range of capital market as they provide the security not only to the investors but also to fixed return. If the company is not able to issue preferred stock which means it will insufficient to create the attraction for the capital from such ordinary types of investors.

Advantages of Preferred Stock – Investors Point of View

- Investors in cumulative preferred stock get a fixed rate of dividend on this stock uniformly even if there is none availability of profit. If there is any arrears regarding dividends is available will be paid in the years of profit.

- Preferred stock carry preference right as regard to the payment of dividend and preferential right as evaluate to paying back of capital in happening of the company's winding up, as a consequence they enjoy lower rate of risk.
- Preference stockholders are provided voting rights in the occurrence that directly affecting their interest, which clearly stated that interest is their protection.
- As the preference stockholders take delights that the preferential rights of their capital's repayment in case of winding up of the company, it provides them protection from capital loses.
- Preferred stock are stated as fair securities for the shareholders during the recession periods when the profits of the company are down.

Disadvantages of Preferred Stock – Company's Point of View

- Company is to pay the dividends at higher rate on these stock than the existing rate of interest on the debentures. As a result it's generally enhances the cost of the capital of the company.
- Generally most of the preferred stock are issued cumulative which means that all the arrears of dividend must be paid on first priority before any can be paid to equity stockholders. It is the responsibility of the company to pay dividend on such kind of shares. Which result in reduction of the profits of the equity shareholders.
- The issue of preferred stock inculpate reduction of equity shareholders affirm over the assets of the company because there is a preferential right available to preference stockholders over the assets of the company in winding up case.
- The debt freeness of the company is extremely influence by the issue of preferred stock. The creditors may anticipated that that the continuity of dividend on stock and adjournment of dividend on equity capital may divest them with regarding to chance of get back their sum amount in full in the happening of cessation of the company, as the preferred capital has the preference right on the assets of the company.
- The amount of preference dividend does not affect any reduction on taxable income.

Disadvantages of Preferred Stock – Investors Point of View

- There is not availability of any voting rights to preference stockholders except in matters directed to affect their interest.
- The dividend on preferred stock other than the participating preferred stock is fixed even if the company is earning higher profits.
- The preference shareholders have no claim over the surplus amount or figure. They can only ask for the return of their capital amount invested in the company.
- Company does not provides any safeguard to the preference capital as is made in case of debentures. Which results non protection of their interest by the assets of the company.

Cost of Preferred Stock

The cost of preference share capital is the rate of return that must be earned on preference capital financed investments, to keep unchanged the earnings available to the equity shareholders. In other words, cost of preferred stock is the rate of return required by the holders of a company's preferred stock.

Cost of Irredeemable Preferred Stock

The cost of irredeemable preferred share capital is the rate of preference dividend, also called the coupon rate divided by net issue proceeds. In case of Irredeemable preferred stock, the cost of irredeemable preferred stock is calculated as:

Cost of Preferred Stock Formula: Kp i.e. cost of preferred stock = Annual dividend of Preferred stock/Net proceeds received from the issue of preferred stock after meeting the issue expenses or Market price of the preferred stock.

Cost of Irredeemable preferred stock Example: XYZ limited has issued 10,000 irredeemable preference share with face value of $ 100 each. The cost of preference share capital is 10 %. The market price of share is currently $ 115. Calculate the cost of preferred share capital.

Annual dividend = $ (100 * 10/100) = $ 10

Kp = $ 10/$ 115 = 8.7 %

Cost of Irredeemable preferred stock Example 2: ABC limited has issued 10,000 irredeemable preference shares of $ 150 each at a coupon rate of 14 % per annum. The flotation cost are $ 15 per share. Calculate cost of preferred share capital.

Cost of Preferred Stock or Kp = 14 % of $ 150/ ($ 150 – $ 15) = $ 21/$ 135 = 0.1555 = 15.55 %.

Cost of Redeemable Preferred Stock

The cost of redeemable preferred stock or redeemable preference capital having fixed maturity date is calculated as follows:

Cost of Preferred Stock Formula: Kp i.e. cost of redeemable preferred stock or shares = [Annual dividend + (Redeemable value – sale value)/number of years of redemption]/ [(Redeemable value of preferred stock or shares + sale value of shares)/2].

Cost of redeemable preferred stock Example: D limited has $ 100 preference share redeemable at a premium of 10 % with 15 years maturity. The coupon rate is 12 %. The flotation cost is 5 %. Sale price is $ 95. Calculate the cost of preferred stock or preference shares.

Redeemable value = $100+ $ 10 = $ 110

Sale value = $ 95 – $ 5 = $ 90

Annual dividend = $ 100 * 12/100 = $ 12

Kp = [12+ (110 -90)/15] / [(110 + 90)/2) = 12 + (20/15) / 200/2 = (12 + 1.33)/100 = 0.133 = 13 % (Appx).

References

- Introduction-to-capital-budgeting, boundless-finance: lumenlearning.com, Retrieved 11 January, 2019
- Investment-criteria-3-things-to-know, criteria, investment: economicsdiscussion.net, Retrieved 18 April, 2019
- Net-present-value-npv, valuation, knowledge, resources: corporatefinanceinstitute.com, Retrieved 27 May, 2019
- Profitability-index-method: strategiccfo.com, Retrieved 21 July, 2019
- Payback-period-discounted-payback-period: wallstreetmojo.com, Retrieved 13 July, 2019
- What-is-preferred-stock: accountingcoach.com, Retrieved 24 March, 2019
- Common-stock, finance, knowledge, resources: corporatefinanceinstitute.com, Retrieved 1 June, 2019
- Convertible-preferred-stock, dictionary: investinganswers.com, Retrieved 21 March, 2019
- Cumulative-preferred-stock: accountingtools.com, Retrieved 12 April, 2019
- Convertible-exchangeable-preferred-stock, investing-dictionary, definitions: money-zine.com, Retrieved 23 June, 2019

6

Fundamental Concepts of Valuation

The process which is used to determine an asset's present value is known as valuation. Some of its fundamental concepts are the time value of money, bond valuation and equity valuation. The topics elaborated in this chapter will help in gaining a better perspective about these key concepts of valuation.

The Time Value of Money

The Time Value of Money concept indicates that money earned today will be more than its intrinsic value in the near future. This is due to the potential earning capacity of the given amount of money. Time Value of Money (TVM) is also referred to as Present Discounted value. Money deposited in a savings bank account earns a certain interest rate to compensate for keeping the money away from them at the current point of time. Hence, if a bank holder deposits $100 in the account, the expectation will be to receive more than $100 after one year.

Future Value of a Single Amount

Suppose one invests $1,000 for 3 years in a Savings account which pays 10% interest per year. If one allows the interest income to be reinvested, the investment shall grow as follows:

Future Value at the End of First Year

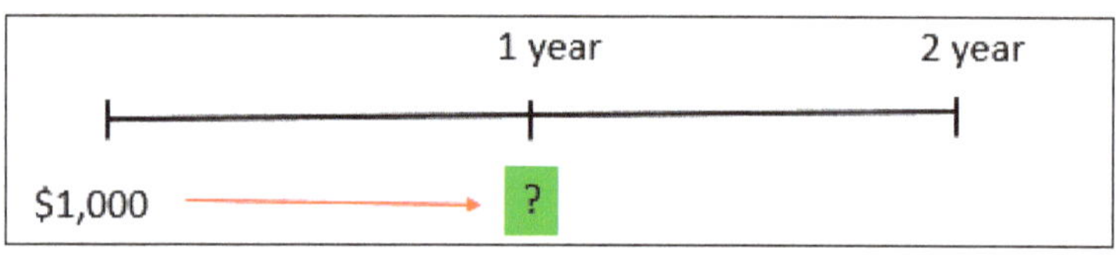

- Principal at the beginning of the year $1,000
- Interest for the year ($1,000 * 0.10) $100
- Principal at the end $1,100

Future Value at the End of Second Year

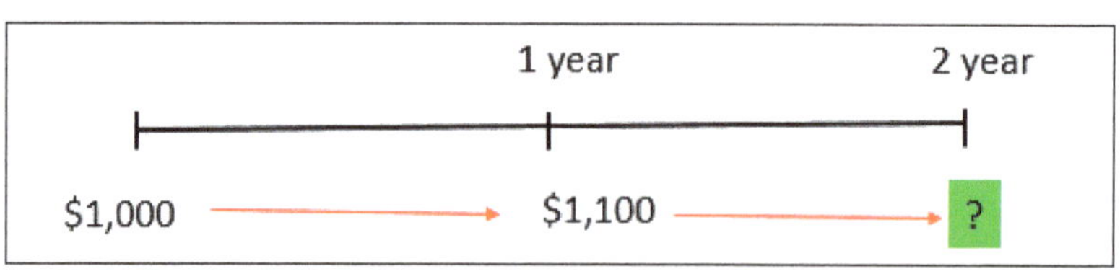

- Principal at the beginning of the year $1,100
- Interest for the year ($1,100 * 0.10) $110
- Principal at the end $1,210

The process of investing money and reinvesting the interest earned is called as Compounding. The future value or compounded value of an investment after "n" year when the interest rate is "r" % is:

$$FV = PV\,(1+r)^n$$

As per the above equation, $(1+r)^n$ is called the future value factor. There are pre-defined tables which specify the rate of interest and its value after 'n' number of years. It can also be utilized with the help of a calculator or an excel spread sheet as well. The below snapshot is an instance of how the rate is computed for different interest rates and at different time intervals.

Hence, taking the above instance, the FV of $1,000 can be used as:

$$FV = 1000\,(1.210) = \$1210$$

Time Value of Money: Doubling Period

The first important aspect in the time value of money (TVM) concept is the doubling period.

Investors are generally keen to know by when their investment can double up at a given Interest. Though a little crude, an established rule is the "Rule of 72" which states that doubling period can be obtained by dividing 72 by the interest rate.

For e.g. if the interest is 8%, the doubling period is 9 years [72/8=9 years].

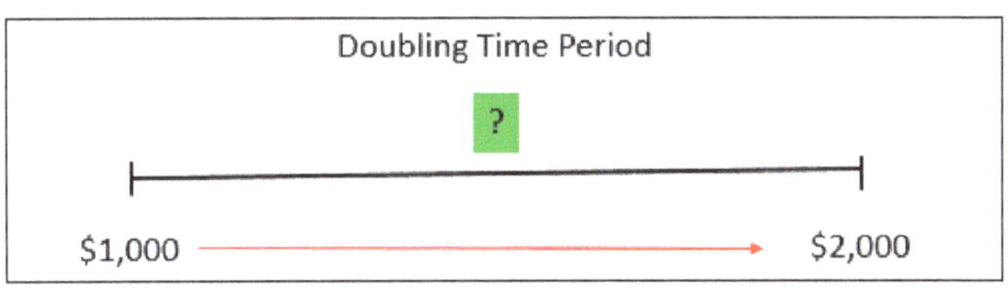

A slightly more calculative rule is the "Rule of 69" which states the doubling period as: 0.35 + 69/ Interest.

Present Value of a Single Amount

The third important point in the time value of money (TVM) concept is to find the present value of a single amount.

This scenario states the Present Value of a sum of money which is expected to be received after a given time period. The process of discounting used for computation of the present value is simply the inverse of compounding. The PV formula can be readily obtained by using the below formula:

$$PV = FV_n\,[1/(1+r)^n]$$

For instance, if a client is expected to receive \$1,000 after 3 years @ 8% ROI its value at the Present time can be computed as:

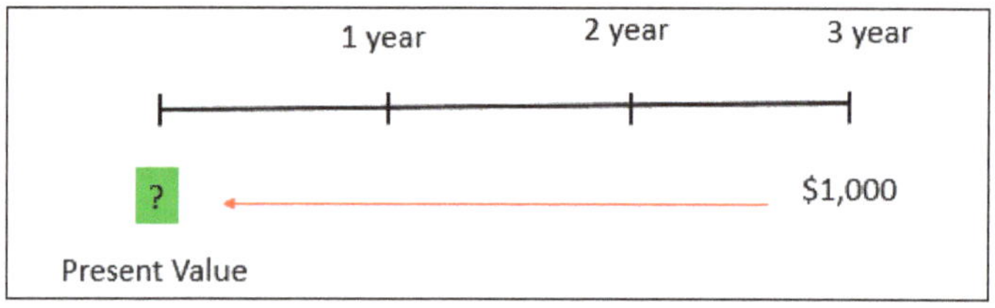

$$PV = 1000\ [1/1.08]^3$$

PV = 1000*0.794 = \$794

Future Value of an Annuity

The fourth important concept in the time value of money (TVM) concept is to calculate the future value of an annuity.

An annuity is a stream of constant cash flows (receipts or payments) occurring at regular time interval. The premium payments of a life insurance policy, for instance, are an annuity. When the cash flows occur at the end of each period, the annuity is called an Ordinary annuity or deferred annuity. When this flow occurs at the beginning of each period, it is called as Annuity due. The formula for an annuity due is simply (1+r) times the formula for corresponding ordinary annuity.

Let's take an example whereby one deposits \$1,000 annually in a bank for 5 years and the deposit is earning a compound interest at 10% ROI, the value of the series of deposits at the end of 5 years:

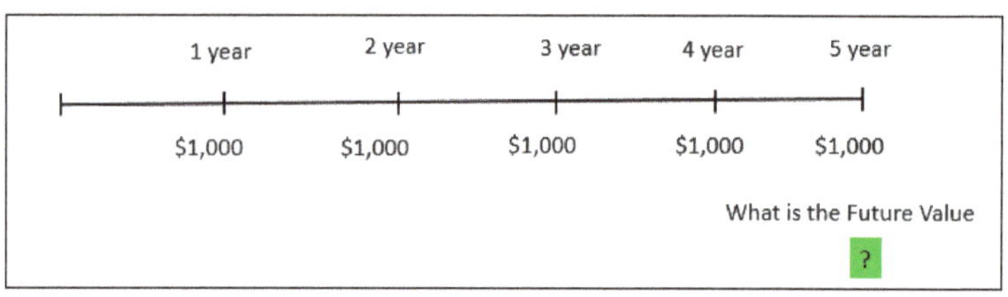

$$\text{Future Value} = \$1,000(1+1.10)^4 + \$1,000(1+1.10)^3 + \$1,000(1+1.10)^2 + \$1,000(1.10) + \$1,000 = \$6,105$$

In general terms the Future value of the annuity is given by the following formula:

- $FVA_n = A\ [(1+r)^n - 1]/r.$
- FVA_n is the FV of annuity having duration of 'n' periods, 'A' is the constant periodic flow, and 'r' is the ROI per period. The term $[(1+r)^n - 1]/r$ is referred as future value interest factor for an annuity.

Present Value of Annuity

The fifth important concept in the time value of money concept is to calculate the present value of an annuity.

This concept is a reversal of the future value of annuity just instead of FV the focus will be on PV. Suppose one is expecting to receive $1,000 annually for 3 years with each receipt occurring at the end of the year, the PV of this stream of benefits at the discount rate of 10% would be computed as below:

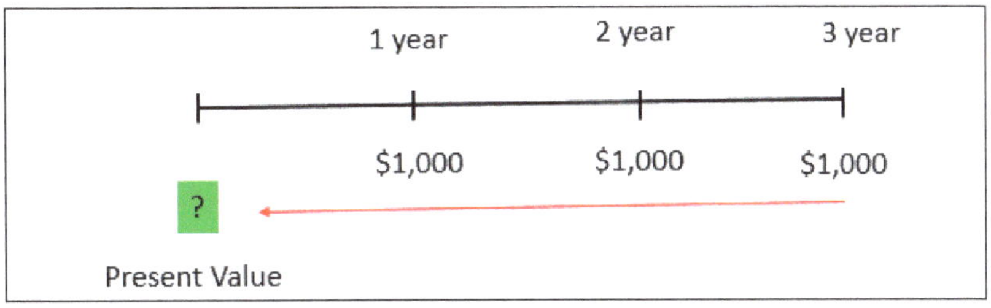

$$\$1,000[1/1.10] + 1,000\,[1/1.10]^2 + 1,000\,[1/1.10]^3 = \$2,486.80$$

In general terms, the present value of an annuity can be expressed as follows:

- $A = [\{1-(1/1+\ r)^n\}/r]$

Present Value of Perpetuity

The sixth concept in the time value of money (TVM) is to find the present value of a perpetuity.

Perpetuity is an annuity of an indefinite duration. For instance, the British government has issued bonds called 'consols' which pay yearly interest throughout its existence. Although the total face value of the perpetuity is infinite and undeterminable, its Present value is not. According to the Time Value of Money (TVM) principle, the Present value of the perpetuity is the sum of the discounted value of each periodic payment of the perpetuity. The formula for computing the Present value of the perpetuity is:

Fixed periodic payment / ROI or the discount rate per compounding period:

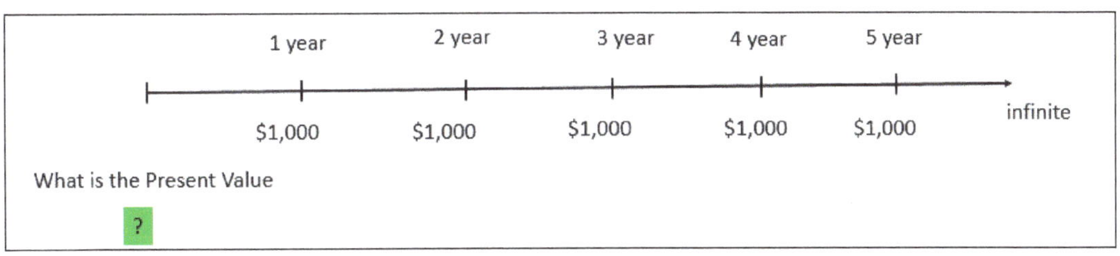

For e.g. calculating the PV on Jan 1, 2015 of a perpetuity paying $1,000 at the end of each month starting from January 2015 with a monthly discount rate of 0.*8% can be shown as:

- PV = $1,000 / 0.8% = $125,000

Growing Perpetuity

This is a scenario in which the perpetuity will keep on changing like Rental payments. For e.g. an office complex is expected to generate a net rental of $3 million for the forthcoming year, which is expected to increase by 5% every year. If we assume that the increase will continue indefinitely, the rental system will be termed as a growing perpetuity. If the discount rate is 10%, the PV of the rental stream will be:

$$PV = \frac{3,00,000}{1.10} + \frac{3,00,000(1.05)^1}{(1.10)^2} + \frac{3,00,000(1.05)^{n-1}}{(1.10)^n}$$

In an algebraic formula, it can be displayed as follows:

- PV = C / r-g, where 'C' is the rental to be received during the year, '*r*' is the ROI and '*g*' is the growth rate.

Time Value of Money – Intra-year Compounding and Discounting

In this case, we consider the case where compounding is done on a frequent basis. Assuming a client deposits $1,000 with a finance company which pays 12% interest on a semi-annual basis which indicates that interest amount is paid every 6 months. The deposit amount will grow as follows:

- irst six months: Principal at the beginning = $1,000.
- Interest for 6 months = $60 ($1,000 * 12%) /2.
- Principal at the end = $1,000 + $60 = $1,060.

Next six months: Principal at the beginning = $1,060

- Interest for 6 months = $63.6 ($1,060 * 12%) /2.
- Principal at the end = $1,060 + $63.6 = $1,123.6.

It is to be noted that if the compounding is done annually, the principal at the end of one year would be $1,000 * 1.12 = $1,120. The difference of $3.6 (between $1,123.6 under semi-annual compounding and $1,120 under annual compounding) represents interest on interest for the second half year.

Time Value of Money Example – Dividend Discount Model

This is a Time value of money real life example of its usage in valuations using Dividend Discount model.

Dividend discount model prices a stock by adding its future cash flows discounted by the required rate of return that an investor demands for the risk of owning the stock.

$$Instrinsic\_value_{stock} = \sum_{t=1}^{\infty} \frac{CF_t}{(1+k)^t}$$

Here the CF = Dividends.

However, this situation is a bit theoretical, as investors normally invest in stocks for dividends as well as capital appreciation. Capital appreciation is when you sell the stock at a higher price then you buy for. In such a case, there are two cash flows:

- Future Dividend Payments.
- Future Selling Price.

Intrinsic Value = Sum of Present Value of Dividends + Present Value of Stock Sale Price.

This DDM price is the intrinsic value of the stock. Let us take an example of Dividend Discount Model here.

Assume that you are considering the purchase of a stock which will pay dividends of $20 (Div 1) next year, and $21.6 (Div 2) the following year. After receiving the second dividend, you plan on selling the stock for $333.3 what is the intrinsic value of this stock if your required return is 15%?

This problem can be solved in 3 steps:

Step 1: Find the present value of Dividends for Year 1 and Year 2.

- PV (year 1) = $\$20/ ((1.15)^{1})$.
- PV (year 2) = $\$20/ ((1.15)^{2})$.
- In this example, they come out to be $17.4 and $16.3 respectively for 1st and 2nd year dividend.

Step 2: Find the Present value of future selling price after two years.

- PV(Selling Price) = $333.3 / (1.15^2)

Step 3: Add the Present Value of Dividends and present value of Selling Price

- $17.4 + $16.3 + $252.0 = $285.8

	Year 0	Year 1	Year 2
Dividend payments	-	$20.0	$21.6
PV (Dividends) @ 15%		$17.4	$16.3
Stock Price			$333.3
PV (Stock) @ 15%			=H17/(1+0.15)^2
Intinsic Value	$0.0	$17.4	$268.4
Total Instrinsic Value	$285.8		

Time Value of Money Example – Loan EMI Calculator

A loan is issued at the beginning of year 1. The principal is $15,000,000, the interest rate is 10% and the term is 60 months. Repayments are to be made at the end of each month. The loan must be fully repaid by the end of the term.

- Principal – $15,000,000.
- Interest Rate (monthly) – 1%.
- Term = 60 months.

To find the Equal Monthly Installment or EMI, we can use the PMT function in Excel. It requires Principal, Interest and term as inputs.

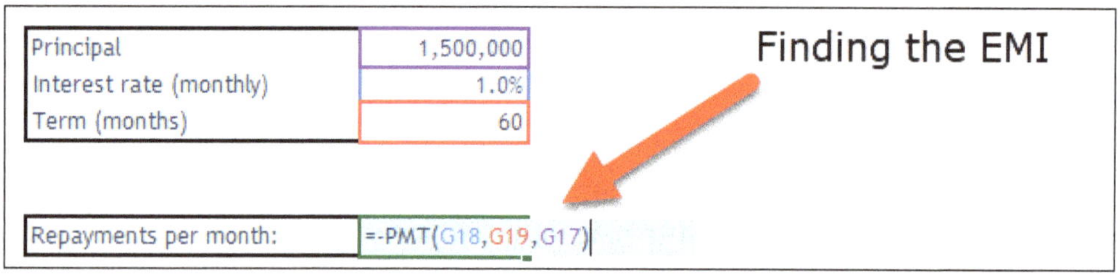

EMI = $33,367 per month

Time Value of Money Example – Alibaba Valuation

Time Value of Money (TVM) concept was applied for valuing Alibaba IPO. For Alibaba valuation, I had done the financial statement analysis and forecast financial statements and then calculate the Free Cash Flow to the Firm. You can download Alibaba Financial Model here.

Presented below is the free cash flow to firm of alibaba. The free cash flow is divided into two parts – a) Historical FCFF and b) Forecast FCFF.

Free Cash flow projections	Historicals		Forcasts				
	Mar-13	Mar-14	Mar-15	Mar-16	Mar-17	Mar-18	Mar-19
(RMB in Million Except per Share Amount)							
EBIT	10,751	26,514	33,072	41,871	53,260	68,042	86,110
Free Cash Flow to Firm							
EBIT x (1 – t)	9,202	24,575	29,103	36,009	45,271	57,155	70,610
Add. Depreciation & Amortization	805	947	2,691	5,069	8,089	11,938	16,831
Less : Capex	(1,046)	(3,010)	(9,225)	(11,679)	(14,855)	(18,979)	(24,018)
Add : Change in working capital	4,285	2,260	3,884	4,861	6,292	8,167	9,982
FCFF	13,246	24,772	26,453	34,261	44,795	58,282	73,405

- Historical FCFF is arrived at from the Income Statement, Balance Sheet and Cash Flows of the company from its Annual Reports.
- Forecast FCFF is calculated only after forecasting the Financial Statements (we call this as preparing the Financial Model) Core Financial Modeling is slightly tricky.
- In order to find the valuation of Alibaba, we must find the present value of all the future financial years (till perpetuity – Terminal value).

Bond Valuation

Bond valuation is a technique for determining the theoretical fair value of a particular bond. Bond valuation includes calculating the present value of a bond's future interest payments, also known as its cash flow, and the bond's value upon maturity, also known as its face value or par value. Because a bond's par value and interest payments are fixed, an investor uses bond valuation to determine what rate of return is required for a bond investment to be worthwhile.

A bond is a debt instrument that provides a steady income stream to the investor in the form of coupon payments. At the maturity date, the full face value of the bond is repaid to the bondholder. The characteristics of a regular bond include:

- Coupon rate: Some bonds have an interest rate, also known as the coupon rate, which is paid to bondholders semi-annually. The coupon rate is the fixed return that an investor earns periodically until it matures.
- Maturity date: All bonds have maturity dates, some short-term, others long-term. When a bond matures, the bond issuer repays the investor the full face value of the bond. For corporate bonds, the face value of a bond is usually $1,000 and for government bonds, the face value is $10,000. The face value is not necessarily the invested principal or purchase price of the bond.
- Current Price: Depending on the level of interest rate in the environment, the investor may purchase a bond at par, below par, or above par. For example, if interest rates increase, the value of a bond will decrease since the coupon rate will be lower than the interest rate in the economy. When this occurs, the bond will trade at a discount, that is, below par. However, the bondholder will be paid the full face value of the bond at maturity even though he purchased it for less than the par value.

Formula of Bond Valuation

Most techniques used to determine bond valuation use a discounted cash flow approach. In general terms, the formula of a bond's fair price is calculated as follows:

$$\text{Bond Price} = \frac{C_1}{(1+r)} + \frac{C_2}{(1+r)^2} + \frac{C_3}{(1+r)^3} + \ldots + \frac{C_N}{(1+r)^N} + \frac{P}{(1+r)^N}$$

or

$$\text{Bond Price} = \sum_{t=1}^{N} \frac{C_t}{(1+r)^t} + \frac{P}{(1+r)^N}$$

where C is a periodic coupon payment, r is the market interest rate or required rate of return, and P is the par value of a bond.

If a bond has a fixed coupon rate, the formula above can be modified as follows:

$$\text{Bond Price} = C \times \frac{1-(1+r)^{-N}}{r} + \frac{P}{(1+r)^{N}}$$

Discounted Cash Flow Approach

The traditional discounted cash flow technique is based on the following assumptions:

- The discount rate used in the model remains fixed, and therefore it applies to each cash flow, including par value paid at maturity.
- Each cash flow is reinvested at a discount rate.

Thus, bond valuation involves three steps:

- Determining the interest rate to be used as a discount rate.
- Estimating expected cash flows.
- Calculating the present value of each expected cash flow by applying the discount rate.

How to Determine a Discount Rate

Determining the discount rate is quite complicated and based on several assumptions. Traditionally, the required rate of return or required yield on a corporate bond can be calculated as follows:

Required Yield = Risk-free Interest Rate + Risk Premium

An on-the-run Treasury bond yield is usually used as a risk-free rate provided it compares with the corporate bond maturity date. In turn, the risk premium is based on the issuer's credit rating. The lower the credit rating, the higher the risk premium and vice versa.

Bond Valuation Example

An investor is considering purchasing a new issue of 5-year bonds of $1,000 par value and an annual fixed coupon rate of 12%, while coupon payments are made semiannually. The minimum semiannual yield that the investor would accept is 6.75%. To find the fair value of a bond, we should calculate the semiannual coupon payment and apply the formula above.

Annual Coupon Payment = $1,000 × 12% = $120

Semiannual Coupon Payment = $120 ÷ 2 = $60

$$\text{Bond Price} = \$60 \times \frac{1-(1+0.0675)^{-10}}{0.0675} + \frac{\$1,000}{(1+0.0675)^{10}} = \$946.71$$

The cash flow is schematically presented in the figure below:

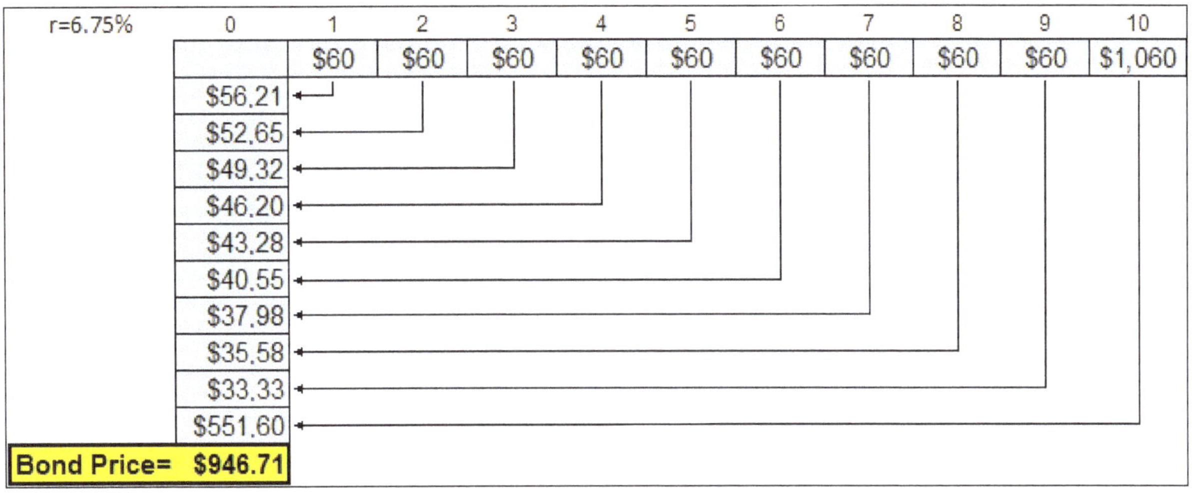

Thus, the highest price affordable for the investor is $946.71.

Zero-coupon Bond Valuation Example

A zero-coupon bond does not have any coupon payments. It is sold at a lower price than the par value, and the par value will be repaid to the investor at maturity. Such a bond has only the cash flow equal to its par value repaid at maturity.

An investor is considering purchasing a 10-year zero-coupon bond of $1,000 par value. Let's calculate the fair value of the bond if the current interest rate for equally risky bonds is 12.4%.

$$\text{Bond Price} = \frac{\$1{,}000}{(1+0.124)^{10}} = \$310.70$$

Floating-rate Bond Valuation

A floating-rate bond, also known as a floating-rate note (FRN), has a coupon rate tied to a benchmark: Treasury bill, LIBOR (London Interbank Offered Rate), and prime rate or inflation rate. The floating coupon rate usually consists of two parts:

- Floating benchmark
- Fixed premium

Coupon Rate = Benchmark + Premium

For example, if coupon payments are made semiannually, the 6-month LIBOR can be used as the floating benchmark. Let's assume that the semiannual risk premium equals 3.75%; thus, the formula for calculating the coupon rate will be as follows:

Coupon Rate = 6 Month LIBOR + 3.75%

As the floating coupon rate follows the current level of interest rates, the current market price of a bond is usually close to its par value. In case of a significant increase or decrease in the issuer's credit rating, the current market price of the floating-rate bond can significantly differ from its par value because the fixed premium depends on the issuer's credit rating.

We should also highlight the inflation-indexed bond, which can have either a floating coupon rate tied to the inflation rate, e.g., CPI (Consumer Price Index) or the principal indexed to the inflation rate. Because the inflation rate has a greater influence on the current level of interest rates such a bond is also usually traded close to its par value.

Bond Valuation Method

The method for valuation of bonds involves three steps as follows:

Step 1: Estimate the expected cash flows.

Step 2: Determine the appropriate interest rate that should be used to discount the cash flows.

Step 3: Calculate the present value of the expected cash flows (step-1) using appropriate interest rate (step- 2) i.e. discounting the expected cash flows.

Bond Valuation Meaning:

- Bond Valuation is method to determine fair value of a bond.

Bond Valuation Method

Step 1: Estimate the expected cash flows.

Step 2: Determine the appropriate interest rate that should be used to discount the cash flows.

Step 3: Calculate the present value of the expected cash flows (Step-1) using interest rate (step-2) i.e. discounting the expected cash flows.

Present Value Formula for Bond Valuation

- Present Value n = Expected cash flows in the period $n/(1 + i)^n$.
- Bond Value = Present Value 1 + Present Value 2 + ... + Present Value n.
- Example.

Why Bond Valuation?

- In order to determine its accurate present value and make informed investment decision

Let's expand and understand each step in detail:

Step-1: Estimating Cash Flows.

Cash flow is the cash that is estimated to be received in future from investment in a bond. There are only two types of cash flows that can be received from investment in bonds i.e. – coupon payments and principal payment at maturity.

The usual cash flow cycle of the bond is coupon payments are received at regular intervals as per the bond agreement, and final coupon plus principle payment is received at the maturity. There are some instances when bonds don't follow these regular patterns. Unusual patterns maybe a result of the different type of bond such as zero-coupon bonds, in which there are no coupon payments. Considering such factors, it is important for an analyst to estimate accurate cash flow for the purpose of bond valuation.

Step-2: Determine the Appropriate Interest Rate to Discount the Cash Flows.

Once the cash flow for the bond is estimated, the next step is to determine the appropriate interest rate to discount cash flows. The minimum interest rate that an investor should require is the interest available in the marketplace for default-free cash flow. Default-free cash flows are cash flows from debt security which are completely safe and has zero chances default. Such securities are usually issued by the central bank of a country, for example, in the USA it is bonds by U.S. Treasury Security.

Consider a situation where an investor wants to invest in bonds. If he is considering to invest corporate bonds, he is expecting to earn higher return from these corporate bond compared to rate of returns of U.S. Treasury Security bonds. This is because chances are that a corporate bond might default, whereas the U.S. Security Treasury bond is never going to default. As he is taking a higher risk by investing in corporate bonds, he expects a higher return. One may use single interest rate or multiple interest rates for valuation.

Step-3: Discounting the Expected Cash Flows.

Now that we already have values of expected future cash flows and interest rate used to discount the cash flow, it is time to find the present value of cash flows. Present Value of a cash flow is the amount of money that must be invested today to generate a specific future value. The present value of a cash flow is more commonly known as discounted value.

The present value of a cash flow depends on two determinants:

- When a cash flow will be received i.e. timing of a cash flow &;
- The required interest rate, more widely known as Discount Rate (rate as per Step-2).

First, we calculate the present value of each expected cash flow. Then we add all the individual present values and the resultant sum is the value of the bond.

Bond Value at Maturity

The formula for calculating a bond's price uses the basic present value (PV) formula for a given discount rate.

$$P = \left(\frac{C}{1+i} + \frac{C}{(1+i)^2} + \ldots + \frac{C}{(1+i)^N} \right) + \frac{M}{(1+i)^N}$$

$$= \left(\sum_{n=1}^{N} \frac{C}{(1+i)^n} \right) + \frac{M}{(1+i)^N}$$

$$= C \left(\frac{1-(1+i)^{-N}}{i} \right) + M(1+i)^{-N}$$

Bond price is the present value of coupon payments and face value paid at maturity.

F = face value, i_F = contractual interest rate, C = F * i_F = coupon payment (periodic interest payment), N = number of payments, i = market interest rate, or required yield, or observed / appropriate yield to maturity, M = value at maturity, usually equals face value, and P = market price of bond.

The bond price can be summarized as the sum of the present value of the par value repaid at maturity and the present value of coupon payments. The present value of coupon payments is the present value of an annuity of coupon payments.

An annuity is a series of payments made at fixed intervals of time. The present value of an annuity is the value of a stream of payments, discounted by the interest rate to account for the payments being made at various moments in the future. The present value is calculated by:

$$\mathrm{PV_A} = \mathrm{PMT_i} \cdot \left(1 - \frac{1}{(1+i)^n} \right)$$

i is the number of periods and n is the per period interest rate.

Par Value at Maturity

Par value is stated value or face value, with a typical bond making a repayment of par value at maturity.

Par value, in finance and accounting, means the stated value or face value. From this comes the expressions at par (at the par value), over par (over par value) and under par (under par value). A bond selling at par has a coupon rate such that the bond is worth an amount equivalent to its original issue value or its value upon redemption at maturity. Corporate bonds usually have par values of $1,000 while municipal bonds generally have face values of $500. Federal government bonds tend to have much higher face values at $10,000.

A typical bond makes coupon payments at fixed intervals during the life of it and a final repayment of par value at maturity. Together with coupon payments, the par value at maturity is discounted back to the time of purchase to calculate the bond price.

Below is the formula for calculating a bond's price, which uses the basic present value (PV) formula for a given discount rate.

$$P = \left(\frac{C}{1+i} + \frac{C}{(1+i)^2} + \ldots + \frac{C}{(1+i)^N} \right) + \frac{M}{(1+i)^N}$$

$$= \left(\sum_{n=1}^{N} \frac{C}{(1+i)^n} \right) + \frac{M}{(1+i)^N}$$

$$= C \left(\frac{1+(1+i)^{-N}}{i} \right) + M(1+i)^{-N}$$

Bond Price Formula: Bond price is the present value of coupon payments and the par value at maturity.

F = face value, iF = contractual interest rate, C = F * iF = coupon payment (periodic interest payment), N = number of payments, i = market interest rate, or required yield, or observed/ appropriate yield to maturity, M = value at maturity, usually equals face value, P = market price of bond.

Par value of a bond usually does not change, except for inflation-linked bonds whose par value is adjusted by inflation rates every predetermined period of time. The coupon payments of such bonds are also accordingly adjusted even though the coupon interest rate is unchanged.

Yield to Maturity

Yield to maturity is the discount rate at which the sum of all future cash flows from the bond are equal to the price of the bond.

The Yield to maturity (YTM) or redemption yield of a bond or other fixed- interest security, such as gilts, is the internal rate of return (IRR, overall interest rate) earned by an investor who buys the bond today at the market price, assuming that the bond will be held until maturity, and that all coupon and principal payments will be made on schedule.

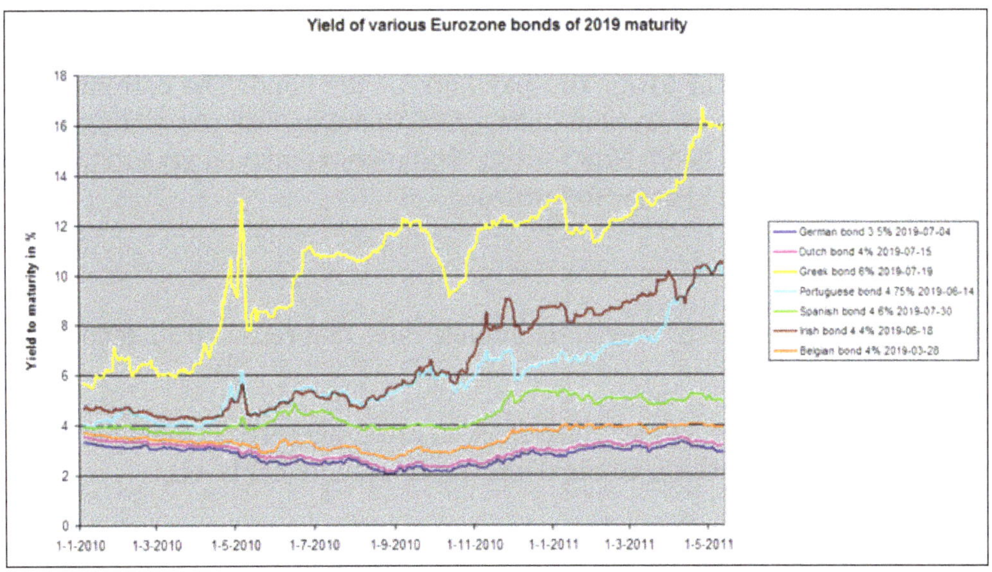

Yield to Maturity: Development of yield to maturity of bonds of 2019 maturity of a number of Eurozone governments.

Contrary to popular belief, including concepts often cited in advanced financial literature, Yield to maturity does not depend upon a reinvestment of dividends. Yield to maturity, rather, is simply the discount rate at which the sum of all future cash flows from the bond (coupons and principal) is equal to the price of the bond. The formula for yield to maturity:

$$\text{Yield to maturity (YTM)} = [(\text{Face value} / \text{Present value})^{1/\text{Time period}}]-1$$

The YTM is often given in terms of Annual Percentage Rate (A.P.R.), but usually market convention is followed: in a number of major markets the convention is to quote yields semi-annually (for example, an annual effective yield of 10.25% would be quoted as 5.00%, because 1.05 x 1.05 = 1.1025).

If the yield to maturity for a bond is less than the bond's coupon rate, then the (clean) market value of the bond is greater than the par value (and vice versa):

- If a bond's coupon rate is less than its YTM, then the bond is selling at a discount.
- If a bond's coupon rate is more than its YTM, then the bond is selling at a premium.
- If a bond's coupon rate is equal to its YTM, then the bond is selling at par.

As some bonds have different characteristics, there are some variants of YTM:

- Yield to call: When a bond is callable (can be repurchased by the issuer before the maturity), the market looks also to the Yield to call, which is the same calculation of the YTM, but assumes that the bond will be called, so the cash flow is shortened.
- Yield to put: Same as yield to call, but when the bond holder has the option to sell the bond back to the issuer at a fixed price on specified date.
- Yield to worst: When a bond is callable, puttable, exchangeable, or has other features, the yield to worst is the lowest yield of yield to maturity, yield to call, yield to put, and others.

For instance, you buy ABC Company bond which matures in 1 year and has a 5% interest rate (coupon) and has a par value of $100. You pay $90 for the bond. The current yield is 5.56% ((5/90)*100). If you hold the bond until maturity, ABC Company will pay you $5 as interest and $100 par value for the matured bond. Now for your $90 investment, you get $105, so your yield to maturity is 16.67% [= (105/90)-1] or [=(105-90)/90].

Inflation Premium

An inflation premium is the part of prevailing interest rates that results from lenders compensating for expected inflation.

An inflation premium is the part of prevailing interest rates that results from lenders compensating for expected inflation by pushing nominal interest rates to higher levels.

In economics and finance, an individual who lends money for repayment at a later point in time expects to be compensated for the time value of money, or not having the use of that money while it is lent. In addition, they will want to be compensated for the risks of the money having less purchasing power when the loan is repaid. These risks are systematic risks, regulatory risks and inflationary risks. The first includes the possibility that the borrower will default or be unable to pay on the originally agreed upon terms, or that collateral backing the loan will prove to be less valuable than estimated. The second includes taxation and changes in the law which would prevent the lender from collecting on a loan or having to pay more in taxes on the amount repaid than originally estimated. The third takes into account that the money repaid may not have as much buying power from the perspective of the lender as the money originally lent, that is inflation, and may include fluctuations in the value of the currencies involved. The inflation premium will compensate for the third risk, so investors seek this premium to compensate for the erosion in the value of their capital, due to inflation.

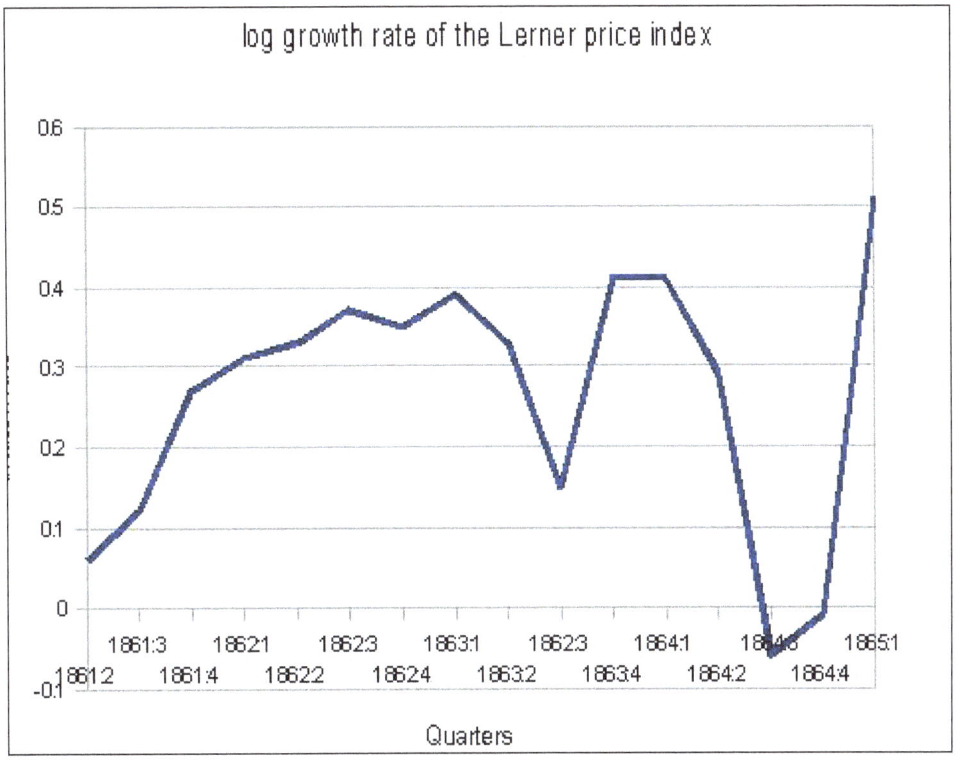

Inflation rate graph: Inflation rate in the Confederacy during the American Civil War.

Actual interest rates (without factoring in inflation) are viewed by economists and investors as being the nominal (stated) interest rate minus the inflation premium.

The Fisher equation in financial mathematics and economics estimates the relationship between nominal and real interest rates under inflation. In economics, this equation is used to predict nominal and real interest rate behavior. Letting r denote the real interest rate, i denote the nominal interest rate, and let π denote the inflation rate, the Fisher equation is: $i = r + \pi$. In the Fisher equation, π is the inflation premium.

For example, if an investor were able to lock in a 5% interest rate for the coming year and anticipates a 2% rise in prices, he would expect to earn a real interest rate of 3%. 2% is the inflation premium. This is not a single number, as different investors have different expectations of future inflation.

Since the inflation rate over the course of a loan is not known initially, volatility in inflation represents a risk to both the lender and the borrower.

Differences between Real and Nominal Rates

Nominal rate refers to the rate before adjustment for inflation; the real rate is the nominal rate minus inflation: $r = R - i$ or, $1 + r = (1 + r)(1 + E(r))$.

In finance and economics, nominal rate refers to the rate before adjustment for inflation (in contrast with the real rate). The real rate is the nominal rate minus inflation. In the case of a loan, it is this real interest that the lender receives as income. If the lender is receiving 8% from a loan and inflation is 8%, then the real rate of interest is zero, because nominal interest and inflation are equal. A lender would have no net benefit from such a loan because inflation fully diminishes the value of the loan's profit.

The relationship between real and nominal rates can be described in the equation:

$$(1 + r)(1 + i) = (1 + R)$$

Real and nominal: The relationship between real and nominal interest rates is captured by the formula.

Where r is the real rate, i is the inflation rate, and R is the nominal rate.

The real rate can be described more formally by the Fisher equation, which states that the real interest rate is approximately the nominal interest rate minus the inflation rate: $1 + i = (1+r)(1+E(r))$, where i = nominal interest rate; r = real interest rate; $E(r)$ = expected inflation rate.

For example, if somebody lends $1,000 for a year at 10%, and receives $1,100 back at the end of the year, this represents a 10% increase in his purchasing power if prices for the average goods and services that he buys are unchanged from what they were at the beginning of the year. However, if the prices of the food, clothing, housing, and other things that he wishes to purchase have increased 20% over this period, he has in fact suffered a real loss of about 12% in his purchasing power.

In this analysis, the nominal rate is the stated rate, and the real rate is the rate after the expected losses due to inflation. Since the future inflation rate can only be estimated, the ex-ante and ex post (before and after the fact) real rates may be different; the premium paid to actual inflation may be higher or lower.

Time to Maturity

"Time to maturity" refers to the length of time that can elapse before the par value (face value) for a bond must be returned to a bondholder. This time may be as short as a few months, or longer than 50 years. Once this time has been reached, the bondholder should receive the par value for their particular bond.

The issuer of a bond has to repay the nominal amount for that bond on the maturity date. After this date, as long as all due payments have been made, the issuer will have no further obligations to the bondholders. The length of time until a bond's matures is referred to as its term, tenor, or maturity. These dates can technically be any length of time, but debt securities with a term of less than one year are generally not designated as bonds. Instead, they are designated as money market instruments.

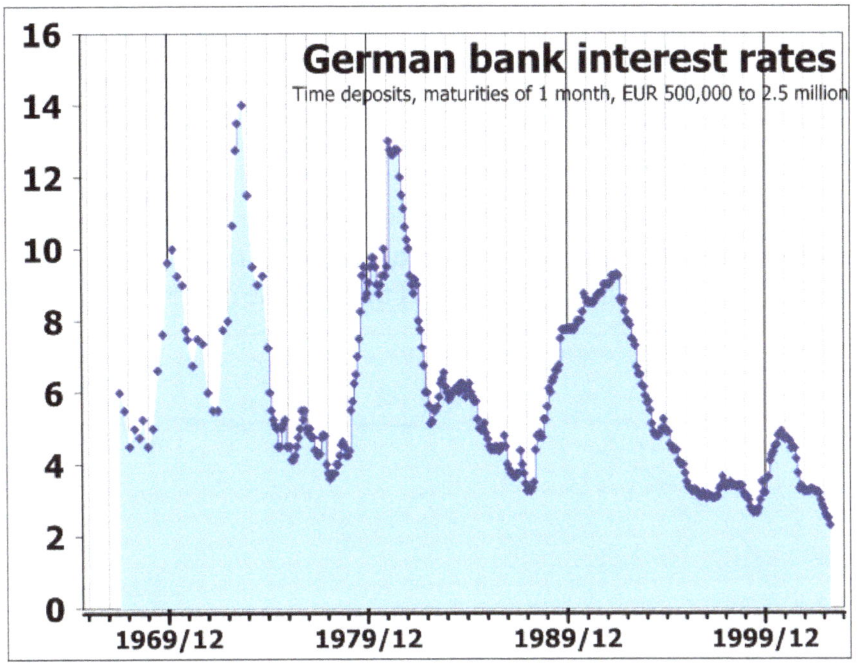

Money market interest rates: Interest rates of one-month maturity of German banks from 1967 to 2003.

Most bonds have a term of up to 30 years. That being said, bonds have been issued with terms of 50 years or more, and historically, issues have arisen where bonds completely lack maturity dates (irredeemables). In the market for United States Treasury securities, there are three categories of bond maturities:

- Short term (bills): maturities between one to five years (Instruments that mature in less than one year are considered Money Market Instruments.).
- Medium term (notes): maturities between six to twelve years.
- Long term (bonds): maturities greater than twelve years.

Because bonds with long maturities necessarily have long durations, the bond prices in these situations are more sensitive to interest rate changes. In other words, the price risk of such bonds is higher. The fair price of a "straight bond," a bond with no embedded options, is usually determined by discounting its expected cash flows at the appropriate discount rate. Although this present value relationship reflects the theoretical approach to determining the value of a bond, in practice, the price is (usually) determined with reference to other, more liquid instruments.

In general, coupon and par value being equal, a bond with a short time to maturity will trade at a higher value than one with a longer time to maturity. This is because the par value is discounted at a higher rate further into the future.

Finally, it is important to recognize that future interest rates are uncertain, and that the discount rate is not adequately represented by a single fixed number (this would be the case if an option was written on the bond in question) stochastic calculus may be employed. Where the market price of a bond is less than its face value (par value), the bond is selling at a discount. Conversely, if the market price of bond is greater than its face value, the bond is selling at a premium.

Calculating yield to Maturity using the Bond Price

The yield to maturity is the discount rate that returns the bond's market price: YTM = [(Face value/Bond price)1/Time period]-1.

YTM

The yield to maturity is the discount rate which returns the market price of the bond. YTM is the internal rate of return of an investment in the bond made at the observed price.

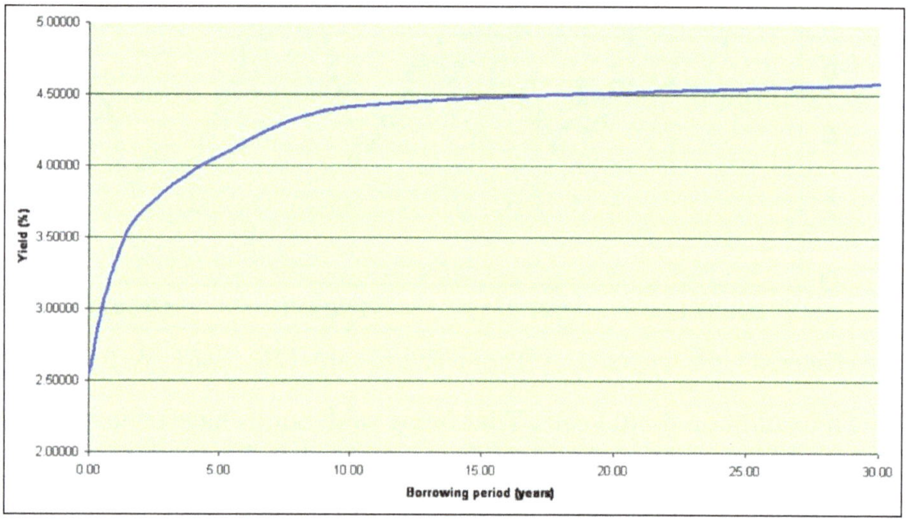

USD Yield Curve: 2005 USD yield curve.

To achieve a return equal to YTM (i.e., where it is the required return on the bond), the bond owner must buy the bond at price Po, hold the bond until maturity, and redeem the bond at par.

If the yield to maturity for a bond is less than the bond's coupon rate, then the (clean) market value of the bond is greater than the par value (and vice versa). If a bond's coupon rate is less than its YTM, then the bond is selling at a discount. If a bond's coupon rate is more than its YTM, then the bond is selling at a premium. If a bond's coupon rate is equal to its YTM, then the bond is selling at par.

Calculating YTM

Formula for yield to maturity: Yield to maturity(YTM) = [(Face value/Bond price)1/Time period]-1.

As can be seen from the formula, the yield to maturity and bond price are inversely correlated.

Consider a 30-year, zero-coupon bond with a face value of $100. If the bond is priced at an annual YTM of 10%, it will cost $5.73 today (the present value of this cash flow, 100/(1.1)30 = 5.73). Over the coming 30 years, the price will advance to $100, and the annualized return will be 10%.

What happens in the meantime? Suppose that over the first 10 years of the holding period, interest rates decline, and the yield-to-maturity on the bond falls to 7%. With 20 years remaining to maturity, the price of the bond will be 100/1.0720, or $25.84. Even though the yield-to-maturity for the remaining life of the bond is just 7%, and the yield-to-maturity bargained for when the bond was purchased was only 10%, the return earned over the first 10 years is 16.25%. This can be found by evaluating (1 +i) from the equation (1 + i) 10 = (25.842/5.731), giving 1.1625.

Over the remaining 20 years of the bond, the annual rate earned is not 16.25%, but rather 7%. This can be found by evaluating (1+i) from the equation (1+i)20 = 100/25.84, giving 1.07. Over the entire 30 year holding period, the original $5.73 invested increased to $100, so 10% per annum was earned, irrespective of any interest rate changes in between.

Impact of Payment Frequency on Bond Prices

Payment frequency can be annual, semi-annual, quarterly, or monthly; the more frequently a bond makes coupon payments, the higher the bond price.

Equity Valuation

Equity valuation refers to the approach and methodology applied to determine the intrinsic value of the shareholders equity in a company. Intrinsic value is the true value of a company based on its fundamentals such as its growth rate, management quality, strategic advantage and other tangible and intangible factors. Shareholders equity (or equity) represents the stake of shareholders in a company. It includes the initial investment, cumulative retained earnings and cumulative other comprehensive income of the company among other things.

Book value of equity equals total assets of the company minus its total liabilities. This fundamental relationship is represented by the accounting equation. In case of listed equity (i.e. stock of companies which are listed on a public stock exchange), market value is readily available. Total market value of all outstanding common stock of the company is referred to as market capitalization and it equals current market price per share multiplied by total number of outstanding shares of common stock.

Intrinsic value is different from market value. While market value represents the value assigned to the company by market forces, intrinsic value is a value that ought to prevail when all investors consider all the information related to the company's business.

Equity valuation models can be broadly categorized into (a) relative valuation and (b) absolute valuation. In relative valuation, a stock's value is determined in relation to market value of comparable stocks. Under this approach, we determine price multiples (such as price to earnings ratio (P/E ratio), price to book ratio, price to sales ratio, etc.) of comparable companies and multiply it with expected earnings, book value and/or sales of the company under valuation.

Models

Under the absolute valuation approach, there are two methods to value equity: (a) determining the total firm value based on free cash flows and subtracting the market value of its debt, in which case the cash flows are discounted using the cost of capital, and (b) determining the value of equity directly by discounting the free cash flows to equity using the cost of equity of the company.

In absolute valuation, value is determined by discounting future cash flows under different models, i.e. single-stage dividend discount model, multi-stage dividend discount model, free cash flows based model, etc. The choice of model depends on whether the equity stake under consideration is a majority holding (>50%) or a minority stake, certainty with which cash flows can be forecasted, the growth stage of the company and whether the stock is listed on an exchange or not.

Formula of Equity Valuation

Under the dividend discount valuation model, value of a company's stock is arrived at using the following formula:

$$\text{Value of a Share} = \frac{\text{Dividend per Share Next Year}}{\text{Required Return on Equity} - \text{Dividend Growth Rate}}$$

Value of Equity = Value per Share × Number of Common Shares Outstanding.

In multi-stage dividend discount model, different level of dividend per share is expected in different periods, each of which is independently discounted. Dividend discount models are appropriate valuation approaches in valuing a minority stage in the company.

In case of majority holding, value of a company is best determined by discounting the free cash flows to firm (FCF) or free cash flows to equity (FCFE) using the cost of capital as follows:

$$\text{Value of a Company} = \frac{\text{Free Cash Flows to Firm Next Year}}{\text{Cost of Capital} - \text{Growth Rate of FCF}}$$

Value of Equity = Value of Company – Market Value of Debt

Value of equity can be determined directly using the following formula:

$$\text{Value of Equity} = \frac{\text{Free Cash Flows to Equity}}{\text{Required Rate of Return on Equity} - \text{Growth Rate of FCFE}}$$

Equity Valuation Methods

Equity valuation methods can be broadly classified into balance sheet methods, discounted cash flow methods, and relative valuation methods. Balance sheet methods comprise of book value, liquidation value, and replacement value methods. Discounted cash flow methods include dividend discount models and free cash flow models. Lastly, relative valuation methods are a price to earnings ratios, price to book value ratios, price to sales ratios etc.

A financial analyst primarily conducts two types of analysis for evaluation of equity investment decisions viz. fundamental and technical analysis. All the above methods are part of the fundamental analysis conducted by a financial analyst. The technical analysis analyses the charts and graphs of the market prices of a stock to understand the sentiments of the market. It believes in a fact that history repeats itself. Many believe that it is used to decide the entry and exit time from the market. On the other hand, fundamental equity valuations methods attempt to find the fair market value of equity share. It involves a study of the assets, earning potential, future prospects, future cash flows, magnitude and probability of dividend payments etc.

Classification/Types of Equity Valuation Methods

Fundamental equity valuation methods are explained in brief under the following categories.

Balance Sheet Methods/Techniques

Balance sheet methods are the methods which utilize the balance sheet information to value a company. These techniques consider everything for which accounting in the books of accounts is done.

Book Value Method

In this method, book value as per balance sheet is considered the value of equity. Book value means the net worth of the company. Net worth is calculated as follows:

Net Worth = Equity Share capital + Preference Share Capital + Reserves & Surplus – Miscellaneous Expenditure (as per B/Sheet) – Accumulated Losses.

Equity valuation methods		
A financial analyst primarily conducts two types of analysis for evaluation of equity investment decisions viz. fundamental and technical analysis		
Type/classification		
Balance sheet method	Earning multiple method	Discounted cash flow method
• Book value Method • Liquidation Value Method • Replacement Cost Method	• Price to Earning Ratio • Price to Book Value Ratio • Price to Sales Ratio	• Dividend Discount Method • Free Cash Flow Method

Liquidation Value Method

Here, in liquidation cost method liquidation value is considered the value of equity. Liquidation value is the value realized if the firm is liquidated today.

Liquidation Value = Net Realizable Value of All Assets – Amounts paid to All Creditors including Preference Shareholders.

Replacement Cost Method

Here, in replacement cost method the value of equity is the replacement value. It means the cost that would be incurred to create a duplicate firm is the value of the firm. It is assumed that the market value and replacement value will coincide in the long run. The famous ratio by James Tobin is Tobin q which tends to become 1. Tobin q is the ratio of market value to replacement cost.

Equity Value = Replacement Cost of Assets – Liabilities.

Discounted Cash Flow Methods/Techniques

Discounted cash flow methods are based on the fact that present value all future dividends and the future price represent the market value of equity.

Dividend Discount Model

This dividend discount model finds the present value of future dividends of a company to derive the present market value of equity. There are various models with different assumptions of a period of dividends and growth in dividends.

Single Period Model

Single Period Model, one of the discounted cash flow models, is an income valuation approach that aims to find the fair value of a stock/firm using single projected cash flow value and then discounting it with an appropriate discount rate. Taking all future streams of cash flow into one single period and discounting is also referred as "Earnings Capitalisation".

This method is a substitute for the traditional discounting of all future cash flows. However since it is a "single period" model, we need a single sum of an amount as the cash flow for all future years or a single sum for 1 year holding period.

Formula for Calculating Value of a Firm/Company using Single Period Model

Value of a firm or company = Net Income / Discounting Rate

Single Period Model Example

To estimate the value of the firm, company or project, stabilized net operating income is divided by an appropriate discount rate. Assuming a stable earning (net of expenses) of USD 300,000 per annum and a discount rate of 12%, the value of the firm can be calculated as follows:

Value = Net Income/Discounting Rate

= $ 300,000/0.12

= $ 2,500,000

If a growth number needs to be adjusted to the model, assuming a constant growth of 5%, the value of the firm can now be calculated as follows:

Value = Net Income/Discounting Rate

= $ 300,000/(0.12 -0.05)

= $ 300,000/0.07

= $ 4,285,714

When the discount rate and growth rate are assumed to remain constant from a day of valuation till perpetuity, the single period model will yield same results as multi-period model.

Example: The same approach under the dividend discount model can be used for calculating the fair value of a stock with a holding period of 1 year. Assuming a \$ 5 dividend is expected after 1 year and the stock price is expected to be \$ 20 after a year, the value of the stock can be calculated assuming a discounting rate of 12% as follows:

Value = D1/ (1+r) + P1/ (1+r)

where,

D1 is the expected dividend after 1 year.

P1 is the expected price after 1 year of holding period.

r is the required rate of return (discounting rate).

Value of the stock = \$ 5 / (1.12) + \$ 20 / (1.12)

= \$ 4.46 + \$ 17.86

= \$ 22.32

Rationale for using Single Period Model

This model is one of the simplest models to understand and calculate the value of a firm/company/project and is still being used, however, certain limitations exist. The key reasons for the wide usage of this model are as follows:

1. Based on Current Year Data

Under the single period model; we do not need to forecast future cash flows and current year data available is enough to value the company under consideration.

2. Suitable for Stable Businesses

This model is best suited for companies where earnings are stable and easily predictable. In such a case, it becomes easy to assume an average earning amount which shall be received for the remaining life of the company.

3. User-friendly and Simple Model

Since an assumption can be made that earnings and expenses will grow at the same rate as the long term growth rate for cash flows; one need not estimate earnings and expenses separately. This makes this model extremely user-friendly as one can take the current financial data from annual reports and attach a constant growth rate to it.

Though the model enjoys simplicity and ease of use; it limits its usage due to some limitations which need to be considered for a thorough understanding of the model.

<table>
<tr><th colspan="2">Single period dcf model</th></tr>
<tr><td colspan="2"><ul><li>Single Period Model is income valuation approach that aims to find fair value of stock/firm using single projected cash flow value and then discounting it with an appropriate discount rate.</li><li>This method is a substitute for the traditional discount of all future cash flows.</li></ul>Formulae : Value of Firm = Net Income / Discounting Rate</td></tr>
<tr><th>Rationale for model</th><th>Limitations</th></tr>
<tr><td>The key reasons for its wide usage are:<ul><li>It is based on the current year's data.</li><li>Suitable for stable businesses.</li><li>It is the most user friendly model.</li><li>It is also the simplest method.</li></ul></td><td><ul><li>Based on single average till perpetuity which can lead to error.</li><li>It is not practical model.</li><li>The discount rate may change over time.</li><li>It is based on a single value and this value is sensitive.</li></ul></td></tr>
</table>

Limitations of Single-period Model

1. Based on Single Average

It assumes a single average and stable net cash flow/income till perpetuity which can lead to substantial errors in valuation if the company under consideration is cyclic or is in growing stage or decline phase or any other case where profitability or cash flows keep fluctuating.

2. Not Practical

The single period model assumes revenues and expenses increase at the same rate and hence considers a constantly grown rate for net income. However, in reality expenditure may in some cases reduce over time due to economies of scale. In some cases, expenditure may increase faster than revenues as companies may incur additional capital expansion or advertisement expenditures. Since the rate at which revenues and expense may not always, in all circumstance, grow at the same rate; this model may face error in valuation due to the impractical approach.

3. Different Discount Rate

The discount rate (also known as the capitalization rate) may change over time. The discount rate calculated using the Capital Asset Pricing Model (CAPM) which pertains to equity may not be the discount rate applicable to the net income in the real world scenario.

4. Sensitivity

Since only one value is estimated and then discounted, the said value is more sensitive than the multi-period model in estimation.

Multi-period Model

Multiple Period Model of Equity Valuation is also a dividend discount model. Like any other discounted cash flow model aims at arriving at the intrinsic/fair value of the stock. The multi-period model takes into account the dividend stream of 'n' years and an expected price at the end of 'n' years. It essentially discounts both dividends and expected price using an appropriate discount rate to arrive at the fair value. This model is appropriate for investors having a holding period in mind. The multi-period model will take those many years into account to arrive at the intrinsic value of the stock.

Brief on Equity Share as an Investment

Equity share is an investment alternative, whereby an investor can take part in a company's capital and share the profits of the company. They also have a claim on assets of the company but they never get their principal back like debt investments. In the case of listed companies, an investor can sell his stake in the market.

Multiple period model	
The multi-period model takes into account the dividend stream of 'n' years and an expected price at the end of 'n' years	
Formulae	Interpretation
Present value of an Equity Share = Present Value of Future Dividends $Po = D1/(1+r) + D2/(1+r)^2 + D3/(1+r)^3 + \ldots\ldots Dn/(1+r)^n$ Where: Po = Price of Equity Share D1 = Expected Dividend 1 Year from now D2 = Expected Dividend 2 Year from now D3 = Expected Dividend 3 Year from now Dn = Expected Dividend n Year from now	• The fair price calculated using this model can be used for investment decisions in the stock market. • It the market price is lower than the value calculated using this model, one can look to buy the stock • When stock is trading higher than value calculated using the model, one may look at short selling the same.

Calculating Stock Price using Multi-period Dividend Discount Model Formula

In essence, the price can be calculated as follows:

Formula for Multi-period Model

For valuing anything using a discounting/present value formula, the first thing that is required is the Cash Inflows. In this case, the cash inflow is the 'Expected Dividend' ought to be received every year. In simple terms, it can be stated as below:

Present Value of an Equity Share = Present Value of Future Dividends.

$$Po = D1/(1+r) + D2/(1+r)^2 + D3/(1+r)^3 + \ldots\ldots Dn/(1+r)^n$$

where,

Po = Price of the equity share.

D1 = expected dividend 1 year from now.

D2 = expected dividend 2 years from now.

Dn = expected dividend n years from now.

r = expected rate of return (cost of equity).

This formula takes into account an infinite number of years, which is difficult to forecast in a real-world situation, and one may use perpetuity as a dividend value after a few years beyond which forecast is difficult. For shorter holding periods, one can use the multi-period to value the stock price as listed in the below example.

Example of Multi-period Model

Let us look at an example where a particular investor with a 5-year horizon wants to calculate the fair value of the stock. Given the expected dividend stream for the next 5 years and expected price after 5 years, one can arrive at the intrinsic value of the stock using an appropriate discount rate. The following information is available:

D1 = \$ 2, D2 = \$ 3, D3 = \$ 4, D4 = \$ 5, D5 = \$ 6

Expected stock price after 5 yrs = \$ 120

Cost of equity (required rate of return) = 10%

Using the information available, the value of the stock can be calculated as follows:

Tenor	Cash Flow	Discount Rate	Present Value
1	\$ 2	10%	$2 / (1+10\%)^1 = 1.82$
2	\$ 3	10%	$3 / (1+10\%)^2 = 2.48$
3	\$ 4	10%	$4 / (1+10\%)^3 = 3.00$
4	\$ 5	10%	$5 / (1+10\%)^4 = 3.42$
5	\$ 6	10%	$6 / (1+10\%)^5 = 3.72$
5	\$ 120	10%	$120 / (1+10\%)^5 = 74.51$

The intrinsic value of the stock will be a summation of all present values and in our case, this sums up to \$ 88.95.

Interpretation of Multi-period Model

The fair price arrived using the multi-period model can be used by investors to make investment decisions in the stock market. If the market price is lower than the value calculated using this model, one can look to buy the stock as the stock is trading undervalued and vice versa when a stock is trading higher than the value calculated using the model, one may look at short selling the same. However, if the market prices seem fair one may need to revisit the estimates of the stock price at the end of the holding period, especially the dividend estimations and the cost of equity. To estimate intrinsic value closer to reality one needs to assume infinite periods and hence one may look at the other multi-period dividend discount models like two-stage growth model, H model or three-stage growth model which will help the investor to reduce the error in the estimation of fair/intrinsic value.

Constant Growth Model

Gordon Growth Model is a part of Dividend Discount Model. This model assumes that both the dividend amount and the stock's fair value will grow at a constant rate. To put in simple words, this model assumes that the dividend paid by the company will grow at a constant percentage.

Formula for Gordon Growth Model/Constant Growth Rate DCF Method

Stock Value (p) = D_1/ (k-g).

Where, p = Intrinsic value of the stock/equity.

k = Investors required rate of return, discount rate.

g = Expected growth rate (It should be assumed to be constant).

D_1= Next years expected annual dividend per share.

When k and g, i.e. investors required rate of return and expected growth rate do not change over the years, so the stocks fair/intrinsic value will increase annually by the rate of dividend increase. To put it in simple words, both the dividend amount and the stock price/value will increase at a constant growth rate.

Let us look at the example below for a better understanding of the concept of constant growth model.

Constant growth rate	
The CONSTANT GROWTH RATE DCF METHOD model assumes that both the dividend amount and the stock's fair value will grow at a constant rate. It is also known as Gorden Dividend Growth Model calculated as P_0 = D_1 / (Ke.g)	
Formulae	Disadvantages
P_0 = D_1 / (Ke.g) Where; P_0 = Intrinsic Value of Stock. Ke = Cost of Equity. G = Growth Rate. D_1 = Next Year's expected annual dividend per share.	• It comes that vague assumption that dividends paid by the company will grow at a constant rate. • Constant Growth rate does not align with the real life scenario. Growth rate may change (increase/ decrease). • Mathematically this model may generate out value as infinity if the cost of growth approaches very close to the Ke.

Example for Calculating Value of Stock using Gordon's Growth Model

Let us say a stock pays a dividend of \$ 5 this year. The dividend has been growing at the rate of 10% annually. Assuming a 15% required rate of return; the value of the stock can be calculated as follows:

Stock Value (p) = D_1/ (k-g)

In the given example;

Current year Dividend Do = $ 5

k = 15% i.e. 0.15

g = 10% i.e. 0.10

Year	Expected Annual Dividend [D]	Discount Rate [k]	Expected Growth Rate [g]	Stock Value [p]
1	$5*(1+0.10) = $5.5	15%	10%	$ 5.5/(0.15-0.10) = $ 110
2	$5.5(1+0.10) = $6.05	15%	10%	$ 6.05/(0.15-0.10) = $ 121
3	$6.05(1+.10) = $6.655	15%	10%	$ 6.655/(0.15-0.10) = $ 133.1
4	$6.655(1+.10) = $7.3205	15%	10%	$ 7.3205/(0.15-0.10) = $ 146.41

Year 1 Dividend will be = $ 5 x $(1+10\%)^1$ = $ 5.50.

Year 2 Dividend will be = $ 5.50 x $(1+10\%)^1$ = $ 6.05.

Year 3 Dividend will be = $ 6.05 x $(1+10\%)^1$ = $ 6.655.

Year 4 Dividend will be = $ 6.655 x $(1+10\%)^1$ = $ 7.3205.

To sum up the calculations, 110*1.1 = 121, 121*1.1 = 133.1 & 133.1*1.1=146.41 respectively for each year. Hence the stock value grows by a constant rate of 1.1 over the next 4 years and will continue to grow by 10% for all the forth coming years. According to the constant growth model, if the stock's value is $110 for the next year, but if the stock is trading at $100 then it is undervalued.

Variations in the Price of the Stock Calculated Under Gordon's Constant Growth Rate DCF Model

- Assuming the company does well in the next year and grows at a growth rate of more than 10% let us say 12%, the price of the stock will be:

  p = $ 5.5/ (0.15-.012) = $ 183.33.

- Conversely, if the company does not do very well and the growth rate goes down, let us assume it goes down to 8%. The price of the stock will be:

  p = $ 5.5/ (0.15-0.08) = $ 78.57.

The model is applied and used for its simplicity and suitability for companies with stable growth and established dividend payout ratios. The model, however, comes with a set of limitations; which one needs to know so as to enable a better understanding of the model.

Disadvantages of Gordon Growth Model

- The constant growth model of equity valuation under discounted cash flow model comes with an assumption that the dividends paid by the company will grow at a constant rate. This is not a true assumption for declining or growing companies.

- Also, constant growth means the company would continue to grow at constant rate till eternity, which does not align with real world scenario and the said approach can lead to estimation errors.
- The growth rate in an industry is the key input. Mathematically this model may generate output value as infinity if the cost of growth approaches very close to the cost of equity and the value may go negative if growth rate goes above the cost of equity.

Two Stage Growth Model

The two-stage dividend discount model takes into account two stages of growth. This method of equity valuation is not a model based on two cash flows but is a two-stage model where the first stage may have a high growth rate and the second stage is usually assumed to have a stable growth rate.

Two-stage Dividend Discount Model

The two-stage model can be used to value companies where the first stage has an unstable initial growth rate and there is stable growth in the second stage, which lasts forever. The first stage may have a positive, negative, or volatile growth rate and will last for a finite period, whereas the second stage is assumed to have a stable growth rate for the rest of the life of the company. In this model, it is assumed that the dividend paid by a company also grows in the same way, i.e., in two stages.

<table>
<tr><th colspan="2">Dividend discount model</th></tr>
<tr><td colspan="2">The two stage model can be used to value companies where the first stage has an unstable initial growth rate and there is stable growth in the second stage which lasts forever. It is assumed that the dividend paid by a company also grows in the exact way i.e. In two such stages

Po = D1 / (Ke - g)</td></tr>
<tr><th>Interpretation</th><th>Limitations</th></tr>
<tr><td>• If MPS of company > model output, it means that our market price is undervalued which in turn means that our estimates for the growth are higher than what market perceives.
• If MPS > model output, it means market expects the company to grow faster than out estimates.</td><td>• Error estimation of higher of the first stage (unstable stage)
• Assuming a direct jump of growth from 12% to say 4%
• Limited to companies which have higher growth rate during the first stage.</td></tr>
</table>

Example Calculating Value of Stock/Share using Two-stage Dividend Discount Model

Let's take the example of a company (ABC Ltd.) that has paid a dividend of $4 this year. Assuming a higher growth for the next 3 years at 15% and stable growth of 4% thereafter, let's calculate the value using a two-stage dividend discount model.

We need to do an adjustment here to arrive at the dividend amount that needs to be discounted after adjusting for the different rates in the different stages. Continuing with the above example and assuming a required rate of return of 10%, we can calculate the value of the stock/firm as follows:

Current Dividend = $ 4.00.

Dividend after 1st year will be = \$ 4.60 (\$ 4 x 1.15 – growing at 15 %).

Dividend after 2nd year will be = \$ 5.29 (\$ 4.60 x 1.15 – growing at 15%).

Dividend after 3rd year will be = \$ 6.0835 (\$ 5.29 x 1.15 – growing at 15%).

Since the growth in the first three years was 15%, the value of the dividend declared after 3 years will be \$6.0835, as calculated above.

The second stage has a growth rate of 4%, so the dividend value after the 4th year will be \$6.0835 x 1.04 = \$6.3268. Assuming this as the constant dividend for the rest of the company's life, we arrive at the present values, as follow:

Po = D/(i – g).

Where Po = Value of the stock/equity.

D = Per-Share dividend paid by the company at the end of each year.

i = Discount rate, which is the required rate of return* that an investor wants for the risk associated with the investment in equity against investment in risk-free security.

g = Growth rate.

*One of the most commonly used ways of calculating the required rate of return is by using the Capital Asset Pricing (CAPM) model.

Now, using the formula for calculating the value of the firm, we can arrive at the present value at the end of 3rd year for all future cash flows as follows:

Value = \$6.3268 / (10% – 4%)

= \$105.45

Table: Showing Present Values.

Tenor	Cash Flow	Discount Rate	Present Value
1	4.6	10%	4.18
2	5.29	10%	4.37
3	6.0835	10%	4.57
3	105.45	10%	79.23
Total Present Value			92.35

Present value calculations in the above table are arrived at as follows:

$\$4.18 = \$4.60 / (1 + 10\%)^1$

$\$4.37 = \$5.29 / (1 + 10\%)^2$

$\$4.57 = \$6.0835 / (1 + 10\%)^3$

$\$79.23 = \$105.45 / (1 + 10\%)^3$

The sum of all the present values will be the value of the firm; in our example, this comes to $92.35. Let's look at how one should interpret the value of the firm from an investor perspective.

Interpreting Firm Value using Two-stage Dividend Discount Model

The comparison of the market price to the value of the firm can help you understand the market perception of the company. If the market price of the company's share is lower than the calculated value using the model, the stock price is undervalued, which could mean that our estimates for the growth of the company are higher than what the market perceives. It can also be interpreted that one needs to revise the growth estimates to align the model value closer to the market price of the stock; this is called the implied growth rate. However, if prices are marginally lower than the model price, one could assume that the stock price is trading cheaper and could be a good investment to make.

On the other hand, if the market price is higher than the model output, it means that the market expects the company to grow faster than our estimates.

Although the model has its benefits and applications; it inherits some limitations as well. Let's look at the limitations faced by the two-stage dividend discount model.

Limitations of the Two-stage Dividend Discount Model

- The model's biggest limitation is the error in estimation that can occur due to the incorrect estimation of the length of the first stage. It is very difficult to estimate the length of the first stage, which could lead to overvaluation or undervaluation of the stock under consideration. A shorter first stage will cause the valuation to be undervalued, while a longer first stage could lead to overvaluation, in the case of a high growth assumption in the first stage.
- Secondly, assuming a direct jump from, for example, 12% in the expansion stage to 4% stable growth in back-to-back years may not be a scenario closer to reality, as, in the real-world scenario, the growth rates will stabilize gradually over a period of time in multiple stages, not just two.
- This model has its usage and applicability limited to companies that have higher growth rates during the 1st phase, which is known and has stable growth rates thereafter. Also, the growth rates in the 1st phase should be closer to growth rates in stage two. Essentially, if there is not much difference between the two stages, the model will yield appropriate results.

There have been other models in use that tend to reduce the estimation error of the two-stage model dividend discount model, such as the H model and three-stage models, such that the valuation could be calibrated close to the market reality. However, the two-stage model is still worthy of application to specific cases and scenarios, as lesser stages require less estimation and business models where high growth lasts only for a few years, after which the reasons for high growth are lost. In the case of an innovation/idea/product, a firm may enjoy high growth rates until the patent expires or competitors jump in. For such cases, a two-stage model is appropriate for use and application.

H Model

H model is another form of Dividend Discount Model under Discounted Cash flow (DCF) method which breaks down the cash flows (dividends) into two phases or stages. It is similar or one can say a variation of a two-stage model however unlike the classical two- stage model, this model differs in how the growth rates are defined in the two stages.

In the two-stage model, it is assumed that the first stage goes through an extraordinary growth phase while the second stage goes through a constant growth phase. In H model, the growth rate in the first phase is not constant but reduces gradually to approach the constant growth rate in the second stage. The key point to note here is that the growth rate is assumed to reduce in a linear way in the initial phase till it reaches stable growth rate in the second stage. The model also makes an assumption that dividend pay-out and cost of equity remain constant. Let us take an example illustrating firm value using H model dividend discount model.

Example of Valuation using H Model – Dividend Discount Model

Let us take an example of a company ABC Ltd. that has paid a dividend of $ 4 this year. Assuming a growth for next 3 years at 13%, 10% and 7% respectively in the first stage and a stable growth of 4% thereafter; let us calculate the firm value using H model dividend discount model.

The dividend values will be as follows:

Current Dividend = $ 4.00

Dividend after 1st year will be = $ 4.52 ($ 4.00 x 1.13 – growing at 13 %).

2nd year will be = $ 4.972 ($ 4.52 x 1.10 – growing at 10%).

3rd year will be = $ 5.32 ($ 4.972 x 1.07 – growing at 7%).

The dividend declared after the first stage will be $ 5.32 as calculated above.

Assuming a stable growth rate of 4% in the second stage; the dividend value after 4th year will be

$ 5.32 x 1.04 = $ 5.5328.

Assuming this as the constant dividend for the rest of the life of the company, we arrive at the present values as follows:

$P0 = D/(i - g)$

where, P0 = Value of the stock/equity

D = per- share dividend paid by the company at the end of each year.

i = discount rate, which is the required rate of return which an investor wants for the risk associated with the investment in equity as against investment in a risk-free security.

g = growth rate.

Now using the formula for calculating the value of the firm, we can arrive at the present value at the end of 3rd year for all future cash flows as follows:

$$\text{Value} = \$\ 5.5328 / (10\% - 4\%)$$

$$= \$\ 92.21$$

Assuming a constant discount rate of 10%, now the value of the firm can be calculated as the present value of future cash flows.

Tenor	Cash Flow	Discount Rate	Present Value
1	4.52	10%	4.11
2	4.972	10%	4.11
3	5.32	10%	3.99
3	92.21	10%	69.28
Total Present Value			81.49

Present value calculations arrived as follows:

$$\$\ 4.11 = \$\ 4.52 / (1 + 10\%)^1$$

$$\$\ 4.11 = \$\ 4.972 / (1 + 10\%)^2$$

$$\$\ 5.32 = \$\ 5.32 / (1 + 10\%)^3$$

$$\$\ 69.28 = \$\ 92.21 / (1 + 10\%)^3$$

The sum of all the present values will be the value of the firm which in our example comes to $81.49.

The H model tries to do away with some of the problems/shortcomings associated with the classical two-stage model; let us have a comparative look to enable the better understanding of the H Model.

<table>
<tr><th colspan="2">H-model dividend discount</th></tr>
<tr><td colspan="2">It breaks down the cash flows (dividends) into two phases or stages. In H model, the growth rate in the first phase is not constant but reduces gradually to approach the constant growth rate in the second stage.</td></tr>
<tr><td>H-model v/s two stage model</td><td>Formulae</td></tr>
<tr><td><ul><li>Two-stage model assumes an extraordinary growth rate (constant) in the initial stage while the H model is free to use an increasing or declining rate in initial phase.</li><li>In two-stage model, growth rate drops suddenly from very high rate to stable rate as stages change, however in H model; growth rate reduce linearly to reach stable growth rate.</li></ul></td><td>Po = D / (I - g)
Where,
Po = Value of Stock
D = Dividend per share
I = Discount Rate
G = Growth Rate</td></tr>
</table>

Risk and Return on Single Asset

The typical object of investment is to make current income from investments in the form of dividends and interest income. The investments should earn reasonable and expected rate of return on investments. Certain investments like bank deposits, public deposits, debentures, bonds etc. will carry a fixed rate of return payable periodically.

In case of investments in shares of companies, the periodical payments in the form of dividends are not assured, but it may ensure higher returns than fixed income investments. But the investments in equity shares of companies carry higher risk than fixed income instruments.

Another form of return is in the form of capital appreciation. This element of return is the difference between the purchase price and the price at which the asset can be sold, it can be a capital gain or capital loss arising due to change in the price of the investment. The rate of return of a particular investment is calculated as follows:

Annual Rate of Return

The annual rate of return of a particular investment can be calculated as follows:

$$\mathrm{R} = \frac{D_1}{P_0} + \frac{P_1 - P_0}{P_0} = \frac{D_1 + (P_1 - P_0)}{P_0}$$

Where, R = Annual rate of return of a share.

D_1 = Dividend paid at the end of the year.

P_0 = Market price of share at the beginning of the year.

P_1 = Market price of share at the end of the year.

The above formula is used for calculation of annual return of an investment in shares. In the above formula, D_1/P_0 represents dividend yield and $(P_1 - P_0)/P_0$ represents capital gain or loss.

Example: Mr. Ravi has purchased 100 shares of \$10 each of Radheshyam Ltd. in 2013 at \$78 per share. The company has declared a dividend @ 40% for the year 2015-16. The market price of share as at 1-4-2015 was \$104 and on 31-3-2016 was \$128. Calculate the annual return on the investment for the year 2015-16.

Solution: Dividend received for 2015-16 = \$ 10 x 40/100 = \$4.

Calculation of Annual Rate of Return on Investment for the Year 2015-16.

$$R = \frac{D_1 + (P_1 - 0)}{P_0} = \frac{4 + (128 - 104)}{104} = 0.2692 \text{ or } 26.92\%$$

Average Rate of Return

The rate of return can also be calculated for a period more than one year. The average rate of return represents the average of annual rates of return over a period of years.

The formula used for calculation of average rate of return is given below:

$$\overline{R} = \frac{1}{n}(R_1 + R_2 + ...R_n)$$

where, $\overline{R}$= Average rate of return.

$R_1, R_2 .....R_n$ = Annual rate of return in period 1, 2,.....

n = Total number of periods.

Example: The average market prices and dividend per share of High-Tech Securities Ltd. for the past 6 years are given below:

Year	Average market price ($)	Dividend per share ($)
2015 – 16	68	3.0
2014 – 15	61	2.6
2013 – 14	50	2.0
2012 – 13	53	2.5
2011 – 12	45	2.0
2010 – 11	38	1.8

Calculate the average rate of return of High Tech Securities Ltd. Shares for past 6 years.

Solution:

Year	Average market price per share ($)	Capital gain (%)	Dividend per share ($)	Dividend Yield (%)	Rate of return (%)
2010 – 11	38	-	1.8	4.74	-
2011 – 12	45	18.42	2.0	4.44	22.86
2012 – 13	53	17.78	2.5	4.72	22.50
2013 – 14	50	-5.66	2.0	4.00	-1.66
2014 – 15	61	22.00	2.6	4.26	26.26
2015 – 16	68	11.48	3.0	4.41	15.89

$$\overline{R} = \frac{1}{5}(22.86 + 22.50 - 1.66 + 26.26 + 15.89) = \frac{1}{5}(85.85) = 17.17\%$$

Risk on Single Asset

The concept of risk is more difficult to quantify. Statistically we can express risk in terms of standard deviation of return. For example, in case of gilt edged security or government bonds, the risk is nil since the return does not vary – it is fixed. But strictly speaking if we consider inflation and calculate real rate of return (inflation adjusted) we find that even government bonds have some amount of risk since the rate of inflation may vary.

Return from unsecured fixed deposits appear to have zero variability and hence zero risk. But there is a risk of default of interest as well as the principal. In such case the rate of return can be negative. Hence, this investment has high risk though apparently it carries zero risk. For other investments like shares, business etc., where the rate of return is not fixed, there may be a schedule of return with associated probability for each rate of return.

The mean of the probable returns gives the expected rate of return and the standard deviation or variance which is square of standard deviation measures risk. Higher the range of the probable return, higher the standard deviation and hence higher the risk. A risk averse investor will look for return where the range is low. Hence, low standard deviation means low risk.

The problem in portfolio management is to minimize the standard deviation without sacrificing expected rate of return. This is possible by diversification. Risk is measured in terms of variability of returns. If Investment 'A' and Investment 'B' whose mean rate of return is same as shown in figure.

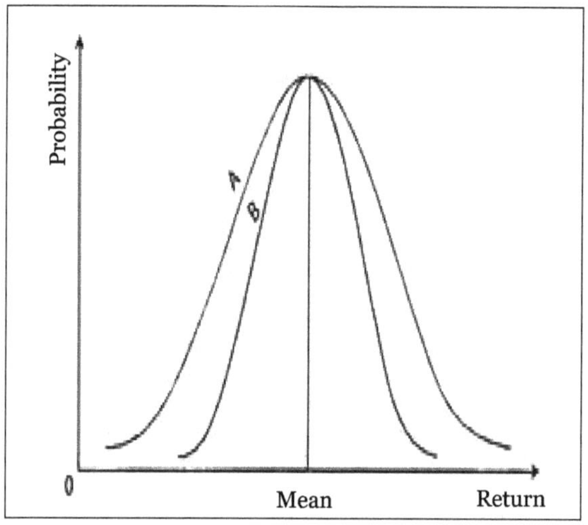

Variability of Return.

The returns of Investment 'A' show more variability than Investment 'B'. In view of the variability of returns, Investment 'A' is more risky, even though both the investments are having the same mean returns. The following illustrations explains the quantification of risk in terms of standard deviation.

Example - The rate of return of equity shares of ABC Steels Ltd. for past six years are given below:

Year	2011	2012	2013	2014	2015	2016
Rate of return (%)	12	18	-6	20	22	24

Calculate the average rate of return, standard deviation and variance.

Solution: Calculation of Average Rate of Return ($\overline{R}$)

$$\overline{R} = \frac{\sum R}{N} = \frac{12+18-6+20+22+24}{6} = 15\%$$

$$\sigma^2 = \frac{\sum\left(R-\overline{R}\right)^2}{N}$$

Year	Rate of Return (%) R	$(R - \bar{R})$	$(R - \bar{R})^2$
2011	12	-3	9
2012	18	3	9
2013	-6	-21	441
2014	20	5	25
2015	22	7	49
2016	24	9	81
			$\sum(R - \bar{R})^2 = 614$

$$Variance\left(\sigma^2\right) = \frac{614}{6} = 102.33$$

$$\sigma = \sqrt{\sigma^2} = \sqrt{Variance} = \sqrt{102.33} = 10.12\%$$

Risk-Return in Portfolio

A portfolio is composed of two or more securities. Each portfolio has risk-return characteristics of its own. A portfolio comprising securities that yield a maximum return for given level of risk or minimum risk for given level of return is termed as 'efficient portfolio'. In their Endeavour to strike a golden mean between risk and return the traditional portfolio managers diversified funds over securities of large number of companies of different industry groups.

However, this was done on intuitive basis with no knowledge of the magnitude of risk reduction gained. Since the 1950s, however, a systematic body of knowledge has been built up which quantifies the expected return and riskiness of the portfolio. These studies have collectively come to be known as 'portfolio theory'.

A portfolio theory provides a normative approach to investors to make decisions to invest their wealth in assets or securities under risk. The theory is based on the assumption that investors are risk averse. Portfolio theory originally developed by Harry Markowitz states that portfolio risk, unlike portfolio return, is more than a simple aggregation of the risk, unlike portfolio return, is more than a simple aggregation of the risks of individual assets.

This is dependent upon the interplay between the returns on assets comprising the portfolio. Another assumption of the portfolio theory is that the returns of assets are normally distributed which means that the mean (expected value) and variance analysis is the foundation of the portfolio.

Portfolio Return

The expected return of a portfolio represents weighted average of the expected returns on the securities comprising that portfolio with weights being the proportion of total funds invested in each security (the total of weights must be 100).

The following formula can be used to determine expected return of a portfolio:

$$\overline{R}_P = \sum_{J=1} Wj\ Rj$$

where $\overline{R}$ = Expected return of a portfolio.

$\overline{P}$ = The proportion, or weight of total funds invested in security j.

Rj = The expected return for security j.

m = The total number of different securities in the portfolio.

Applying formula $\overline{R}_P = \sum_{J=1} Wj\ Rj$ to possible returns for two securities with funds equally invested in a portfolio, we can find the expected return of the portfolio as below:

	Security X	Security Y
Expected Return, Rj	15.0%	12.6%
Standard deviation, σj	10.7	1.5

The expected return of the portfolio is = (.5)15.0% + (.5)12.6 = 13.8%

Portfolio Risk

Unlike the expected return on a portfolio which is simply the weighted average of the expected returns on the individual assets in the portfolio, the portfolio risk, σp is not the simple, weighted average of the standard deviations of the individual assets in the portfolios.

It is for this fact that consideration of a weighted average of individual security deviations amounts to ignoring the relationship, or covariance that exists between the returns on securities. In fact, the overall risk of the portfolio includes the interactive risk of asset in relation to the others, measured by the covariance of returns. Covariance is a statistical measure of the degree to which two variables (securities' returns) move together. Thus, covariance depends on the correlation between returns on the securities in the portfolio.

Covariance between two securities is calculated as below:

1. Find the expected returns on securities.
2. Find the deviation of possible returns from the expected return for each security.
3. Find the sum of the product of each deviation of returns of two securities and respective probability.

The formula for determining the covariance of returns of two securities is:

$$COVAB = \sum^{n} \left[RA - E(R_A)\right]\left[R_B - E(R_B)\right] \times pi$$

Where COVAB = The covariance of return on securities A and B.

R_A and R_B = Return on securities A and B.

$E(R_A)$and $E(R_B)$ = Expected return of A and B.

Pi = Probability of occurrence of the state of economy.

Let us explain the computation of covariance of returns on two securities with the help of the following illustration:

Table: Covariance of Return on Securities A and B.

State of Economy	Probability	Return		Derivations from Expected Returns		Product of deviation and probability
		A	B	A	B	
Highly Buoyant	0.1	-2	10	-10	5	-50
Buoyant	0.2	8	-5	6	-10	-120
Normal	0.3	6	4	4	-2	-2.4
Recession	0.2	4	10	0	6	0.0
Depression	0.2	-3	10	-8	12	-19.2
		$E(R_A)$3.8%		$E(R_B)$5.2%		Cover = - 38.6

So far as the nature of relationship between the returns of securities A and B is concerned, there may be three possibilities, viz., positive covariance, negative covariance and zero covariance. Positive covariance shows that on an average the two variables move together.

A's and B's returns could be above their average returns at the same time or they could be below their average returns at the same time. This signifies that as the proportion of high return and high risk assets is increased, higher returns on portfolio come with higher risk.

Negative covariance suggests that, on an average, the two variables move in opposite direction. It means A's returns could be above its average returns while B's return could be below its average returns and vice-versa. This implies that it is possible to combine the two securities A and B in a manner that will eliminate all risk.

Zero covariance means that the two variables do not move together either in positive or negative direction. In other words, returns on the two securities are not related at all. Such situation does not exist in real world. Covariance may be non-zero due to randomness and negative and positive terms may not cancel each other.

In the above example, covariance between returns on A and B is negative i.e., -38.6. This suggests that the two returns are negatively related.

The above discussion leads us to conclude that the riskiness of a portfolio depends much more on the paired security covariance than on the riskiness (standard deviations) of the separate security holdings. This means that a combination of individually risky securities could still comprise a moderate-to-low-risk portfolio as long as securities do not move in lock step with each other. In brief, low covariance's lead to low portfolio risk.

Diversification

Diversification is venerable rule of investment which suggests "Don't put all your eggs in one basket", spreading risk across a number of securities.

Diversification may take the form of unit, industry, maturity, geography, type of security and management. Through diversification of investments, an investor can reduce investment risks.

Investment of funds, say, $ 1 lakh evenly among as many as 20 different securities is more diversified than if the same amount is deployed evenly across 7 securities. This sort of security diversification is naive in the sense that it does not factor in the covariance between security returns.

The portfolio comprising 20 securities could represent stocks of one industry only and have returns which are positively correlated and high portfolio returns variability. On the other hand, the 7-stock portfolio might represent a number of different industries where returns might show low correlation and, hence, low portfolio returns variability.

Meaningful diversification is one which involves holding of stocks of more than one industry so that risks of losses occurring in one industry are counterbalanced by gains from the other industry. Investing in global financial markets can achieve greater diversification than investing in securities from a single country. This is for the fact that the economic cycles of different countries hardly synchronize and as such a weak economy in one country may be offset by a strong economy in another.

In figure below portrays meaningful diversification. It may be noted from the figure that the returns overtime for Security X are cyclical in that they move in tandem with the economic fluctuations. In case of Security Y returns are moderately counter cyclical. Thus, the returns for these two securities are negatively correlated.

If equal amounts are invested in both securities, the dispersion of returns, up, on the portfolio of investments will be less because some of each individual security's variability is offsetting. Thus, the gains of diversification of investment portfolio, in the form of risk minimization, can be derived if the securities are not perfectly and positively correlated.

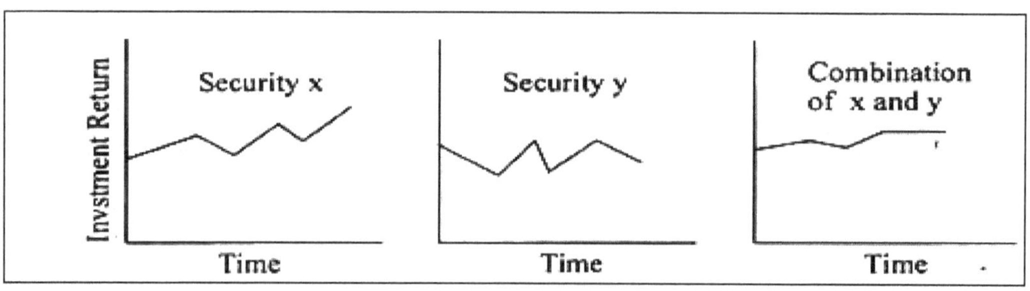

Systematic and Unsystematic Risk

Thus, the variance of returns on a portfolio moving in inverse direction can minimize portfolio risk. However, it is not possible to reduce portfolio risk to zero by increasing the number of securities in the portfolio. According to the research studies, when we begin with a single stock, the risk of the portfolio is the standard deviation of that one stock.

As the number of securities selected randomly held in the portfolio increase, the total risk of the portfolio is reduced, though at a decreasing rate. Thus, degree of portfolio risk can be reduced to a large extent with a relatively moderate amount of diversification, say 15-20 randomly selected securities in equal-rupee amounts.

Portfolio risk comprises systematic risk and unsystematic risk. Systematic risk is also known as non- diversifiable risk which arises because of the forces that affect the overall market, such, as changes in the nation's economy, fiscal policy of the Government, monetary policy of the Central bank, change in the world energy situation etc.

Such types of risks affect securities overall and hence, cannot be diversified away. Even if an investor holds well diversified portfolio, he is exposed to this type of risk which is affecting the overall market. This is why, non-diversifiable or unsystematic risk is also termed as market risk which remains after diversification.

Another risk component is unsystematic risk. It is also known as diversifiable risk caused by such random events as law suits, strikes, successful and unsuccessful marketing programmes, winning or losing a major contract and other events that are unique to a particular firm.

Unsystematic risk can be eliminated through diversification because these events are random, their effects on individual securities in a portfolio cancel out each other. Thus, not all of the risks involved in holding a security are relevant because part of the risk can be diversified away. What is relevant for investors is systematic risk which is unavoidable and they would like to be compensated for bearing it. However, they should not expect the market to provide any extra compensation for bearing the avoidable risk, as is contended in the Capital Asset Pricing Model.

Figure displays two components of portfolio risk and their relationship to portfolio size.

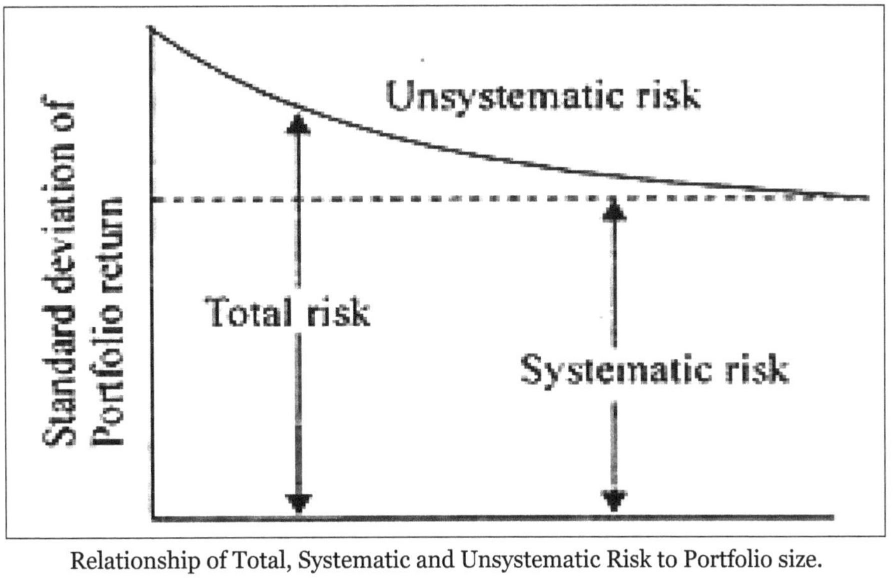

Relationship of Total, Systematic and Unsystematic Risk to Portfolio size.

Illustrative Problems

1. An investor has two investment options before him. Portfolio A offers risk-free expected return

of 10%. Portfolio B offers an expected return of 20% and has standard deviation of 10%. His risk aversion index is 5. Which investment portfolio the investor should choose?

Solution: The following equation can be used to measure utility score of a portfolio,

$$U = E(r) - 0.005A\sigma^2$$

$$U(A) = 10 - 0.005 \times 5 \times (10 - 0) = 10\%$$

$$U(B) = 20 - 0.005 \times 5(10)^2 = 20 - 2.5 = 17.5\%$$

2. Companies X and Y have common stocks having the expected returns and standard deviations given below:

	X	Y
Expected return (Rj)	.10	.05
Standard deviation (oj)	.06	.04

The expected correlation coefficient between the two stocks is – 35.

You are required to calculate the risk and return for a portfolio comprising 60% invested in the stock of Company X and 40% invested in the stock of Company Y.

Solution:

i) Rp = (.60)(.10) + (.40)(.06) = 8.4%.

ii) op = $[(.6)^2 (1.0)(.05)^2 + 2(.6) (.4) (-35) (.05) (.04) + (.4)^2 (1.0) (.04)^2)]^{1/2}$

$= [.00082)^{1/2} = 2.86\%$.

Risk-Return Trade-off

The risk-return trade-off is the concept that the level of return to be earned from an investment should increase as the level of risk increases. Conversely, this means that investors will be less likely to pay a high price for investments that have a low risk level, such as high-grade corporate or government bonds. Different investors will have different tolerances for the level of risk they are willing to accept, so that some will readily invest in low-return investments because there is a low risk of losing the investment. Others have a higher risk tolerance and so will buy riskier investments in pursuit of a higher return, despite the risk of losing their investments. Some investors develop a portfolio of low-risk, low-return investments and higher-risk, higher-return investments in hopes of achieving a more balanced risk-return trade-off.

Special Considerations

Measuring Singular Risk in Context

When an investor considers high-risk-high-return investments, the investor can apply the risk-return trade-off to the vehicle on a singular basis as well as within the context of the portfolio as a whole. Examples of high-risk-high return investments include options, penny stocks and leveraged exchange-traded funds (ETFs). Generally speaking, a diversified portfolio reduces the risks presented by individual investment positions. For example, a penny stock position may have a high risk on a singular basis, but if it is the only position of its kind in a larger portfolio, the risk incurred by holding the stock is minimal.

Risk-Return Trade-off at the Portfolio Level

That said, the risk-return trade-off also exists at the portfolio level. For example, a portfolio composed of all equities presents both higher risk and higher potential returns. Within an all-equity portfolio, risk and reward can be increased by concentrating investments in specific sectors or by taking on single positions that represent a large percentage of holdings. For investors, assessing the cumulative risk-return trade-off of all positions can provide insight on whether a portfolio assumes enough risk to achieve long-term return objectives or if the risk levels are too high with the existing mix of holdings.

References

- Time-value-money: wallstreetmojo.com, Retrieved 3 August, 2019
- Bond-valuation: investopedia.com, Retrieved 19 May, 2019
- Bond-valuation: financialmanagementpro.com, Retrieved 28 April, 2019
- Bond-valuation, investment-decisions: efinancemanagement.com, Retrieved 8 August, 2019
- Equity-valuation-methods, investment-decisions: efinancemanagement.com, Retrieved 9 May, 2019
- Risk-and-return-on-single-asset-investments-financial-management, risk-and-return-investment, investment: businessmanagementideas.com, Retrieved 26 July, 2019
- Concept-of-risk-return-in-portfolio-context-with-formulas, financial-management: yourarticlelibrary.com, Retrieved 5 February, 2019
- Risk return tradeoff: investopedia.com, Retrieved 19 April, 2019

7

International Financial Management

The management of finance in an international business environment is known as international financial management. It is mainly involved in trading and making money through the exchange of foreign currency. All the diverse aspects of international financial management such as the international monetary system and foreign exchange market have been carefully analyzed in this chapter.

International Finance

International Finance discusses the issues related with monetary interactions of at least two or more countries. International finance is concerned with subjects such as exchange rates of currencies, monetary systems of the world, foreign direct investment (FDI), and other important issues associated with international financial management.

Like international trade and business, international finance exists due to the fact that economic activities of businesses, governments, and organizations get affected by the existence of nations. It is a known fact that countries often borrow and lend from each other. In such trades, many countries use their own currencies. Therefore, we must understand how the currencies compare with each other. Moreover, we should also have a good understanding of how these goods are paid for and what is the determining factor of the prices that the currencies trade at.

Importance of International Finance

International finance plays a critical role in international trade and inter-economy exchange of goods and services. It is important for a number of reasons; the most notable ones are listed here:

- International finance is an important tool to find the exchange rates, compare inflation rates, get an idea about investing in international debt securities, ascertain the economic status of other countries and judge the foreign markets.

- Exchange rates are very important in international finance, as they let us determine the relative values of currencies. International finance helps in calculating these rates.
- Various economic factors help in making international investment decisions. Economic factors of economies help in determining whether or not investors' money is safe with foreign debt securities.
- Utilizing IFRS is an important factor for many stages of international finance. Financial statements made by the countries that have adopted IFRS are similar. It helps many countries to follow similar reporting systems.
- IFRS system, which is a part of international finance, also helps in saving money by following the rules of reporting on a single accounting standard.
- International finance has grown in stature due to globalization. It helps understand the basics of all international organizations and keeps the balance intact among them.
- An international finance system maintains peace among the nations. Without a solid finance measure, all nations would work for their self-interest. International finance helps in keeping that issue at bay.
- International finance organizations, such as IMF, the World Bank, etc., provide a mediators' role in managing international finance disputes.

International Financial Management

International financial management deals with the financial decisions taken in the area of international business. It is a popular concept which means management of finance in an international business environment, it implies, doing of trade and making money through the exchange of foreign currency. The international financial activities help the organizations to connect with international dealings with overseas business partners- customers, suppliers, lenders etc.

Basic Functions

- Acquisition of funds: This function involves generating funds from internal as well as external sources. The effort is to get funds at the lowest possible cost.
- Investment decisions: It is concerned with the investment of acquired funds in an optimum manner so as to maximize shareholders' as well as stakeholders' wealth.

Features of International Finance

- Foreign exchange risk.

- Political risk.
- Expanded opportunity set.
- Market imperfections.

Oreign exchange risk: In a domestic economy this risk is generally ignored because a single national currency serves as the main medium of exchange within a country. However, when different national currencies are exchanged, there is definite risk of volatility in foreign exchange rates. Variability of exchange rates is widely regarded as the most serious international financial problem facing policymakers and corporate managers.

Political risk: It is risk of loss (or gain) from unforeseen government action or other events of political character, such as acts of terrorism.

Expanded opportunity set: When firms go global, they get benefited from the expanded opportunities available globally. They can locate production in any country or region to maximize their performance and raise funds in any capital market where the cost of capital is the lowest. They can also gain from greater economies of scale when tangible and intangible assets are deployed on a global basis.

Market imperfections: The world markets are highly imperfect, in the sense that a variety of barriers still hamper free movements of people, goods, services, and capital across national boundaries.

Importance of International Financial Management (IFM)

Compared to national financial markets international markets have a different shape and analytics. Proper management of international finances can help the organization in achieving same efficiency and effectiveness in all markets, hence without IFM sustaining in the market can be difficult. Companies are motivated to invest capital in abroad for the following reasons:

- Efficiently produce products in foreign markets than that domestically.
- Obtain the essential raw materials needed for production.
- Broaden and diversify markets.
- Yield will be high.

The International Monetary System

International monetary system refers to a system that forms rules and standards for facilitating international trade among the nations. It helps in reallocating the capital and investment from one nation to another.

It is the global network of the government and financial institutions that determine the exchange rate of different currencies for international trade. It is a governing body that sets rules and regulations by which different nations exchange currencies with each other.

With the growing complexity in the international trade and financial market, the international monetary system is necessary to assign a standard value of the international currencies. The rules and regulations set by the international monetary system to regulate and control the exchange value of the currencies are agreed upon by the respective governments of the nations. Thus, the government's stand may affect the decision making of the international monetary system. For example, change in the trade policy of a government may affect the international trade of goods and services.

Foreign Exchange Market

The Foreign Exchange Market is a market where the buyers and sellers are involved in the sale and purchase of foreign currencies. In other words, a market where the currencies of different countries are bought and sold is called a foreign exchange market.

The structure of the foreign exchange market constitutes central banks, commercial banks, brokers, exporters and importers, immigrants, investors, tourists. These are the main players of the foreign market, their position and place are shown in the figure below.

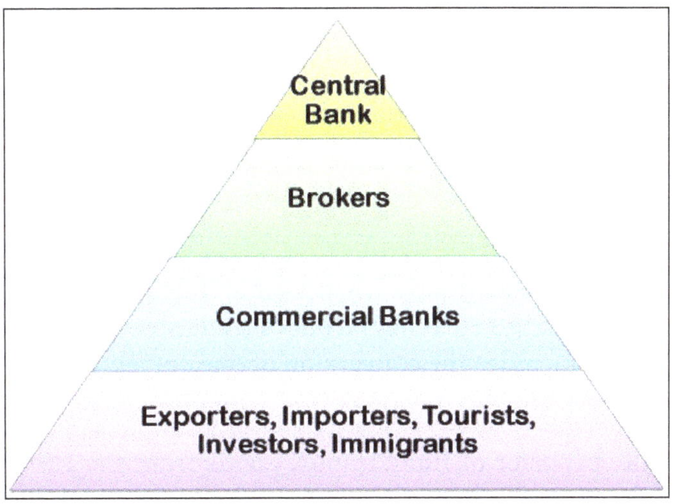

At the bottom of a pyramid are the actual buyers and sellers of the foreign currencies- exporters, importers, tourist, investors, and immigrants. They are actual users of the currencies and approach commercial banks to buy it.

The commercial banks are the second most important organ of the foreign exchange market. The banks dealing in foreign exchange play a role of "market makers", in the sense that they quote on a daily basis the foreign exchange rates for buying and selling of the foreign currencies. Also, they function as clearing houses, thereby helping in wiping out the difference between the demand for and the supply of currencies. These banks buy the currencies from the brokers and sell it to the buyers.

The third layer of a pyramid constitutes the foreign exchange brokers. These brokers function as a link between the central bank and the commercial banks and also between the actual buyers and commercial banks. They are the major source of market information. These are the persons who do not themselves buy the foreign currency, but rather strike a deal between the buyer and the seller on a commission basis.

The central bank of any country is the apex body in the organization of the exchange market. They work as the lender of the last resort and the custodian of foreign exchange of the country. The central bank has the power to regulate and control the foreign exchange market so as to assure that it works in the orderly fashion. One of the major functions of the central bank is to prevent the aggressive fluctuations in the foreign exchange market, if necessary, by direct intervention. Intervention in the form of selling the currency when it is overvalued and buying it when it tends to be undervalued.

Functions of Foreign Exchange Market

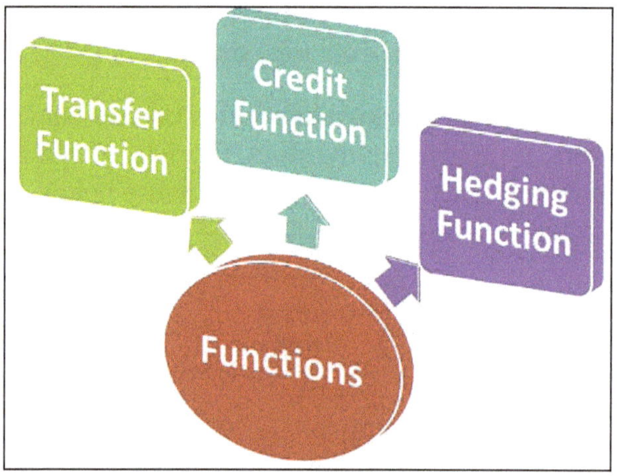

- Transfer Function: The basic and the most visible function of foreign exchange market is the transfer of funds (foreign currency) from one country to another for the settlement of payments. It basically includes the conversion of one currency to another, wherein the role of FOREX is to transfer the purchasing power from one country to another.

  For example, If the exporter of India import goods from the USA and the payment is to be made in dollars, then the conversion of the rupee to the dollar will be facilitated by FOREX. The transfer function is performed through a use of credit instruments, such as bank drafts, bills of foreign exchange, and telephone transfers.

- Credit Function: Forex provides a short-term credit to the importers so as to facilitate the smooth flow of goods and services from country to country. An importer can use credit to finance the foreign purchases. Such as an Indian company wants to purchase the machinery from the USA, can pay for the purchase by issuing a bill of exchange in the foreign exchange market, essentially with a three-month maturity.

- Hedging Function: The third function of a foreign exchange market is to hedge foreign exchange risks. The parties to the foreign exchange are often afraid of the fluctuations in the exchange rates, i.e., the price of one currency in terms of another. The change in the exchange rate may result in a gain or loss to the party concerned.

Thus, due to this reason the Forex provides the services for hedging the anticipated or actual claims/liabilities in exchange for the forward contracts. A forward contract is usually a three month contract to buy or sell the foreign exchange for another currency at a fixed date in the future at a price agreed upon today. Thus, no money is exchanged at the time of the contract.

Characteristics of the Foreign Exchange Market

Characteristics of the Foreign Exchange Market.

To understand what a forex market is, we must first go through its essential features. Discussed below are the various characteristics of the foreign exchange market which differentiates it from other financial markets:

- Market Transparency: It is effortless to monitor the fluctuations in the value of currencies of different countries in a forex market easily through account tracking and real-time portfolio, without the involvement of brokers.
- Dollar is Extensively Traded Currency: The USD, which is paired with almost every country's currency and listed on the forex, is the most widely traded currency in the world.
- Most Dynamic Market: The value of the currencies in the forex market keeps on changing every second and function twenty-four hours a day. This makes it one of the most active markets in the world.
- International Network of Dealers: The foreign exchange market establishes a medium among the dealers and also with the customers. There are dealer's institutions located globally to carry out the exchange and trading activities.
- "Over-The-Counter" Market: In different countries, the forex market is the highly unregulated market initiating over the counter trade by the banks through telex and telephone.
- High Liquidity: The currency is considered to be the most widely traded financial instrument across the globe, making the forex market highly liquid.

- Twenty-Four Hour Market: The foreign exchange market is operational for twenty-four hours of the day, initiating the active trade and exchange of currencies at any time.

Transactions in Foreign Exchange Market

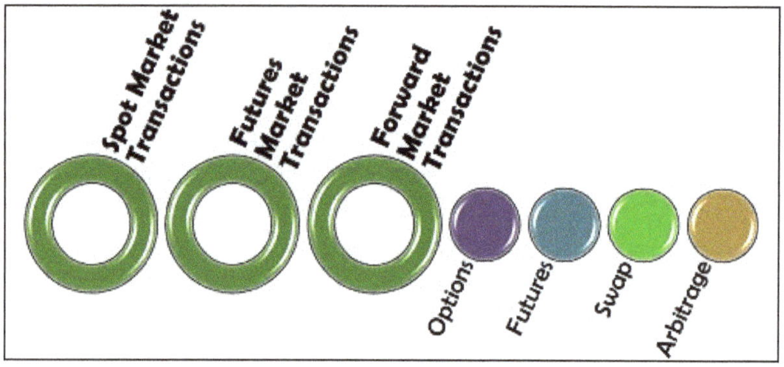

Transactions in Foreign Exchange Market.

A forex market performs three significant operations which are explained in detail below:

Spot Market Transactions

The forex transactions which are executed immediately, or usually within two days, is known as the spot transaction. Such a forex market is termed as a spot market, and the rate of exchange is called a spot rate.

Futures Market Transactions

The market in which the exchange of currencies involves a future delivery and payment and the rate of exchange for the same is pre-determined is called a futures forex market. Such exchange rate is known as a future rate. It protects the buyer from the risk of a rise in the value of the currency.

Forward Market Transactions

A forward forex market is however very similar to the futures market, but here, the terms of the contract are negotiable and can be amended by any of the parties involved.

- Options: In an options contract, the holder is not bound to but have the right to buy or sell the specified asset quantity at the pre-determined price on the specific future.
- Futures: In a future contract, the quantity of an asset, date of execution and price of the contract is fixed and standardized.
- Swap: Usually, commercial banks adopt swap contracts if they perform forward exchange business operations. Here, they sell off a particular currency in the spot market to buy that same currency in the forward market.
- Arbitrage: The rigorous buying and selling of different currencies in the forex market to fetch gains out of such transactions are called arbitrage.

Advantages of Foreign Exchange Market

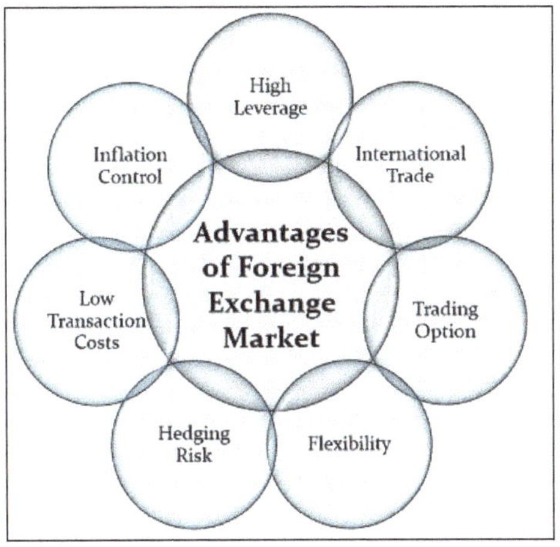

As we know that 'trade makes everyone better-off' and so goes for the exchange or trade of currencies.

- High Leverage: A forex investor can avail the facility of leverage or loan of up to 20 or 30 times of his/her capacity, for trading in the forex market.
- International Trade: Every country has its currency and therefore, to facilitate trade activities between two countries, the forex market is essential.
- Trading Option: For the speculators or traders, foreign exchange market is just like other financial markets where they can make money on short term fluctuations in the currencies.
- Flexibility: We know that the forex market is a twenty-four-seven market, and there is no minimum or maximum limit of the exchange amount. It provides the flexibility of investment or exchange to the traders.
- Hedging Risk: The forex market provides for hedging the risk of loss on currency fluctuations while carrying global business operations and trading in foreign currency.
- Low Transaction Costs: Since brokers are not very much entertained in the forex market, the transaction cost (called as 'spread') charged by the dealers is reasonably low if compared to other financial markets.
- Inflation Control: To maintain the economic stability in the country and control situations like inflation, the central bank maintains a forex reserve which consists of currencies of different countries around the world.

  It adopts other means too, like decreasing bank lending rates and selling out domestic currency for foreign currency.

Disadvantages of Foreign Exchange Market

A forex market is not always favourable and involves various kinds of risks. These can be seen as its drawbacks and are elaborated below:

- Leverage Risks: Leverage refers to loan in other terms. Forex market initiates the leverage of up to 20 to 30 times the investment capacity of the traders or speculators, which may even lead the loss of the entire amount of the investor.

- Counterparty Risks: The forex is highly unregulated with no central authority for currency exchange or trading risk mitigation. Thus, it may encounter the risk of non-fulfilment of the obligations by any of the parties involved in such a contract.
- Operational Risks: Since forex is a twenty-four hours market, it is difficult to manage its operations by humans. As a result, the traders and MNCs rely on the algorithms, and trading desks spread, respectively, to safeguard their investment in their absence.

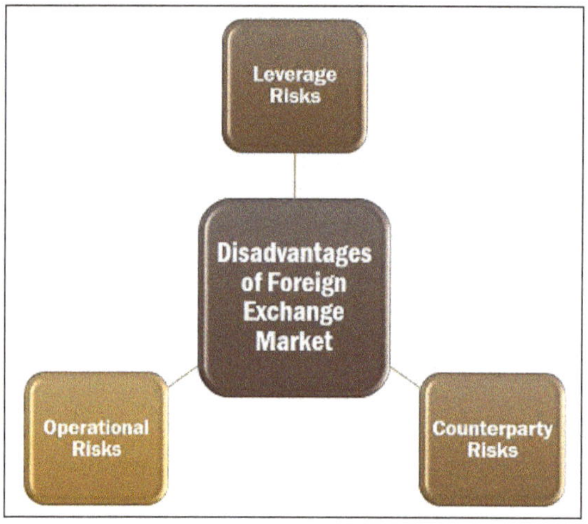

Foreign Direct Investment

Foreign direct investment (FDI) is an investment made by a firm or individual in one country into business interests located in another country. Generally, FDI takes place when an investor establishes foreign business operations or acquires foreign business assets in a foreign company. However, FDIs are distinguished from portfolio investments in which an investor merely purchases equities of foreign-based companies.

How a Foreign Direct Investment Works

Foreign direct investments are commonly made in open economies that offer a skilled workforce and above-average growth prospects for the investor, as opposed to tightly regulated economies. Foreign direct investment frequently involves more than just a capital investment. It may include provisions of management or technology as well. The key feature of foreign direct investment is that it establishes either effective control of or at least substantial influence over the decision-making of a foreign business.

Types of Foreign Direct Investment

Foreign direct investments are commonly categorized as being horizontal, vertical or conglomerate. A horizontal direct investment refers to the investor establishing the same type of business operation in a foreign country as it operates in its home country, for example, a cell phone provider based in the United States opening stores in China.

A vertical investment is one in which different but related business activities from the investor's main business are established or acquired in a foreign country, such as when a manufacturing company acquires an interest in a foreign company that supplies parts or raw materials required for the manufacturing company to make its products.

A conglomerate type of foreign direct investment is one where a company or individual makes a foreign investment in a business that is unrelated to its existing business in its home country. Since this type of investment involves entering an industry in which the investor has no previous experience, it often takes the form of a joint venture with a foreign company already operating in the industry.

Examples of Foreign Direct Investments

Examples of foreign direct investments include mergers, acquisitions, retail, services, logistics, and manufacturing, among others. Foreign direct investments and the laws governing them can be pivotal to a company's growth strategy.

In 2017, for example, U.S.-based Apple announced a $507.1 million investment to boost its research and development work in China, Apple's third-largest market behind the Americas and Europe. The announced investment relayed CEO Tim Cook's bullishness toward the Chinese market despite a 12% year-over-year decline in Apple's Greater China revenue in the quarter preceding the announcement.

China's economy has been fueled by an influx of FDI targeting the nation's high-tech manufacturing and services, which according to China's Ministry of Commerce, grew 11.1% and 20.4% year over year, respectively, in the first half of 2017. Meanwhile, relaxed FDI regulations in India now allows 100% foreign direct investment in single-brand retail without government approval. The regulatory decision reportedly facilitates Apple's desire to open a physical store in the Indian market. Thus far, the firm's iPhones have only been available through third-party physical and online retailers.

Types of FDI

Strategically, FDI comes in three types:

- Horizontal: In case of horizontal FDI, the company does all the same activities abroad as at home. For example, Toyota assembles motor cars in Japan and the UK.
- Vertical: In vertical assignments, different types of activities are carried out abroad. In case of forward vertical FDI, the FDI brings the company nearer to a market (for example, Toyota buying a car distributorship in America). In case of backward Vertical FDI, the international integration goes back towards raw materials (for example, Toyota getting majority stake in a tyre manufacturer or a rubber plantation).
- Conglomerate: In this type of investment, the investment is made to acquire an unrelated business abroad. It is the most surprising form of FDI, as it requires overcoming two barriers simultaneously – one, entering a foreign country and two, working in a new industry.

FDI can take the form of Greenfield entry or takeover.

- Greenfield entry refers to activities or assembling all the elements right from scratch as Honda did in the UK.
- Foreign takeover means acquiring an existing foreign company – as Tata's acquisition of Jaguar Land Rover. Foreign takeover is often called mergers and acquisitions (M&A) but internationally, mergers are absolutely small, which accounts for less than 1% of all foreign acquisitions.

This choice of entry in a market and its mode interacts with the ownership strategy. The choice of wholly owned subsidiaries against joint ventures gives a 2x2 matrix of choices – the options of which are:

- Greenfield wholly owned ventures,
- Greenfield joint ventures,
- Wholly owned takeovers, and
- Joint foreign acquisitions.

These choices offer foreign investors options to match their own interests, capabilities, and foreign conditions.

Importance of FDI

FDI is an important source of externally derived finance that offers countries with limited amounts of capital get finance beyond national borders from wealthier countries. For example, exports and FDI are the two key ingredients in China's rapid economic growth.

According to the World Bank, FDI is one of the critical elements in developing the private sector in lower-income economies and thereby, in reducing poverty.

Vehicles of FDI

- Reciprocal distribution agreements: This type of strategic alliance is found more in trade-based verticals, but in practical sense, it does represent a type of direct investment. Basically, two companies, usually within the same or affiliated industries, but from different nations, agree to become national distributors for each other's products.
- Joint venture and other hybrid strategic alliances: Traditional joint venture is bilateral, involving two parties who are within the same industry, partnering for getting some strategic advantage. Joint ventures and strategic alliances offer access to proprietary technology, gaining access to intellectual capital as human resources, and access to closed channels of distribution in select locations.
- Portfolio investment: For most of the 20th century, a company's portfolio investments were not considered a direct investment. However, two or three companies with "soft" investments in a company could try to find some mutual interests and use their shareholding for management control. This is another form of strategic alliance, sometimes called shadow alliances.

Basic Requirements of FDI

As a minimum requirement, a firm will have to keep itself abreast of global trends in its industry. From a competitive perspective, it is important to be aware if the competitors are getting into a foreign market and how they do that.

It is also important to see how globalization is currently affecting the domestic clients. Often, it becomes imperative to expand for key clients overseas for an active business relationship.

New market access is also another major reason to invest in a foreign country. At some stage, export of product or service becomes obsolete and foreign production or location becomes more cost effective. Any decision on investing is thus a combination of a number of key factors including:

- Assessment of internal resources,
- Competitiveness,
- Market analysis, and
- Market expectations.

References

- International-finance-introduction, international-finance: tutorialspoint.com, Retrieved 25 February, 2019
- International-financial-management: myassignmenthelp.net, Retrieved 16 January, 2019
- International-monetary-system: economicsdiscussion.net, Retrieved 29 March, 2019
- Foreign-exchange-market: businessjargons.com, Retrieved 30 April, 2019
- Functions-of-foreign-exchange-market: businessjargons.com, Retrieved 14 July, 2019
- Characteristics, foreign-exchange-market: theinvestorsbook.com, Retrieved 29 June, 2019
- Foreign-direct-investment, international-finance: tutorialspoint.com, Retrieved 11 January, 2019

Permissions

All chapters in this book are published with permission under the Creative Commons Attribution Share Alike License or equivalent. Every chapter published in this book has been scrutinized by our experts. Their significance has been extensively debated. The topics covered herein carry significant information for a comprehensive understanding. They may even be implemented as practical applications or may be referred to as a beginning point for further studies.

We would like to thank the editorial team for lending their expertise to make the book truly unique. They have played a crucial role in the development of this book. Without their invaluable contributions this book wouldn't have been possible. They have made vital efforts to compile up to date information on the varied aspects of this subject to make this book a valuable addition to the collection of many professionals and students.

This book was conceptualized with the vision of imparting up-to-date and integrated information in this field. To ensure the same, a matchless editorial board was set up. Every individual on the board went through rigorous rounds of assessment to prove their worth. After which they invested a large part of their time researching and compiling the most relevant data for our readers.

The editorial board has been involved in producing this book since its inception. They have spent rigorous hours researching and exploring the diverse topics which have resulted in the successful publishing of this book. They have passed on their knowledge of decades through this book. To expedite this challenging task, the publisher supported the team at every step. A small team of assistant editors was also appointed to further simplify the editing procedure and attain best results for the readers.

Apart from the editorial board, the designing team has also invested a significant amount of their time in understanding the subject and creating the most relevant covers. They scrutinized every image to scout for the most suitable representation of the subject and create an appropriate cover for the book.

The publishing team has been an ardent support to the editorial, designing and production team. Their endless efforts to recruit the best for this project, has resulted in the accomplishment of this book. They are a veteran in the field of academics and their pool of knowledge is as vast as their experience in printing. Their expertise and guidance has proved useful at every step. Their uncompromising quality standards have made this book an exceptional effort. Their encouragement from time to time has been an inspiration for everyone.

The publisher and the editorial board hope that this book will prove to be a valuable piece of knowledge for students, practitioners and scholars across the globe.

Index

P

R

S

T

V

W

CPSIA information can be obtained
at www.ICGtesting.com
Printed in the USA
LVHW060901030122
707669LV00002B/287

9 781641 726184